HIKING COLORADO'S WESTERN SLOPE

HELP US KEEP THIS GUIDE UP TO DATE

Every effort has been made by the author and editors to make this guide as accurate and useful as possible. However, many things can change after a guide is published—regulations change, facilities come under new management, and so forth.

We would love to hear from you concerning your experiences with this guide and how you feel it could be improved and kept up to date. While we may not be able to respond to all comments and suggestions, we'll take them to heart, and we'll also make certain to share them with the author. Please send your comments and suggestions to falconeditorial@rowman.com.

Thanks for your input!

HIKING COLORADO'S WESTERN SLOPE

SECOND EDITION

Bill Haggerty

FALCONGUIDES

ESSEX, CONNECTICUT

To Patricia Maeve Bennett, my precious granddaughter

FALCONGUIDES®

An imprint of The Globe Pequot Publishing Group, Inc.
64 South Main Street
Essex, CT 06426
www.globepequot.com

Falcon and FalconGuides are registered trademarks and Make Adventure Your Story is a trademark of The Rowman & Littlefield Publishing Group, Inc.

Distributed by NATIONAL BOOK NETWORK

Copyright © 2025 The Globe Pequot Publishing Group, Inc.
Photos by Bill Haggerty unless noted otherwise.
Maps by The Globe Pequot Publishing Group, Inc.

British Library Cataloguing in Publication Information available

Library of Congress Cataloging-in-Publication Data available

ISBN 978-1-4930-7545-4 (paper: alk. paper)
ISBN 978-1-4930-7546-1 (electronic)

Printed in India

The author and The Globe Pequot Publishing Group, Inc., assume no liability for accidents happening to, or injuries sustained by, readers who engage in the activities described in this book.

CONTENTS

THE HIKES

MEET YOUR GUIDE

I love hiking in western Colorado for the cool mountain air and bright desert heat, for the diminutive roar of a rushing high-mountain brook, and the vibrant colors of desert wildflowers in the spring . . . the way the light changes across the canyons, the alpenglow on the peaks at sunset, the smell of fresh pine after a rainstorm, pupils dilated, skin tingling, all the senses alive and contributing to the feeling of wonder that Mother Nature has provided.

Hiking in these environments soothes my soul, makes me aware and alive, and keeps me in the moment. When I return home, I can breathe easier, think more clearly, and deal with the issues of life with a smile and not a frown.

Hiking makes me happy. It keeps me grounded and allows me to be grateful every day for where I live and what I do and who I love.

"'Tis a privilege to live in Colorado," my dear mother always said. Mom was always right.

As you check out this book, you'll notice that a lot of "classic" hikes on the western slope are not included. There are no hikes into the Maroon Bells, one of the most scenic and rugged places in the entire Rocky Mountains. That's because it's so crowded, you have to take a shuttle bus to get there. Hanging Lakes in Glenwood Canyon is drop-dead gorgeous, but the parking lot in the canyon is closed by 9 a.m. all summer because it's already full.

Another reason some "classic" hikes are not included is because there must be 200 of them. You can only put so much in one book!

The hikes that are included here, for the most part, remain off the beaten path and they're spread across the western slope, so you can discover your own favorite part on the bright side of the Continental Divide. All these hikes are marked with GPS waypoints. How accurate are GPS apps? It depends. Cheap apps, satellite geometry, signal blockage, atmospheric conditions, and receiver quality all play a role. Accuracy worsens near buildings, bridges, trees, canyons and mountains. Some publications note a .001 difference could mean a 4–6 feet (1.5 meters) difference. Generally, however, you should be in the right neighborhood with GPS coordinates listed in this book.

Be careful, stay safe and enjoy yourselves.

Happy Trails!

—Hag

(**Editor's Note:** Mr. Haggerty has been writing about outdoor issues in western Colorado for more than four decades, first as a newspaper reporter/photographer, then as information specialist for the Colorado Division of Wildlife, and more recently as an outdoor columnist. This is the second edition of his second book for Falcon. His first Falcon book, entitled *Best Easy Day Hikes Grand Junction/Fruita*, was published in 2015 as part of Falcon's popular "Where To Hike" Series. Haggerty also authored *Discovering the Colorado Plateau: A Guide to the Region's Hidden Wonders*, published by Falcon in 2021.)

HOW TO USE THIS GUIDE

Each hike features **The Rundown**. This summary describes where the trail begins, how long it is, and how long it will take to hike. You'll also find degree of difficulty, elevation, canine compatibility, nearest towns, maps, and other pertinent information. This section is designed to give you a feel for the hike.

Difficulty ratings, for example, give a general sense of how strenuous a hike is. The ratings correspond to elevation gain, tempered by the grade, length, and hiking surface.

Easy: can be completed with little difficulty by hikers of all abilities.

Moderate: may be challenging due to elevation gain or other factors.

Strenuous: may tax even experienced hikers.

Very strenuous: will be difficult even for experienced hikers.

Elevation gain shows the high and low points on the trail, usually at the trailhead and trail-end. However, you may gain or lose a lot more in elevation depending upon terrain.

Some routes may be marked with rock cairns, wooden posts, or fiberglass stakes and follow intermittent sections of tread laid down by hikers' feet, but they are rough and may be difficult to follow in places. "Cross-country" or "bushwhacking" refers to travel following a line of geography like a stream or ridgeline without any marking or tread to follow.

NOTES ON MAPS

Topographic maps are an essential companion to the activities in this guide. Falcon has partnered with National Geographic to provide the best mapping resources. Each activity is accompanied by a detailed map and the name of the National Geographic TOPO! map (USGS), which can be downloaded for free from natgeomaps.com.

If the activity takes place on a National Geographic Trails Illustrated map it will be noted. Continually setting the standard for accuracy, each Trails Illustrated topographic map is crafted in conjunction with local land managers and undergoes rigorous review and enhancement before being printed on waterproof, tear-resistant material. Trails Illustrated maps and information about their digital versions, that can be used on mobile GPS applications, can be found at natgeomaps.com.

TRAIL FINDER

	BEST PHOTOS	FAMILY FRIENDLY	WATER FEATURES	DOG FRIENDLY	FINDING SOLITUDE
ROUTT NATIONAL FOREST, INCLUDING MOUNT ZIRKEL WILDERNESS					
1. North Lake Trail	●	●	●	●	●
2. Three Island Lake	●		●	●	●
3. Mica Basin	●		●	●	●
DINOSAUR NATIONAL MONUMENT/					
4. Harpers Corner Trail	●	●	●	●	●
5. Browns Park National Wildlife Refuge	●	●	●	●	●
6. Slide Mandall Lake	●		●	●	●
7. Carhart Trail around Trappers Lake	●		●	●	●
8. Skinny Fish Trail	●	●	●	●	
9. Storm King Fourteen Memorial Hike	●			●	●
WEST ELKS/RAGGEDS WILDERNESS					
10. Oh-Be-Joyful Trail	●	●	●	●	
11. Ruby Anthracite Trail	●		●	●	●
12. Dark Canyon Trail to Anthracite Creek	●	●	●	●	●
13. Fryingpan Lakes	●		●	●	●
14. Lost Man Trail	●		●	●	
15. Nolan Lake Trail	●		●	●	●
CENTRAL COLORADO PLATEAU/COLORADO RIVER DRAINAGE					
16. Rattlesnake Canyon Arches Trail	●	●		●	●
17. Mee Canyon	●			●	●
18. Monument Canyon Trail	●	●			●
19. Mt. Garfield Trail	●				●
20. Dominguez Canyon Trail	●		●	●	●

	BEST PHOTOS	FAMILY FRIENDLY	WATER FEATURES	DOG FRIENDLY	FINDING SOLITUDE
21. Juanita Arch	•		•	•	•
22. Dolores River Canyon Trail	•	•	•	•	•
23. Wildcat Trail	•			•	•
24. Crag Crest Trail	•		•	•	•
25. West Bench Trail	•	•	•	•	•
26. Lake of the Woods Trail to Bull Basin	•	•	•	•	•
27. Drop Off Trail	•	•	•	•	•
BLACK CANYON OF THE GUNNISON					
28. Deadhorse Trail—North Rim of the Black Canyon of the Gunnison	•	•	•	•	•
29. Ute Park—South Rim into Gunnison Gorge NCA	•		•	•	•
30. Bobcat Trail into the Black Canyon of the Gunnison River	•		•	•	•
SOUTHERN ROCKIES					
31. Powderhorn Lakes	•		•	•	•
32. Fall Creek Trail	•	•	•	•	•
33. Handies Peak	•		•	•	
34. Piedra River Trail	•	•	•	•	•
35. Fourmile Trail to Fourmile Falls	•	•	•	•	•
36. Geyser Spring	•	•	•	•	•
37. Petroglyph Point—Mesa Verde National Park	•	•			
38. Sand Canyon—Canyon of the Ancients National Monument	•	•			•
39. Cutthroat Castle—Hovenweep National Monument	•	•			•

TOP 5 HIKES

1. HIKE 9: STORM KING FOURTEEN MEMORIAL HIKE

1. HIKE 9: STORM KING FOURTEEN MEMORIAL HIKE

This is not the most stunning hike in the book. Yet, its rugged, nasty terrain and the memorials it leads to for the fourteen firefighters who perished here are a constant reminder of the fragility of our environment and the bravery of those who tried to protect us from its fiery power of destruction.

2. HIKE 17: MEE CANYON

2. HIKE 17: MEE CANYON

Mother Nature carved an incredible canyon here, and this is such a fun hike—crawling through rock windows in the sky, climbing down Navajo-style ladders, tightroping across narrow ledges, and dropping into one of the largest alcoves in the canyon lands. This hike is a must!

3. HIKE 3: MICA BASIN

3. HIKE 3: MICA BASIN

Stunning. Simply stunning! Nestled in a basin with the 11,233-foot Little Agnes Mountain to the west, the Sawtooth Range looming to the north, and the 12,059-foot Big Agnes Mountain to the east, Mica Lake is a less traveled path into the Zirkel Wilderness—once you get 1.5 miles away from the parking area and main trails!

4. HIKE 31: POWDERHORN LAKES

4. HIKE 31: POWDERHORN LAKES

Wildflowers are found in abundance along the trail to Powderhorn Lakes. Situated in the heart of one of the largest unbroken expanses of alpine tundra in the United States, this wilderness sits above 12,000 feet in elevation. The lakes are about 115 feet below that!

5. HIKE 38: SAND CANYON—CANYON OF THE ANCIENTS NATIONAL MONUMENT

5. HIKE 38: SAND CANYON—CANYON OF THE ANCIENTS NATIONAL MONUMENT

Incredible Native Puebloan ruins, unspoiled and remote!

BEFORE YOU HIT THE TRAIL

WESTERN SLOPE OVERVIEW

I grew up in Colorado and studied its geography and geology in college. It was hard. I became a journalist instead.

I left the eastern slope (we call it "the Dark Side" over here) and came to the western slope because of its lack of people and plethora of gnarly mountains and cool canyons.

How's that for geography/geology?

I loved cool afternoon mountain breezes and warm spring mornings in the desert, and I could find it all within a short distance from where I lived. Plus, I found a job, and a life.

But, could I remember that geology stuff?

No way.

That's why I hang out with people who have better memories than me—folks like the biologists at the Division of Wildlife who taught me so much about wildlife and habitat, and folks like my geologist buddy, Ray, who understands the physiography of western Colorado and remembers it. (Physiography, says Ray, is the study of features and attributes of the earth's surface, and hiking with Ray is like having someone read *Roadside Geology* aloud as you trek through this gorgeous country!)

Here's what Ray says about the physiography of western Colorado:

- The Continental Divide bisects the state of Colorado, acting as the ridgeline of the roof of the western United States. It sheds water, causing streams on the eastern side to flow to the Atlantic Ocean or Gulf of México. Water collecting on the western side flows home to the Pacific.

- The western half of Colorado hosts diverse scenery encompassing craggy mountains, flattop mesas, high deserts, and deep canyons. It includes terrain that can be deeply covered by snow in the winter and blanketed by grasses and flowering plants in the warm months of the year.

- The geologic history of western Colorado is complex and underlies the captivating landforms we see today. Our scenic vistas were shaped by geologic processes over 1.8 billion years or more that deposited thick packages of sediment, intruded by injections of molten rocks, draped by volcanic flows, uplifted, folded, faulted, and deeply incised by relentless flowing water.

- While exploring western Colorado, you cannot avoid the beauty of the glaciated mountain ranges juxtaposed to deep canyons cradling streams and rivers that are carving through the eons of history using only water and bits of rock to chisel the scenery you see.

- The dry wind of the high desert sculpts cliff faces into yawning overhangs or graceful arches, and the sparse and tough plant and animal life have adapted to the dry steppe climate.

Yea, what he said!

You'll notice that hikes in this book are grouped by certain geographic areas and characterized by similar landforms. Ray helped me with that.

These areas correspond to physiographic provinces that were identified and named by the early explorers, geologists, and geographers who ventured west of the Continental Divide to survey the wealth of the territory. The early explorers recognized these physiographic provinces by the differences they could see in the landforms, and changes in elevations and environment.

There are four physiographic provinces in western Colorado: the Middle Rocky Mountains, the Wyoming Basin, the Southern Rockies, and the Colorado Plateau.

Within these provinces, climate interacts with the land to provide unique environments and habitat where indigenous species of vegetation and animals thrive.

So, these are the basics. Enjoy the gnarly mountains and gentle canyons and know it's been a couple billion years in the making.

By the way, Raymond C. Pilcher, P.G., lives in Grand Junction, Colorado. His company, Raven Ridge Resources, is known worldwide for its technical assistance in the reduction of methane gas emissions from coal mining.

WEATHER

Colorado receives 310-plus days of sun or partial sun each year. So, expect it. The weather along the Utah/Colorado border on the Colorado Plateau comes from the west and blows toward the east. However, the Rocky Mountains—within their corresponding physiographic provinces—create their own weather. The prime example of this is the rainstorm you're sure to get caught in if you're in the high country on any given summer afternoon.

In general, with an increase in elevation comes a decrease in temperature and an increase in precipitation. The desert country of the Colorado Plateau is hot and dry in the summer months while the mountains are cool and refreshing. Conversely, the mountains are full of snow and nasty weather in the winter—great for skiing—while the desert country is quite amenable to hiking.

Wintertime temperatures in the mountains can reach 50°F below 0, while wintertime temperatures in the canyons of western Colorado along the Utah border rarely dip below 0 and are usually in the 30s and 40s.

Above 7,000 feet, the nights are quite cool throughout the summer, while bright sunshine makes the days comfortably warm. Summertime temperatures in the mountains can range from 32°F at night to about 65°F or 70°F during the day, although on some days, temperatures can reach the 80s or 90s.

A note about timberline: It's usually found in Colorado between 11,500 and 12,000 feet in elevation, approaching the higher altitude only on the north-facing slopes.

In the high-desert regions of western Colorado below 7,000 feet in elevation, summertime temperatures may dip into the 60s or 70s at night, but they'll reach the 90s and into the 100s in the daytime.

Check on local weather conditions by going to the internet and clicking on the town nearest your destination. Those towns are listed on every hike. You may or may not get accurate information, but it'll give you a starting point. Also, call the trail contact listed in each hike to find out about trail conditions as well as local weather conditions. Some trails in this book are covered in snow well into June in some years, while they may be snow-free by late April in other years.

FLORA AND FAUNA

The flora and fauna of western Colorado are as diverse as its physiographic provinces: collared lizards in the desert and moose in the mountains, yellow prickly pear cactus in the lowlands, and blue columbines in the high country.

Colorado is made up of eight distinct ecosystems, seven of which are found on the western slope. An ecosystem is the physical environment and all the organisms in a given area. Each ecosystem is unique. It has its own elevation and latitude, its own geology and climate that's unique for the plants and animals that live there.

(The one Colorado ecosystem that does not exist in western Colorado is the Grassland Zone. It lies between 4,000 to 10,000 feet in elevation, covers the eastern third of Colorado, and is made up primarily of short-grass species.)

Western Colorado ecosystems include:

- The Alpine (tundra) zone: 11,400 feet and above—where only tundra grasses, mosses, sedges, and lichens grow. You'll find perennial wildflowers here, but they're no more than a couple of inches tall because of the rugged nature of the region. Plants must be able to handle months of being covered in snow and then being exposed to strong winds and intense sunlight. The American pika and yellow-bellied marmot make their living here.

- Subalpine (forest) zone: 9,000 to 11,400 feet—heavy forests leading up to timberline, which is generally 11,000 to 12,000 feet, collect the heaviest snow accumulation that during spring thaw provide all the water we receive to fill our lakes and reservoirs and all the water that flows into the southwest United States, providing irrigation and water to nearly 40 million people. Mammals such as black bears, Canada lynx, pine squirrels, and Rocky Mountain bighorn sheep and elk live here.

- Montane (forest) zone: 5,600 to 9,000 feet—here, you'll find ponderosa pines, Douglas firs, lodgepole pines, spruce, aspen—and lots of wildflowers in the summer. This zone is where the heaviest effects of human encroachment occur. We build our ski areas here, at approximately 8,500 feet in elevation, and the towns associated with those areas encroach on the wild black bear populations that happen to live in this transitional zone between timber and shrubland. This is where the berries and nuts are—high-protein, high-calorie foods needed for bear survival into the following year. This is also where their dens are located. Besides bears, you'll also find porcupines, pine martens, red fox, bobcats, and mule deer in this zone.

- Montane (shrubland) zone: 5,500 to 10,000 feet—still the transitional zone, these dry, rocky foothills provide a mix of vegetation from grasses to Gambel oak. You'll find chipmunks, cottontail rabbits, and raccoons along with gopher snakes and golden eagles.

- Pinyon-juniper woodland: 5,500 to 8,000 feet—the ground cover here between the trees is sparse with a variety of grasses, shrubs, and flowering plants. This zone is also called the high desert, which describes most of the Colorado Plateau.

- Semidesert shrubland: up to 7,000 feet—the soil is very alkaline here. It has poor water infiltration and high runoff. Sagebrush, pinyon pine, and Utah juniper survive on little water. Burrowing owls eat prairie dogs and steal their homes while Gambel's quail scurry about living off the seeds of desert grasses and shrubs.

- Riparian zones: the areas that interface with a river or stream and the landscape it supports. The western slope has low-altitude, medium-altitude, and high-altitude riparian zones that are extremely important, as 90 percent of all wildlife will use riparian zones at one time of the year or another. The rare canyon tree frog, which actually lives on the ground and not in trees, is only found in a few moist canyons in western Colorado, while the native Colorado River cutthroat trout thrives in our high-mountain lakes and streams.

WILDERNESS REGULATIONS AND RESTRICTIONS

Motorized equipment and equipment used for mechanical transport are prohibited in all the wilderness areas listed in this book. Also, camping is prohibited within 100 feet of any lake, stream, or trail. (There is a quarter-mile camping restriction in the Zirkel Wilderness.) All wilderness areas require dogs to be always under control. The areas that require your dog to be *on a leash* at all times include the Hunter-Fryingpan, Eagles Nest/Holy Cross, Mt. Sneffels, Powderhorn, Raggeds, and Uncompahgre Wilderness Areas.

There's a maximum group size of fifteen people or a combined total of twenty-five people and pack or saddle animals allowed in all wilderness areas, and each wilderness area may have other restrictions. Check first before traveling into a wilderness area. A trail contact is listed on each of these hikes.

Finally, practice "Leave No Trace" (LNT) ethics. Take only pictures. Leave only footprints.

NATIONAL PARK REGULATIONS AND RESTRICTIONS

For the Colorado National Monument, Black Canyon National Park, and Mesa Verde National Park, dogs are not allowed on any trail.

THREE DEADLY KILLERS:

There are three main issues Colorado search and rescue teams and hospital emergency personnel caution Colorado backcountry users about: hypothermia, altitude sickness, and staying put if you're lost.

Hypothermia is a potentially dangerous drop in body temperature, usually caused by prolonged exposure to cold temperatures. The risk increases in winter, but if you're exposed to cold temperatures on a spring hike or stuck in a rainstorm in the mountains in the middle of the summer, you can also be at risk of hypothermia.

Normal body temperature averages 98.6°F. With hypothermia, core temperature drops below 95°F. In severe hypothermia, core body temperature can drop to 82°F or lower.

When you get wet and begin to chill, you gasp (torso reflex). Your skin begins to cool, and your body constricts surface blood vessels to conserve heat for your vital organs. Blood pressure and heart rate increase. Muscles tense and shiver; this produces more body heat but results in a loss of dexterity and motor control.

Signs that a person is nearing a hypothermic state include shivering, poor coordination, and mental sluggishness. Resisting help and acting irrational or confused are common indicators. As hypothermia progresses, shivering ceases, coordination is severely impaired, and confusion is coupled with incoherence and irrationality.

If your core temperature drops dangerously low, you may become semiconscious, then unconscious. Stress, shock, and low core temperatures may cause cardiac and respiratory failure.

This potentially life-threatening condition needs immediate emergency medical attention. If medical care isn't immediately available,

- Remove any wet clothes, hats, gloves, shoes, and socks.
- Protect the person against wind, drafts, and further heat loss with warm, dry clothes and blankets.
- Move gently to a warm, dry shelter as soon as possible.
- Begin rewarming the person with extra clothing. Use warm blankets. Use hot packs, if available, on the torso, armpits, neck, and groin. Be careful. These can burn the skin.
- Use your own body heat if nothing else is available.
- Offer warm liquids, but avoid alcohol and caffeine, which speed up heat loss.

How do you prevent hypothermia? Don't get wet. Most Colorado survival experts have three rules for dressing for a potentially chilly day outdoors:

1. No cotton. When wet it is worthless as an insulator and it becomes extremely heavy.
2. Layer your clothing. Wear a wicking fabric next to your skin, an insulating layer of fleece or wool on top of that, then an outer layer made of windproof, watertight materials.
3. No cotton—seriously!

Altitude sickness occurs when you cannot get enough oxygen at high altitude. It affects the lungs and brain and causes symptoms such as headaches, loss of appetite, and trouble sleeping. It happens most often when people who are not used to high altitudes go quickly from lower elevations to 8,000 feet (2,438 meters) or higher. It also can happen to people who are used to altitude, but who are not adequately hydrated.

Mild altitude sickness is common. Experts don't know who will get it and who won't. Neither your fitness level nor being male or female plays a role in whether you get altitude sickness.

The symptoms of altitude sickness include a throbbing headache that gets worse during the night and when you wake up; being confused; not walking straight (ataxia); loss of appetite; feeling sick to your stomach; feeling weak and tired to the point you don't have the energy to eat or dress yourself; feeling faint or dizzy; having blue or gray lips or fingernails.

Watch for these symptoms in yourself and others in your hiking group. If anyone shows signs of altitude sickness, get them to a lower elevation immediately.

The best way to prevent altitude sickness is to hydrate, hydrate, hydrate . . . and move up slowly in elevation—acclimate—if you're not used to it.

Stay put if you're lost: We all get a little turned around now and then. Sometimes, we get lost, even though we may know where we're headed. Maybe we get caught in a freak blizzard in Colorado's high country or wander down a canyon we don't recognize on the Colorado Plateau. Hopefully, that won't happen to you. If you're confident with your use of map and compass, you understand how your GPS unit operates, or if you're with someone who's already familiar with the area, you'll be fine. But, if you do get lost or separated from your group, don't panic. Build a fire and STAY PUT! The fire will keep you company until someone comes to find you.

Surely, you told someone where you were going and when you're expected back? They'll notify the authorities and OUR SEARCH AND RESCUE TEAMS WILL FIND YOU! But don't make it any tougher on them by moving around. Build a fire, spell out "Help" in large letters in the snow, or with logs and rocks. Then, keep warm, keep dry, and STAY PUT!

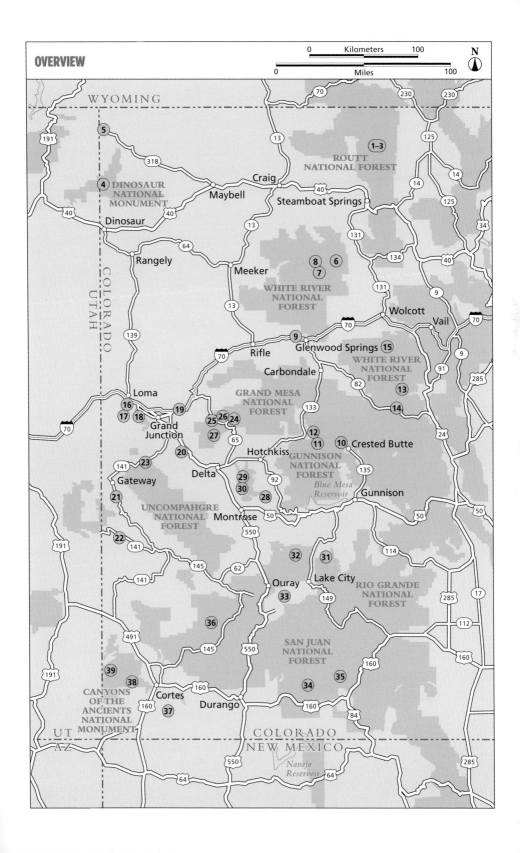

MAP LEGEND

Municipal

Interstate Highway

US Highway

State Road

Local Road

Unpaved Road

Trails

Featured Trail

Trail

Water Features

Body of Water

River/Creek

Spring

Waterfall

Land Management

National Park/Forest

National Monument/Wilderness

Symbols

Bridge

Building/Point of Interest

Campground

Caves

Inn/Lodging

Parking

Pass/Gap

Peak

Ranger Station/Park Office

Restrooms

Scenic View

Ski Area

Town

Trailhead

Tunnel

Visitor/Information Center

ROUTT NATIONAL FOREST, INCLUDING MOUNT ZIRKEL WILDERNESS

In 1905 President Theodore Roosevelt proclaimed this area the "Park Range Forest Reserve." In 1908, he changed the name to Routt in honor of Colonel John Routt, the last territorial governor and first elected governor of Colorado, which officially became the 38th State of the Union in 1876.

The hikes in this section lie within Routt National Forest boundaries. The Continental Divide follows the Park Range from the Wyoming border to Rabbit Ears Pass, near Steamboat Springs and the world-famous Steamboat Springs Ski Area. Its diverse topography of high plateaus, rolling foothills, and mountains creates long, snowy winters and short, cool summers on the Routt.

The 160,000-acre Zirkel Wilderness lies in the midst of all this splendor. This volcanically uplifted area was constantly modified during glacial periods over the last 2.5 million years. It's also been modified by more recent erosional processes, such as water, rock- and mudslides, fires, deforestation, drought, and winds. Erosion in recent years has been caused by a combination of all the above.

In the 1940s, this part of the state experienced drought, which in turn enabled a native parasite, the spruce beetle, to take hold and thrive. (See the sidebar on spruce and pine beetles in Hike 1: North Lake Trail.)

The spruce beetle epidemic killed large swaths of forest throughout the Zirkels. It was ripe for fire, which can be beneficial to the long-term health of a forest. In the short term and on a massive scale, however, fire denudes the landscape and increases debris flow and erosion at a tremendous rate. That's especially true here on the edge of the Southern Rockies, where it's so steep.

As described in the North Lake hike, it was wind and fire that destroyed thousands of acres in the Zirkels. In 1997, a 120-mph microburst of wind knocked down 20,000 acres of trees here. The Burn Ridge and Hinman Fires in 2002 destroyed another 30,000 acres.

Yet, the forest keeps coming back, as you'll see in the following pages and on your upcoming hikes.

Creeks in the Zirkels flow clean and clear by midsummer but may be
a raging mess early in the spring!

1 NORTH LAKE TRAIL

North Lake Trail into the Zirkel Wilderness is an eerie trip into an incredibly resilient forest. You'll see thousands of acres of spruce destroyed by spruce beetle in the 1940s, and thousands more literally knocked over in the Routt Divide Blowdown of 1997—a microburst that produced 120-mph winds. The Burn Ridge and Hinman Fires in 2002 destroyed 30,000 acres around here. The Wolverine Fire, ignited by lightning in 2005, burned another 460 acres. You'll see all this, but you'll also see the rebirth of a forest, with wildflowers galore and emerald green grasses, as well as deer, elk, moose, marmots, and bighorn sheep.

Start: From North Lake Trailhead (FS Trail #1164)
Elevation gain: 8,455 feet to 10,373 feet (1,918 feet)
Distance: 8.0 miles out and back
Difficulty: Moderate to strenuous
Hiking time: 5+ hours
Seasons/schedule: June to Sept
Fees and permits: None
Trail contacts: USFS Hahns Peak/ Bears Ears Ranger District, 925 Weiss Dr., Steamboat Springs, CO 80487-9315; (970) 870-2299; www.fs.usda .gov/mbr
Canine compatibility: Dogs permitted under voice command (it is unlawful for pets to chase wildlife!)
Trail surface: Dirt and rock backcountry trail with lots of deadfall
Land status: Routt National Forest

Nearest towns: Clark, Steamboat Springs
Other trail users: Some horseback use
Nat Geo TOPO! map (USGS): Mt. Zirkel, CO
National Geographic Trails Illustrated map: #116, Hahns Peak/Steamboat Lake, #117, Clark/Buffalo Pass
Other maps: Routt National Forest Service map
Special considerations: Standing dead trees (snags) and live trees may fall at any time. Use caution and pay attention to weather forecasts for high wind. Locate campsites away from all snags.
Other: You have to stop at the Clark Store for ice cream after this trip. It's a must!

FINDING THE TRAILHEAD

From Steamboat Springs, take US 40 west and turn right (north) onto CR 129, the Elk River Road. Travel north 18 miles to the Seedhouse Road (FR 400/CR 64) and turn right. It's just past Clark, CO and historic Glen Eden Resort. Drive 10 miles and turn right onto FR 443 (North Lake Road). Continue 1.4 miles past Three Island Lake Trailhead (Hike 2) to the end of the road at North Lake Trailhead (FS Trail #1164).
Trailhead GPS: N40 45.2140' / W106 43.9527'

THE HIKE

From the spruce beetle to fire to massive blowdowns to acid rain, this forest has seen its problems. But it is resilient and is attempting a comeback after decades of hardship. The spruce beetle began devastating this area as far back as the early 1940s. With all the dead standing spruce, it was ripe for fire, but it was a gale-force wind that brought it to its knees in 1997. That's when 120-mph winds blew in from the east, "spun off the backside of a massive low-pressure system that was blanketing the plains in snow, crested the Continental Divide, then knocked over trees like dominoes," according to the *High Country News*. About 20,000 acres of trees were knocked down.

Then, it was fire's turn. The Burn Ridge, Hinman and Wolverine Fires all took their turn at roughing up this forest. Yet, the wilderness remains. While regrowth may take a hundred years or more, it's on its way.

Acid rain along the Continental Divide remains a major issue for this and all watersheds in Colorado, and research continues on this important topic.

This trail begins at the end of FR 443, the North Lake Road. It heads south from the parking lot and within three-tenths of a mile, you'll find your first set of major switchbacks that lead you into the wilderness. The North Lake Trail, like most trails in the Zirkels, begins with a steep climb to the rim, beyond which lies its treasure trove of glacial lakes, snowfields, rockslides, and snowmelt springs. In fact, many rock glaciers here may have been active during the Little Ice Age (roughly AD 1300–1850).

Rock glaciers are distinctive topographic landforms. Some develop from the melting of an ice glacier that was covered by a landslide, an ice glacier that encountered a mass of rock debris blocking its valley, or simply the rock debris left from a retreating ice glacier. You can actually see them here in the Zirkels.

North Lake, situated at 10,373 feet in elevation, is loaded with wild fighting brook trout.

Horseback riders

By the time you reach the first mile, you'll have climbed 1,200 feet to where the trail levels off—briefly—and a plethora of wildflowers will line your path. Your climb continues, leading in a more easterly direction now. In 2 miles, you can look through the dead trees to your right for a view of the Dome, an 11,739-feet rocky peak that dominates views to the south.

At 3.4 miles, you'll cross a tributary to the South Fork of the Elk River. This may be difficult in June because of spring runoff. By mid-July, however, there are numerous logs both up- and downstream where you may safely ford the creek without getting too wet. You want dry feet because in another 0.1 mile, you'll head up another steep set of switchbacks before reaching the Wolverine Basin Cutoff, a barely visible unmarked trail to your right (south). The trail levels off now for the next 0.2 mile to the shores of North Lake.

This 5.5-acre brook trout lake provides numerous good, dispersed camping spots for those who backpacked. Just remember, no camping or campfires within ¼ mile of the lake, stream, or trail here.

You could continue on this trail for another 7 miles to the Wyoming Trail, which follows the Continental Divide from here to Buffalo Pass, but our track ends here. We needed to rest up for our next hike.

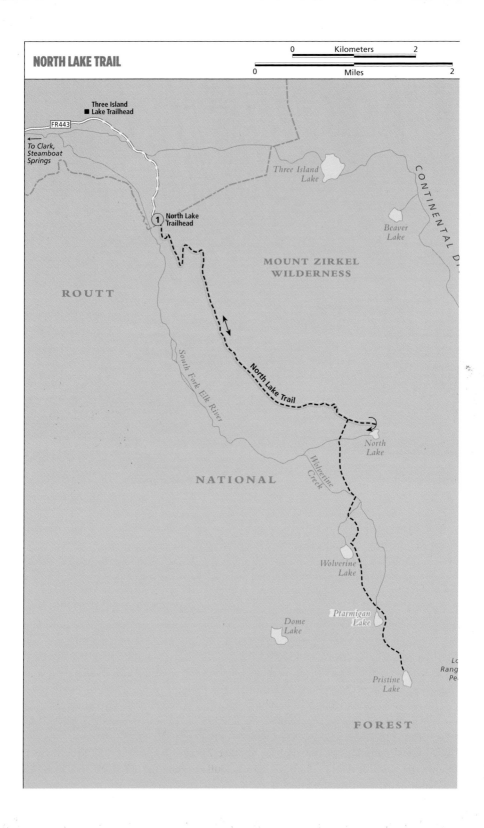

NORTH LAKE TRAIL

0 Kilometers 2
0 Miles 2

Three Island
Lake Trailhead

FR443

To Clark,
Steamboat
Springs

North Lake
Trailhead

1

Three Island
Lake

CONTINENTAL DI

Beaver
Lake

MOUNT ZIRKEL
WILDERNESS

ROUTT

South Fork Elk River

North Lake Trail

North
Lake

NATIONAL

Wolverine Creek

Wolverine
Lake

Ptarmigan
Lake

Dome
Lake

Lo
Rang
Pe

Pristine
Lake

FOREST

MILES AND DIRECTIONS

0.0 Start from North Lake Trailhead (FS #1164).

0.3 Hit the switchbacks.

0.9 Trail levels off briefly—take a breather.

1.0 The trail climbs a little more gently—for about 30 yards!

2.0 Trail levels and you can see the Dome.

3.4 Cross a tributary to the South Fork of the Elk River.

3.5 The trail hits another set of switchbacks and climbs again.

3.8 Pass the barely visible Wolverine Basin cutoff. **N40 43.5296' / W106 41.7675'**

4.0 Arrive at North Lake. **N40 43.4730' / W106 41.4551'**

8.0 After backtracking, arrive back at the trailhead.

SPRUCE BEETLES AND PINE BEETLES— BOTH DEADLY INFESTATIONS!

Forests throughout the Rocky Mountain region are currently suffering from both pine beetle and spruce beetle infestations.

Though spruce beetles and pine beetles are related, the two insects mostly attack only the type of trees they are named for. Both kill trees by destroying the thin layer of tissue below the bark that transports nutrients.

Beetle outbreaks are natural occurrences and the trees and beetles have evolved together over millions of years. However, researchers believe a combination of drought, warmer winters, high-wind events and large amounts of older trees growing close together have intensified the beetle outbreaks throughout the Rockies, from Canada to Mexico.

By 2014 in Colorado, it appeared spruce beetles were killing more spruce while pine beetles were killing fewer pine, perhaps because the pine beetle is running out of live trees to infest.

The greatest problems with spruce beetles continue to occur in southwest Colorado's San Juan Mountains, while major pine beetle infestations have occurred in northern Colorado on both sides of the Continental Divide.

Between 1996 and 2014, the mountain pine beetle outbreak had affected about 5,300 square miles in Colorado, Forest Service officials say. (By comparison, the entire state of Connecticut is 5,543 square miles.)

The total area affected in Colorado by the spruce beetle during that same time had increased to 2,200 square miles (about the size of West Virginia).

Is there anything that can be done to stop these infestations? While numerous treatments have been tried for years—from massive timber operations to chemical treatments—nothing has worked effectively. "Nature will run its course," according to researchers.

New forests will develop and grow. New stands of aspen will fill in for old stands of pine or spruce. Those aspen stands, in turn, will grow, and then die before new spruce or pine forests regenerate. This process will take decades, perhaps centuries.

More reading:
https://www.fs.usda.gov/Internet/FSE_DOCUMENTS/stelprdb5340736.pdf

http://www.summitdaily.com/news/15037891-113/in-colorado-spruce-bug-epidemic-eclipses-mountain-pine-beetle-blight

2 THREE ISLAND LAKE

A trek into the Zirkel Wilderness Area takes hikers back in time, both geologically and historically. Geologically speaking, this wilderness includes 36 miles of the Continental Divide. Its numerous lakes owe their existence to Pleistocene glaciation 15,000 years ago. Historically, the Zirkel Wilderness is one of the five original Colorado wilderness areas designated by the 1964 Wilderness Act. This short trail presents all the normal challenges of hiking into this wilderness—in other words, hiking along these glaciated valleys is easy, but routes into them may be a bit more difficult.

Start: From Upper Three Island Lake Trailhead #1163

Elevation gain: 8,422–9,906 feet (1,484 feet)

Distance: 6.0 miles out and back

Difficulty: Moderate to strenuous due to relatively steep climb entering the wilderness

Hiking time: 1.5–2.5 hours each way

Seasons/schedule: Late spring, summer, early fall

Fees and permits: None

Trail contacts: USFS Hahns Peak/Bears Ears Ranger District, 925 Weiss Dr., Steamboat Springs, CO 80487-9315; (970) 870-2299; www.fs.usda.gov/mbr

Canine compatibility: Yes, however dogs must be under control at all times

Trail surface: Backcountry singletrack dirt and rock path

Land status: USFS, Routt National Forest (Zirkel Wilderness Area)

Nearest towns: Clark, Steamboat Springs

Other trail users: Anglers and horseback riders; hunters during fall big game hunting seasons

Nat Geo TOPO! maps: Mt. Zirkel, CO

National Geographic Trails Illustrated map: #116

Other maps: Routt National Forest Service map

Special considerations: Because of all the lakes in this area, mosquitoes can be nasty during the summer. Be prepared. Also, plan on hiking early in the day. Afternoon thundershowers can dampen your parade—and it's very dangerous on these ridges in a storm.

Other: Three organizations of note in this area: Friends of Wilderness, PO Box 771318, Steamboat Springs, CO 80477, www.friendsofwilderness.com; Hahns Peak Area Historical Society, www.hahnspeakhistoric.com; and, Yampatika, a nonprofit environmental education organization with the mission to inspire environmental stewardship through education, www.yampatika.org.

FINDING THE TRAILHEAD

From Steamboat Springs, take US 40 (Lincoln Avenue) northwest. Turn right (north) on the Elk River Road, Routt CR 129. Travel 18 miles to the Clark General Store. This is your last chance to purchase forgotten hiking/camping items. Continue on CR 129 for another 0.8 mile past the store, and then turn right (east) onto Seedhouse Road/Routt CR 64. This becomes FSR 400. Continue 8.5 miles and follow the signs to Seedhouse Campground. In 0.7 mile, turn right onto FR 443 and continue another 3.2 miles to the trailhead. You'll pass a lower trailhead for Three Island Lake Trail in 1.2 miles from Seedhouse Campground but continue another

2 miles to the main (upper) trailhead on the north side of the road near the Forest Service information kiosk.

Trailhead GPS: N40 45.9919' / W106 44.7285'

THE HIKE

The Three Island Lake Trail is an excellent introductory hike into the famous Zirkel Wilderness. It climbs immediately through a beautiful aspen grove, then in and out of dark timber and aspen, with magnificent wildflowers showing their colors throughout the summer months.

Generally following the north fork of Three Island Creek, it climbs to a switchback, then climbs to another switchback, then climbs again, from an elevation of 8,422 feet at the trailhead to a peak elevation of 9,906 feet. This type of ascent is quite common in the Zirkel as it's difficult to enter these long, glaciated valleys. Once you have entered, however, travel is much less strenuous.

It's easy to spot the reddish-brown summer pelage of mule deer along this trail as they browse at dawn and dusk, mainly on shrubs. Mule deer in Colorado molt twice a year. While their summer coats are reddish-brown, their winter coats are dull gray. And, while their eyesight is good, deer rely on their large ears for defense. They can pick up far-off sounds, and a quick, elusive gait allows them to avoid danger.

Three tiny islands dot this picturesque lake high in the Zirkel Wilderness north of Steamboat Springs.

Chest-high thimbleberry, *Rubus parviflorus*, lines the trail to Three Island Lake.

A backpacker stops to admire one of the tremendous granite outcroppings found here that was thrust upward beneath sedimentary shales and limestones that have long since eroded from the surrounding peaks more than 15,000 years ago.

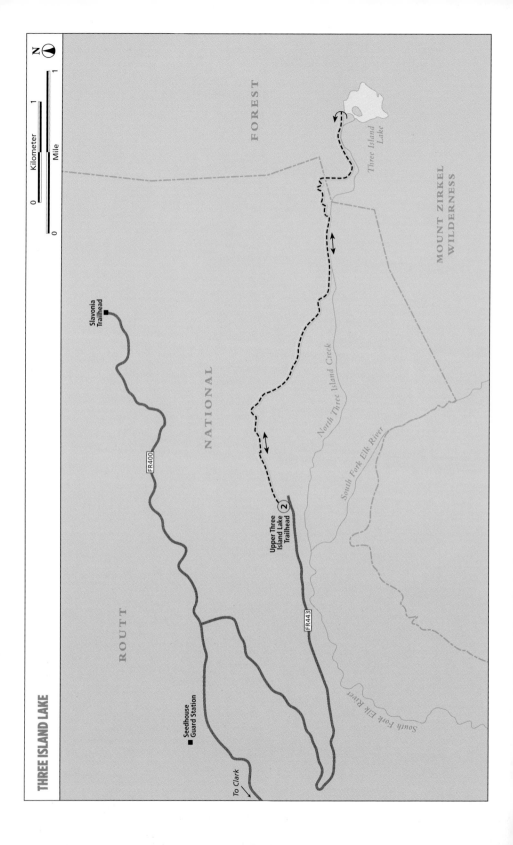

THREE ISLAND LAKE

Seedhouse
Guard Station

To Clark

ROUTT

FR400

Slavonia
Trailhead

NATIONAL

FOREST

Upper Three
Island Lake
Trailhead ②

FR443

North Three Island Creek

South Fork Elk River

South Fork Elk River

MOUNT ZIRKEL
WILDERNESS

Three Island
Lake

N

Kilometer

0   1

0   1
Mile

Elk are numerous in this area, but much more difficult to find, and bighorn sheep also roam the rocky cliffs of the Park Range looming over the wilderness.

The creek flowing out of Three Island Lake provides a hypnotic sound in the quiet of the wilderness. While small, it is very fast moving and narrow in places, with numerous short waterfalls beneath which lie pockets and pools where big game animals can water, and where small brook trout can congregate and eat without being swept away in the current. This creek flows into the North Fork of the Elk River about a mile southeast of the Three Island Lake trailhead.

This trail receives much less pressure than the more famous Gilpin/Gold Creek loop trail just to the north, even though this trail is much shorter. In the summertime, it may see twenty to thirty hikers on the weekends, fewer during the week.

Three Island Lake (yes, there are three tiny islands) is a wonderful lake to backpack into, as most visitors here are day-hikers or anglers. Remember, though, that once you arrive at the lake, you must backtrack for a quarter-mile—or continue past the lake for a quarter-mile—in order to camp. That's one of the special regulations that govern this area. In most wilderness areas, there's a 100-foot camping limit from any water or trail.

The Colorado Division of Parks and Wildlife stocks native cutthroat trout fingerlings in this and many other lakes in the Zirkels from an airplane every third or fourth year. Nonetheless, the bulk of the fish population in the lake and stream are wild, feisty brook trout.

MILES AND DIRECTIONS

0.0   Start at the Three Island Lake Trailhead across the road from the parking pull-out, 20 feet east of the Forest Service information kiosk (elevation 8,422 feet).

0.5   Reach the first of many switchbacks.

0.8   Cross seep and continue through aspen grove.

0.9   Cross creek and continue east.

1.1   Scenic overlook.

1.3   Trail leads back into the dark timber.

1.6   Another switchback; get used to them.

1.7   Trail now meanders next to Three Island Creek.

2.1   Trail switches back and away from the creek.

2.4   Trail wanders back toward the creek.

2.5   Zirkel Wilderness Area boundary.

3.0   Arrive at lake (backtrack 0.25 mile if you plan on camping overnight!).
      N40 45.7229' / W106 41.9925'

6.0   After backtracking, arrive back at the trailhead.

3 MICA BASIN

According to *The Historical Guide to Routt County*, gold prospector Robert McIntosh named Big Agnes Mountain in 1875—but it doesn't say who Agnes was. Mica Basin lies between Big Agnes and Little Agnes Mountains, in one of the prettiest cirques in this entire wilderness area, so I'm guessing Agnes must have been fairly special to old Robert McIntosh. Yet, while they're beautiful, these are rugged and rocky peaks with a range called "Sawtooth" between them, so I don't know. You'll have to decide for yourself about Agnes, but Robert sure found a gorgeous place to prospect for gold.

Start: Mica Basin Trailhead (FS Trail #1162)
Elevation gain: 8,359–10,459 feet (2,100 feet)
Distance: 8.6 miles out and back
Difficulty: Moderate to strenuous due to length and elevation gain
Hiking time: +/- 6 hours
Seasons/schedule: June to Sept—possibly later depending on the snow
Fees and permits: None
Trail contacts: USFS Hahns Peak/Bears Ears Ranger District, 925 Weiss Dr., Steamboat Springs, CO 80487-9315; (970) 870-2299; www.fs.usda.gov/mbr
Canine compatibility: Dogs permitted under voice command or on a leash (it is unlawful for pets to chase wildlife!)
Trail surface: Dirt and rock backcountry trail with some deadfall
Land status: Routt National Forest, Zirkel Wilderness
Nearest town: Clark, Steamboat Springs
Other trail users: Some horseback use
Nat Geo TOPO! map (USGS): Mt. Zirkel, CO

National Geographic Trails Illustrated map: #116
Other maps: Routt National Forest Service map
Special considerations: Because of all the lakes in this area, mosquitoes can be nasty during the summer. Be prepared. Also, plan on hiking early in the day. Afternoon thundershowers can dampen your parade—and it's very dangerous on these ridges in a storm.
Other: Friends of Wilderness is an all-volunteer not-for-profit organization that assists the USFS in managing and protecting wilderness areas in the Routt National Forest and parts of the White River National Forest. That's their sole purpose. In conjunction with the Forest Service, they recruit, train, equip, and field volunteers to serve as rangers and trail crew to educate the public and provide other appropriate support to help manage these wilderness areas, which are popular and heavily used. Want to volunteer? Go to www.friendsofwilderness.com.

FINDING THE TRAILHEAD

From Steamboat Springs, take US 40 west and turn right (north) onto CR 129, the Elk River Road. Travel north 18 miles to the Seedhouse Road (FR 400/CR 64) and turn right. It's just past Clark and historic Glen Eden Resort. There are private residences for the first few miles. Watch your speed for loose dogs and children. At 5.7 miles, the pavement ends and the road becomes FR 400. Continue for another 6.3 miles to the end of the road at the Slavonia Trailhead parking area.
Trailhead GPS: N40 46.9927' / W106 43.3716'

Boulders of metamorphic rock along the trail

THE HIKE

Seeing the reflection of Little Agnes and the Sawtooth Range in the glassy waters of Mica Lake makes this trip worth it all by itself. Nestled in a basin with the 11,233-foot Little Agnes to the west and northwest, the Sawtooth Range looming to the north, and the 12,059-foot Big Agnes Mountain to the northeast and east, this trail is also less traveled than the popular Gilpin Lake–Gold Creek loop, although they share the trailhead and parking area, and follow the Gilpin Trail into the wilderness area.

You'll begin your hike from the Slovania trailhead on Gilpin Trail #1161, heading up through a lovely aspen forest with mixed Engelmann spruce, subalpine fir, and lodgepole pine. There are also some healthy 12- to 14-foot-tall willows here.

In a tenth of a mile, you'll come to the Wilderness sign-in. Gold Creek Trail #1150 leads to the right here, while Gilpin Trail #1161 goes to the left. Go left and at 0.3 mile, the trail opens to the first of many scenic mountain meadows while continuing its steady ascent north and east.

At 0.7 mile, you'll cross a small creek. Stay left here following the main trail. At 0.9 mile, you'll cross another tributary and at the 1-mile mark, you'll discover an opening where you can see the water in Gilpin Creek carving its own canyon straight down to your right. To the left, you can now clearly see the ragged edge of the Zirkels as you head for the gap, or low spot in these rugged hills.

You'll reach the Zirkel Wilderness boundary in 1.4 miles and in another 0.1 mile, you'll come to Mica Basin Trail #1162. Turn left (north) on the Mica Basin Trail. The Gilpin Trail continues to the right (northeast).

As you continue to gain altitude, you'll soon come to a delightful cascading Mica Creek as it slices through the rocky upheaval of an uplift you're about to climb. By the 2.2-mile mark, you'll be huffing and puffing up a 16 percent grade. It's worth it, though, as you'll catch another nice view of the cascading creek to your right at the 2.6-mile mark. You'll then hike between two colorful, rocky knolls before the trail finally levels off, if only for a short distance.

You're now at 9,784 feet (you've gained 1,425 feet from the trailhead by now) and you'll soon cross Mica Creek and hike through a marshy willow-filled meadow as the trail remains somewhat level for the next 0.4 mile. It then travels up and through intricate rock and wildflower-strewn saddles in the landscape twice more before you reach the 4-mile mark. One final climb, and you can take a breather for the last short stretch to the lake, at 4.3 miles.

It's time to gawk, stare, gaze, contemplate, observe . . . whatever. It's time!

MILES AND DIRECTIONS

0.0   Start from Slovania Trailhead to the right of the kiosk.

0.1   Wilderness boundary sign-in; go left on Gilpin Trail #1161.

0.3   Trail leads to an open meadow.

0.4   Cruise on a more gradual grade.

0.7   Cross the creek and head to the left following the main trail.

0.9   The trail swings to the right, crosses another tributary, then winds back to the left.

The "Sawtooth" between Little Agnes and Big Agnes

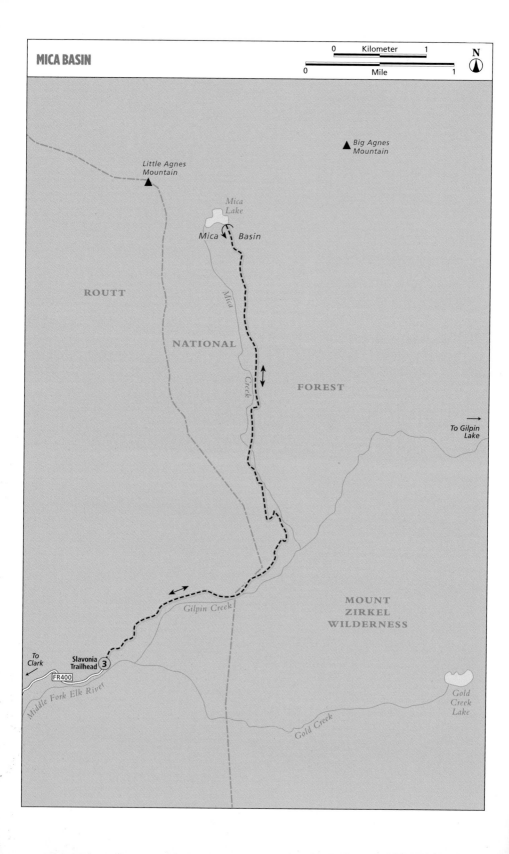

MICA BASIN

0 Kilometer 1
0 Mile 1

N

Big Agnes
Mountain

Little Agnes
Mountain

Mica
Lake

Mica   Basin

ROUTT

Mica

Creek

NATIONAL

FOREST

To Gilpin
Lake

MOUNT
ZIRKEL
WILDERNESS

Gilpin Creek

To
Clark

Slavonia
Trailhead 3

FR400

Middle Fork Elk River

Gold Creek

Gold
Creek
Lake

1.0 Pop into an opening with views of Gilpin Creek cutting into its canyon down to your right.

1.4 Reach the wilderness boundary.

1.5 The trails split; go left (north) on Mica Basin Trail #1162.

1.7 Mica Creek flows into Gilpin Creek below you and to your right.

1.8 Waters cascade down Mica Creek; there's a big switchback coming.

2.3 Prepare for another set of switchbacks.

2.6 Photo op! Nice view of the cascading creek.

2.7 Cross the creek and hike through a marshy, willow-filled meadow.

3.2 The trail climbs again next to the stream, then up the next rise.

3.6 10,087 feet, and the trail levels out a bit.

4.0 A last little climb to 10,459 feet before the trail descends to the lake.

4.3 Arrive at Mica Lake at 10,428 feet in elevation. It's OK to stare! This is your turn-around point.

8.6 Arrive back at the trailhead.

DINOSAUR NATIONAL MONUMENT AND BROWNS PARK

Old homestead on Beaver Creek

The ancestral Upper Green River once flowed east to the North Platte River in what is now southeast Wyoming. During the Tertiary Period—66.4 million years ago to 2 million years ago—erosion of the lower Green River combined with the uplift of the Rocky Mountains and caused this drainage to flow southward, as it does today.

Uniquely, three physiographic regions, the Colorado Plateau, the middle Rocky Mountains, and the Wyoming basin all meet here. The movement of the river, combined with the influences of the physiographic region known as the Great Basin, just to the west, greatly enhanced the biological diversity of the park's ecosystem.

Earl Douglass, a paleontologist with the Carnegie Museum of Natural History, discovered a massive dinosaur fossil bed near Jensen, Utah, in 1909. President Woodrow Wilson declared the original 80-acre tract surrounding the dinosaur quarry in Utah a national monument on October 4, 1915. That was expanded to 210,000 acres in Utah and Colorado in 1938, to encompass the spectacular canyons of the Green and Yampa Rivers.

Typical of high deserts, summer temperatures can be extremely hot while winter temperatures can be very cold. Rainfall rarely exceeds 10 inches per year.

All the while, the Green and Yampa Rivers continue to knife their way through twenty-three colorful rock layers that exist on the Colorado Plateau. Their grinding and cutting and scouring has exposed sheer cliffs and steep canyons that create habitats for a startling diversity of plant and animal life.

4 HARPERS CORNER TRAIL

Dinosaur National Monument is spread across 210,000 acres along the Colorado/Utah border. The Colorado side is known for spectacular canyon country while the famous Dinosaur Quarry and Visitor Center resides in Utah. The Harpers Corner Road begins in Colorado and swings into Utah, then back into Colorado along a 32-mile scenic drive that includes overlooks of the Yampa and Green Rivers. The short Harpers Corner Trail at road's end offers great photographic opportunities of the Green and Yampa Rivers flowing toward Steamboat Rock where they converge into a much larger Green River that flows downstream into Whirlpool Canyon. (That is, if the weather cooperates! Even on a rainy, snowy, cloudy sort of day, though, the photo opportunities are still there.)

Start: From the end of Harpers Corner Road, 32 miles north of the Canyon Visitor Center
Elevation loss: 7,582 feet at trailhead; 7,493 feet at trail's end
Distance: 2.0 miles out and back
Difficulty: Easy to moderate
Hiking time: 1–2 hours
Seasons/schedule: Apr to Oct, but best in spring and fall. The monument is open 24 hours per day, all year, but some roads and facilities are closed during the winter months. In Colorado, the Canyon Visitor Center, 2 miles east of Dinosaur, CO, is open weekends in Apr and early May, and remains open daily from mid-May to early Oct (depending on weather and road conditions.) The Harpers Corner Road is closed to traffic in the winter, but it is open to cross-country skiing. It is plowed and opened as early as possible, usually in mid- to late Mar.
Fees and permits: $25 per private vehicle and motorcycle, $10 per person (bicycle or walk-in) for a seven-day pass; $45 for a Dinosaur National Monument annual pass; or, $80 for an annual Interagency Pass (good nationwide); free annual pass for all active-duty military personnel and dependents (with appropriate ID).
Trail contacts: Dinosaur National Monument, 4545 E Hwy. 40, Dinosaur, CO 81610, (435) 781-7700 (phone manned only in summer); www.nps.gov/dino/contacts.htm
Canine compatibility: Dogs are not permitted on this trail or in the monument's backcountry (see sidebar)
Trail surface: Rock and dirt path, easy to follow
Land status: National Park Service, Dinosaur National Monument
Nearest towns: Dinosaur, CO, Jensen, UT
Other trail users: None
Nat Geo TOPO! map (USGS): Jones Hole, UT
National Geographic Trails Illustrated map: #220, Dinosaur National Monument
Other maps: Dinosaur National Monument map; Map MRC: 40109E1; Canyon of Lodore South, Map MRC: 40108E8
Special considerations: Be prepared for desert hiking: Take a hat, sunscreen, and water—a minimum of 2 quarts of water per person is recommended in the summer; let someone know where you are going and when you are due back; wear comfortable shoes. Open-toed shoes are not recommended; use caution near cliffs and keep a close eye on small children; watch for thunderstorms during the summer afternoons.

FINDING THE TRAILHEAD

From Rangely, go west on CO 64 for 18 miles to Dinosaur. Turn right (east) onto E. Brontosaurus Blvd./US 40. In 1.9 miles, turn left at the Dinosaur National Monument sign and the Canyon Visitor Center. This is the Harpers Corner Road. Continue past the Visitor Center for 32 miles to the end of the road and the trailhead. (Watch your speed on this paved but sometimes rough 45 mph road. You don't want to miss the elk, golden eagles, red-tailed hawks, or sudden curves in the road.)

Trailhead GPS: N40 31.4432' / W109 01.1792'

THE HIKE

You may have noticed the residents of Dinosaur are pretty proud of their dinosaurs, with streets named Tyrannosaurus Trail and Allosaurus Lane. And then, there are those huge painted dinosaurs placed strategically through town.

If you're looking for real dinosaur bones, however, you need to drive over to the Utah side of the national monument outside Vernal, Utah. If you want to see some spectacular scenery, this drive and this hike is the place to be.

The drive to the trailhead winds along a shallow ravine, then crosses a grassy plain before climbing to the top of a plateau. In about 4 miles, you'll find the shelters for Plug Hat Rock picnic area. Here, you'll find great views of the west rim of the plateau and the wooded canyons toward Jensen and the Green River. The road takes you out of the national monument and into Utah before heading back east. Soon, you'll catch more great views of the expansive wilderness leading east toward the Yampa Bench, Yampa River Canyon, and Cross and Diamond Mountains. The drive only gets better as the road reenters Colorado and Dinosaur National Monument, leading to the trailhead.

This short, well-marked trail begins at the northeast end of a large parking area with vault toilets and picnic tables. It descends a short distance to a sharp switchback to the left. This turn is marked with a self-guided tour post labeled #1. (Toss a dollar into the trailhead stand and fish out a full-color trail guide keyed to sixteen numbered points of interest along the trail. It's very informative!)

A couple more quick, short switchbacks follow this first one before the trail becomes fairly level, with a few moderate ups and downs.

The trail winds along the top of a ridgeline high above a tremendous oxbow bend on the Green River, to your left and downstream from the confluence of the Yampa and Green Rivers. To your right, you'll see the long draw of Echo Park stretch out to the northeast. It's there where the two great rivers converge.

In a half-mile, the trail splits briefly. If you follow the left-hand trail, you'll be rewarded by spectacular views of Whirlpool Canyon downstream. Even on a cloudy day, you can see well into Utah. In less than a hundred yards, the trails converge as it continues to its terminus.

The Green River continues its course downstream and west toward Utah.

Notice the hard granite cut with rocks from the Bishop Conglomerate at the end of this trail. You stand on fossils of ocean life that now rest 2,500 feet—762 meters—above the river. Here, at the end of the trail, you'll find sweeping views of the river canyons. To your right, the Green River rushes down from the northwest and Wyoming while the muddy Yampa flows into Echo Park from due east, originating along the Continental Divide above Steamboat Springs, Colorado.

Although you can't see it, the Green cuts south and converges with the Yampa behind Steamboat Rock, that large rock formation you see directly before you to the east. What you see in the foreground is the now enlarged Green as it winds around Steamboat Rock from Echo Park. Odds are the Yampa, coming in from the east, and the Green, from the northeast, will eventually erode Steamboat Rock—but not in our lifetimes.

A great conservation struggle occurred here in the 1950s when a proposal to construct a dam in Echo Park was defeated, thus saving the Yampa as the only naturally flowing river in the entire Colorado River system. A dam was built instead upriver on the Green River, at Flaming Gorge, in 1964.

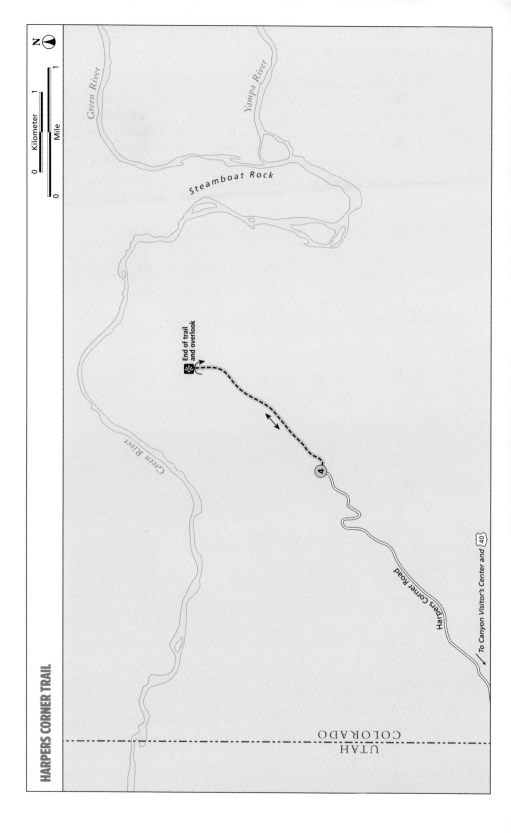

HARPERS CORNER TRAIL

Green River

Yampa River

Steamboat Rock

Green River

End of trail
and overlook

④

Harpers Corner Road

To Canyon Visitor's Center and ⑳40

UTAH
COLORADO

N

0 Kilometer 1

0 Mile 1

MILES AND DIRECTIONS

0.0   Start at Harpers Corner Trailhead.

0.1   Trail marker #2 marks an ancient pinyon tree, and a few feet farther, trail marker #3 stands before an ancient juniper.

0.5   The trail splits briefly. Go to the left, following the arrow on the trail marker, for views downstream of the Green River, looking west toward Utah.

0.6   A bench near viewpoint #8 looks back toward the southeast and Echo Park.

1.0   **N40 32.0686' / W109 00.4782'** Trail ends at an expansive guardrail overlooking the Green River. Views to the west display the Green River downstream; views to the east show the Green River winding its way around Steamboat Rock.

2.0   Arrive back at your vehicle.

WATCH YOUR PET!

While your pet is welcome in the monument, pets are not allowed on most trails, in the monument's backcountry, or in public buildings. Due to the hot summer temperatures, do not leave pets in a vehicle for any amount of time.

5 BROWNS PARK NATIONAL WILDLIFE REFUGE

Hiking is permitted throughout the 12,150-acre Browns Park National Wildlife Refuge. The 1.2-mile trail described here leads from the refuge office along Beaver Creek to a historic homesteader cabin. It's well worth stretching your legs after the long drive. And, since you've come this far, you are encouraged to explore Browns Park on your own—on foot. Anywhere. Meander at will. This area became part of our National Wildlife Refuge System in 1965 "to provide sanctuary for migratory birds, conserve endangered and threatened species, and offer wildlife-dependent recreational opportunities." Enjoy it, but please avoid disturbing animals by getting too close.

Start: From Beaver Creek Trailhead at the Browns Park Refuge Office and Visitor Center
Elevation: 5,464 feet
Distance: 1.2-mile lollipop loop
Difficulty: Easy
Hiking time: About 40 minutes
Seasons/schedule: Year-round, but best from Apr to Nov
Fees and permits: None
Trail contacts: Browns Park National Wildlife Refuge, 1318 Hwy. 318, Maybell, CO 81640, (970) 365-3613; www.fws.gov/refuge/browns_park
Canine compatibility: Dogs permitted, on leash
Trail surface: Wide grass and dirt path
Land status: US Fish and Wildlife Service
Nearest towns: Maybell, Craig, CO; Dutch John, UT
Other trail users: Mule deer, magpies, beaver, elk, moose

Nat Geo TOPO! map (USGS): Lodore School, CO
Other maps: Bureau of Land Management (BLM) Canyon of Lodore 1:100,000 quad
Special considerations: Because of the remoteness of the refuge, visitors should bring sufficient water, food, and fuel for their visit. Visitor services are not available nearby. Cellphone coverage is sporadic at best in this area and should not be counted on in an emergency. Notify a friend or family member of your location in case you need to be contacted in an emergency.
Other: This area is listed as "Family Friendly." That's true, but it's a LONG DRIVE FROM ANYWHERE to get here, so be prepared! Also, don't forget your binoculars and camera and remember: Take only pictures, leave only footprints!

FINDING THE TRAILHEAD

From Craig, travel west for 31 miles on US 40 to Maybell. Turn right CO 318 and continue another 60 miles to the Browns Park National Wildlife Refuge headquarters, approximately 1 mile east of the Colorado and Utah border.
Trailhead GPS: N40 51.7663' / W109 01.3393'

THE HIKE

On the drive into this unique 12,000-acre "park," you're sure to see elk, pronghorn antelope, and mule deer. If you look up, you'll likely see turkey vultures, golden eagles, and osprey. And that's if you're not paying attention.

A visit to the Browns Park National Wildlife Refuge in the very northwest corner of Colorado is a trip back into time.

Prehistoric people were present here from 8,000 to 10,000 years ago, probably chasing big game. About 3,500 years ago, prehistoric farmers grew corn here.

Native American tribes inhabited the area for at least 1,000 years. In 1832, Fort Davy Crockett was established and began trading with the tribes who once roamed this region. During the height of the fur trading business in the Rocky Mountains, this was the location—back then known as Brown's Hole—of some of the greatest mountain man rendezvous ever held. Soon thereafter, the area was settled by ranchers and frequented by outlaws like Butch Cassidy.

Historically, waterfowl were given "management priority" here, and within a hundred yards of the Beaver Creek Trailhead, you have probably already kicked up a few mallard ducks.

Current management is now focused on maintaining the rich diversity of native wildlife habitats found in Browns Park. This has not only benefited waterfowl, but it's improved the flyway for all migrating birds and improved habitat for threatened and endangered species and species of special concern.

Within a few hundred yards of the trailhead as you approach an active beaver dam along this diminutive creek, notice the rich diversity of grasses and shrubs in this riparian zone—the green ribbon of life alongside a stream. Today, the refuge supports sixty-eight species of mammals, fifteen species of reptiles and amphibians, and at least 223 species of

A sweeping view of Browns Park

birds. In fact, birders from all over the world come here to view pied-billed grebes, lazuli buntings, Wilson's warblers, American bitterns, Bullock's orioles, and white-faced ibises.

As you can imagine, water is key to everything around here. In 0.3 mile, the trail splits. While you'll want to go right, notice how water is used to irrigate the meadow on your left (east) to maintain a vigorous stand of grasses and forbs for grassland-dependent species such as northern harriers and short-eared owls.

At times, irrigation is as necessary as fire to manage this habitat. That's because water development has altered this riparian zone tremendously over time. The building of Flaming Gorge Dam upstream in Utah was the largest environmental change that's occurred here in literally thousands of years (see "Before the Dam").

At 0.6 mile, you'll have reached an old settler's cabin, depicting a homestead from the mid-1800s. It was not an easy life, especially if you had to share your low-slung one-room family cabin with the likes of Butch Cassidy and his Wild Bunch, or the outlaw Tom Horn.

Once you've rounded the cabin, stay to the right until you reach the head of the lollipop loop you passed at 0.3 mile, and follow the main trail back to the trailhead. Then, hop in your vehicle and follow the signs to River's Edge Wildlife Drive. Here, you'll find numerous spots to pull off and take a hike. A few waypoints for stops are listed below in "Miles and Directions."

MILES AND DIRECTIONS

0.0 Start from Beaver Creek Trailhead at Refuge Office.

0.2 Cross a tiny footbridge along nature trail.

0.3 Cross another footbridge as the creek meanders to the south toward the Green River; a couple hundred feet past that, you'll reach a trail split. Take the trail leading to your right (west). There's an irrigated field on your left.

0.4 The nicely mowed trail turns to dirt going through the sagebrush.

0.5 A resting bench sits on an elbow in the creek and you'll soon come to an old set of corrals. The trail splits again. Stay right.

0.6 **N40 51.3141' / W109 01.3970'** Another bench sits in front of the corrals and cabin near a sign that reads: "Early homesteaders." The trail winds around this old homestead, then heads back up the irrigated field toward the ranger station.

0.7 You've circled the corral and homestead back to the irrigated field; now continue to the right (east) and complete the lollipop loop.

0.9 You're back on the main trail. **N40 51.5257' / W109 01.3797'**

1.2 Back to the trailhead. Now, hop in the vehicle and drive down the River's Edge Wildlife Drive for more meandering at the following waypoints:

#1 **N40 49.8376' / W109 01.7061'**

#2 **N40 49.6639' / W109 00.5457'**

#3 **N40 50.0958' / W108 59.1027'**

#4 **N40 50.1037' / W108 58.8872'**

#5 **N40 49.9601' / W108 58.0865'**

#6 **N40 49.4556' / W108 57.7635'**

#7 **N40 48.5747' / W108 55.3983'**

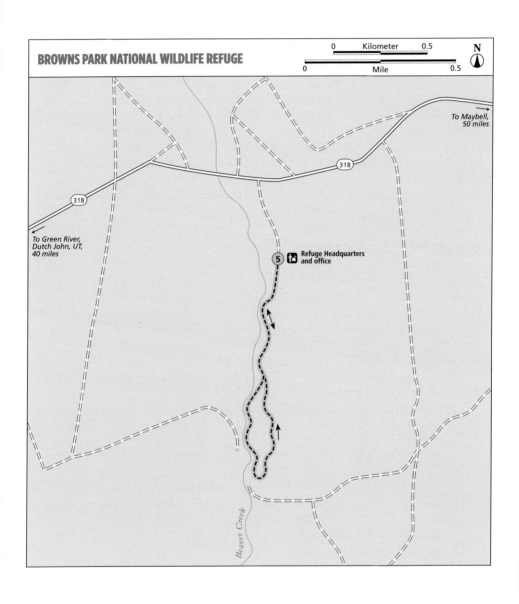

BROWNS PARK NATIONAL WILDLIFE REFUGE

Kilometer
0   0.5

Mile
0   0.5

N

318

To Maybell,
50 miles

318

To Green River,
Dutch John, UT,
40 miles

5 Refuge Headquarters
and office

Beaver Creek

BEFORE THE DAM

Before Flaming Gorge Dam and Reservoir were completed in 1965, the Green River's water levels responded only to Mother Nature and her constant floods and droughts. Flooding occurred in spring, with river flows reduced dramatically in late summer and fall. That spring flooding was the primary source of water for the natural wetlands bordering the river and the two creeks that flow into it at Browns Park—Beaver Creek and Vermillion Creek farther to the east.

Seasonal floods also created backwater ponds and natural nursery basins for the native fish that used to live in this rich riparian zone. Today, only four native species remain—the Colorado pikeminnow, humpback chub, bonytail chub, and razorback sucker. All four are on the endangered species list because flooding has been controlled, the waterway channelized, spawning migration runs have been blocked, and the water flowing from the bottom of Flaming Gorge Dam is too cold. In addition, there are now more than fifty non-native fish species that compete for food and space with the native fish.

Mule deer scurry across the area formerly known as Brown's Hole, where some of the greatest mountain man rendezvous ever were held in the late 1830s.

FLAT TOPS WILDERNESS

In 1919, the first full-time landscape architect for the USFS, Arthur Carhart, surveyed the area around Trappers Lake in the White River National Forest near Meeker, Colorado. He was supposed to plot several homesites on the shores of Trappers, the second-largest natural lake in the state.

After weeks of work, Carhart recommended that no development be permitted, insisting that the best use of the area was for wilderness recreation.

That idea—that unprecedented notion—eventually led to The Wilderness Act of 1964.

In 1920, the year following Carhart's suggestion that Trappers Lake remain primitive, the Forest Service designated Trappers Lake as an undeveloped, roadless area. In 1932, the Flat Tops Primitive Area was established.

Carhart went on to work with conservationist Aldo Leopold and lay the foundation of the modern wilderness. Finally, on September 3, 1964, 45 years after Carhart first conceived the idea, the US Congress created The Wilderness Act. You can read all about "The Cradle of Wilderness" at the end of Hike 7: Carhart Trail around Trappers Lake.

The 235,406-acre Flat Tops Wilderness was established on December 12, 1975, and is the second-largest wilderness area in Colorado. The Carhart Trail travels around the lake where it all began.

The historic Trappers Lake cabins have been used to store equipment for the native cutthroat trout spawn-taking operation and to house the crews manning the fish traps since 1914.

6 SLIDE MANDALL LAKE

The Flat Tops, a flattened dome of sedimentary rock capped with lava, form a series of flat-topped ridges and summits on the White River Plateau. There are more than 110 lakes on the Flat Tops with huge amphitheater-like rock escarpments surrounded by broad high-mountain parks and meadows.

Today, 160 miles of hiking trails cross this wilderness. Mandall Lakes Trail (FS #1121) is one of the lesser-used trails leading to Slide Mandall Lake, the destination of our hike, and continuing to Black Mandall Lake and Mandall Pass.

Start: From Mandall Lakes Trailhead (FS #1121) opposite the Bear Lake Campground
Elevation gain: 9,800–10,815 feet (1,015 feet)
Distance: 6.6 miles out and back
Difficulty: Moderate to strenuous
Hiking time: 3+ hours
Seasons/schedule: June to Oct
Fees and permits: None
Trail contacts: USFS, Yampa Ranger District, 300 Roselawn Ave., PO Box 7, Yampa, CO 80483, (970) 638-4516
Canine compatibility: Dogs permitted but must be under control at all times. It's illegal for dogs to chase wildlife.
Trail surface: Rough dirt and rock singletrack backcountry trail
Land status: USFS, Flat Tops Wilderness Area
Nearest town: Yampa
Other trail users: Some horseback use

Nat Geo TOPO! map (USGS): Orno Peak
National Geographic Trails Illustrated map: #150, Flat Tops North
Special considerations: Be prepared for mosquitoes!
Other: Find out what's local from the locals! Before you hit the trail, head to Montgomery's General Merchandise, 24 Main St., Yampa, CO 80483, (970) 638-4531, where you'll find information as well as groceries, clothing, sporting goods, and more. While you're at it, check out these fine organizations:
Friends of Wilderness: PO Box 771318, Steamboat Springs, CO 80477, www.friendsofwilderness.com;
Yampatika: a nonprofit environmental education organization with the mission to inspire environmental stewardship through education, www.yampatika.org.

FINDING THE TRAILHEAD

From Yampa, follow CR 7 west for 6.4 miles to FR 900. Continue on FR 900 for 5.6 miles to the trailhead. Park on the left-hand (south) side of the road. The trailhead is just across the road.
Trailhead GPS: N40 02.7586' / W107 04.5462'

THE HIKE

This hike begins with a lovely uphill trek through a quaking aspen forest before reaching the wilderness boundary in 1.3 miles. By then, you'll have already climbed from 9,800 feet to 10,073 feet in elevation—eventually reaching 10,815 feet by the time you reach Slide Mandall Lake in another 2 miles. Maybe that's why this is a little-used trail, although

the most heavily used trail on the east side of the Flat Tops, the Devil's Causeway, climbs even more in a shorter distance.

The difference is that the causeway itself is roughly 50 feet long and only 3 feet wide in some spots, with 60- to 80-foot cliffs on both sides and steep talus slopes dropping another 600–800 feet to the drainages below. So, people climb—or crawl—across that "land bridge" just for the thrill, then hustle back to Steamboat Springs to soak their nerves in the hot springs.

Devil's Causeway trailhead is only a few miles past the Mandall Lakes Trailhead, so this is a good place to stop. Let everyone else go to the causeway. You'll get plenty of exercise here, you'll see far fewer people, and because of that, you'll probably see more wildlife.

The parking area for this trailhead is on the north side of Bear Lake—also labeled Upper Stillwater (Yampa) Reservoir on the maps.

Park here and walk 40 paces across FSR 900 to a narrow path that leads into a shimmering aspen forest and begin to climb. (***Note:*** Parking may be limited on busy weekends, but most people are here to recreate on the lake and not hike up the trail. Additional parking is available at the Bear Lake day use area.)

In 0.6 mile, you'll reach the first of a series of switchbacks that will lead you to the wilderness boundary at the 1.3-mile mark. Designated a wilderness area in 1975 and nicknamed "The Cradle of Wilderness," the Flat Tops is the second-largest wilderness area in Colorado (see the sidebar for Hike 7: Carhart Trail).

At 1.6 miles, you'll reach 10,500 feet in elevation before giving it all back up as you drop into a long, broad mountain park full of grasses and wildflowers. You can hear the rush of water as you cross a small tributary flowing into Mandall Creek from the north.

Brook trout are abundant in Slide Mandall Lake.

At 2.1 miles, you'll cross Mandall Creek itself. This may be tricky early in the spring, but there are plenty of dead logs to cross over most of the hiking season (June to October).

In another 0.1 mile, you'll cross another creek that drops in from the southwest. It's coming from Mud Mandall and Twin Mandall Lakes, which lie in a small bench below Slide Mandall Lake.

By the time you reach the 3.1-mile mark, you'll be hiking up a 9–13 percent grade, eventually popping up to a beaver dam just below Slide Mandall Lake. Veer left above the top beaver dam before entering a boggy wet meadow. Watch for a Forest Service "no camping" sign that shows you're at your destination.

If you've got the time and stamina—and the weather holds—this trail continues to Black Mandall Lake and Mandall Pass. The last section up to Mandall Pass climbs 450 feet in 0.5 mile to the top of that 12,000-foot ridge above the lakes. The maintained trail ends here, but you can access Orno Peak to the east and the Devil's Causeway area to the southwest by navigating cross-country. A map and compass, and/or GPS coordinates are necessary to find either one.

MILES AND DIRECTIONS

- 0.0   Start from parking area on FR 900, cross the road 40 paces to the trail.
- 0.6   Begin switchbacks and climb through a lovely aspen forest.
- 1.0   Continue climbing, from 9,800 feet at trail start to 10,329 feet, where the trail finally levels a bit, before climbing again.
- 1.3   Wilderness boundary. **N40 02.8411' / W107 05.0769'**
- 1.6   Climb to this point at about 10,500 feet, then give up all that elevation gain!
- 1.8   Drop to 10,300 feet into a long, broad mountain park.
- 1.9   Cross a tributary that flows into Mandall Creek from the north.

Water cascades down from Slide Mandall Lake.

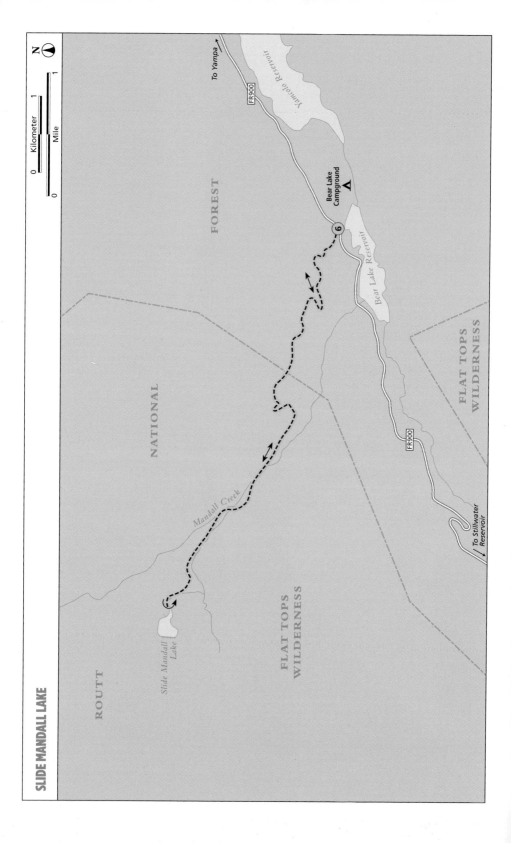

SLIDE MANDALL LAKE

2.1 Cross Mandall Creek and continue northwest—you're now on the southwest side of the creek.

2.2 Cross another creek that flows from the southwest, coming from Mud Mandall and Twin Mandall Lakes.

2.8 Big climb at 10,500 feet.

3.1 9 percent to 13 percent grade hiking next to Mandall Creek.

3.2 The trail pops up to the beaver dams just below Side Mandall Lake; trail is mucky, veer to left above top beaver dam before you enter a boggy wet meadow. Watch for Forest Service "no camping" sign to your left at Slide Mandall Lake.

3.3 Arrive at Slide Mandall Lake. **N40 03.7164' / W107 07.1937'**

6.6 Arrive back at the trailhead.

7 CARHART TRAIL AROUND TRAPPERS LAKE

This is "the Cradle of Wilderness" where that grand and noble notion was born—that fundamental realization that we should set aside certain places in our country and never develop them, just because they're too pristine, too special.

The Carhart Trail is named for Albert Carhart who, in 1919, insisted the best use of this area was for wilderness. In 1964—45 years later—The Wilderness Act was born (see "The Cradle of Wilderness").

This trail circumnavigates historic Trappers Lake, the second-largest natural lake in Colorado. Eerily beautiful, it is not the same as when Carhart first visited nearly 100 years ago. A devastating fire in 2002 changed the landscape dramatically.

Start: Outlet Trailhead
Elevation gain: 9,622–9,956 feet (334 feet)
Distance: 6.0 miles round-trip
Difficulty: Easy to moderate (some scrambling over Cabin Creek and Frasier Creek)
Hiking time: 2–3 hours
Seasons/schedule: Late spring to early fall
Fees and permits: None
Trail contacts: White River National Forest, Blanco Ranger District, 220 East Market St., Meeker, CO 81641, (970) 878-4039; https://www.fs.usda.gov/recarea/whiteriver/recreation/recarea/?recid=40411
Canine compatibility: Yes, as long as pets are under strict leash or voice command
Trail surface: Backcountry singletrack dirt trail

Land status: White River National Forest, Flat Tops Wilderness Area
Nearest town: Meeker
Other trail users: Hiking and horseback only; hunters on foot or horseback during fall big game hunting seasons
Nat Geo TOPO! map (USGS): Devils Causeway and Trappers Lake
National Geographic Trails Illustrated map: #150, Flat Tops North
Other maps: White River National Forest map
Special considerations: The crossings at Cabin and Frasier Creeks can be tricky, especially during spring runoff and into the summer. It's wise to carry wading gear with you, or expect to take your boots off to make the crossings.

FINDING THE TRAILHEAD

From Meeker, take CO 13 east for 1 mile; turn right (east) on Rio Blanco CR 8 and proceed 39 miles. Turn south (right) on the Trappers Lake Road (FR 205) and travel 10 miles to the Outlet Trailhead.
Trailhead GPS: N39 59.9289' / W107 13.8485'

THE HIKE

This trailhead is located near the Trappers Lake outlet where the North Fork of the White River originates. Start near the posted sign and immediately traverse a hillside on the western edge of the parking area. The trail splits at the wilderness boundary in 0.1 mile. Go left (southeast) to the shores of Trappers Lake heading toward Cabin Creek.

This lake holds the world's largest naturally breeding population of Colorado River cutthroat trout. Fishing here can be excellent and special fishing regulations apply. (Go to www.cpw.state.co.us or check for fishing regulations at Wyatt's Sports Center in Meeker.)

Within 0.5 mile, you'll spy the historic Trappers Lake cabins (see "Historic Cabins"). The trail passes the cabins before crossing Cabin Creek and heading along the northeast shore of the lake. A rushing creek and fallen timber make this route difficult without getting wet. You may have to bushwhack upstream to find a safe crossing.

The downed timber here is due to two large weather events. One was a drought in the 1940s that led to a pine beetle infestation killing thousands of lodgepole pine trees. Then, in 2002, that dried wood became fodder for one of the largest lightning-ignited wildfires ever seen in this area—the 17,000-acre Big Fish Fire.

You'll reach the Flat Tops Wilderness boundary in a tenth of a mile from the parking area. From here, the Carhart Trail circumnavigates Trappers Lake, the second-largest natural lake in Colorado behind Grand Lake near Granby.

Trappers Lake, the second-largest natural lake in Colorado, seen through dead-standing pine scorched in the 2002 Big Fish Fire.

In 1.2 miles, the trail meanders away from the lake and around a beautiful knoll at about 9,900 feet in elevation. Before you can see the lake again, you'll find the lush, willow-filled Frasier Creek inlet and a trail crossing at 2.1 miles. Trappers Lake Trail #1816 continues up the Frasier Creek Valley to the south. The Carhart Trail leads to the right (southwest). In another 0.1 mile, the trail winds into a lovely pine grove that somehow escaped the 2002 fire and hikers can experience the forest as it once was.

Unfortunately, that experience lasts for only a few hundred feet. Rounding the next corner and heading northwest, you'll see hundreds of very large burnt trees uprooted after being blown down following the fire. Pay attention through here, especially if it's windy. Don't get hit by a falling snag.

At 2.3 miles, you'll begin to hear water trickle through the tall grasses and willows and 0.1 mile farther, you must find a crossing to Frasier Creek. You'll be wet if you didn't bring wading gear, so you may want to take your boots off!

At 2.7 miles, the trail crosses through more mountain seepage before heading back toward the lake at 3 miles, where it magically appears to your right. For the next mile, you'll stroll beneath "the Wall" and Wall Lake, about 1,500 feet directly above you to the left (southwest).

The trail passes a few small ponds and other grassy areas that look ripe for moose, and then at the 4-mile mark, it crosses Wall Lake Trail #1818. Continue to the right (northeast) toward Trappers.

In a half-mile, the trail leads into the Scotts Lake area and Trappers Lake Campground. These areas lie just outside the wilderness boundary. Numerous social trails exist, but stick to the trail leading to the right, along the northwest flank of Trappers Lake. (To make this a true 6-mile hike, however, follow the directions listed below and hike through the Scotts Lake area to add about 0.2 mile to your trip.)

Soon, you'll reach a hiking bridge that crosses the crystal-clear outlet. Hike up the hill in front of you, angling slightly to the left and in 0.1 mile, you'll return to the main trail. Go left to reach the parking area.

MILES AND DIRECTIONS

0.0   Start at Outlet trailhead/Carhart Trail # 1815. **N39 59.9289' / W107 13.8485'**

0.1   Trail splits prior to wilderness boundary; go left.

0.5   Trail splits, go left above the cabin.

0.7   Trail splits above cabin; the lower trail to the right continues on Carhart Trail #1815 (Stillwater Trail #1814, to the left, leads to Coffin Lake, Little Trappers Lake, and beyond).

0.8   Reach Cabin Creek, cross, get feet wet or bash upstream.

1.2   Start wandering away from lake.

1.7   Trail leads up a long draw to the left and away from the lake.

2.1   Trail tops out and leads back to Frasier Creek drainage. You can't see the lake from here, but you can hear water trickling in the huge, marshy meadow in front of you; within a hundred yards, the trail splits. Trappers Lake Trail #1816 continues up the Frasier Creek valley. Carhart Trail leads to the right.

2.2   The trail slashes across a muddy stretch and into a nice pine forest that didn't get burned in the fire.

2.4 As you come to the creek, wade or crawl across logs just downstream from the trail, or find a short crossing above. Throughout most of the year, you'll be wet without wading gear.

2.5 After crossing the creek, the trail wanders toward "the Wall" on the opposite side of Trappers Lake from the historic cabins. Here, fields of wildflowers bloom in stark contrast to the tall, spindly, burned, standing pines.

3.0 Trappers magically appears on your right as you head down a little hill toward the lake.

3.9 As you travel through a meadow with tall grass and downed timber, a great view of "the Wall" opens to the left and slightly behind you. Notice how it wraps around to your left (west) then directly in front of you (north) toward the parking area and outlet.

4.0 Trail crossing: To the left and southwest is Wall Lake Trail #1818. Go right to continue on the Carhart Trail.

4.4 Pass three small ponds to the right as you approach the wilderness boundary.

4.6 Wilderness boundary; you'll encounter numerous social trails from here. The main trail cuts right toward a narrow strip of land between Scotts Lake and Trappers. To extend the trip somewhat and make sure you get a good 6-mile hike in, go left. That trail takes you west and north around Scotts Lake.

5.5 Reach wilderness boundary sign and Carhart Trail; continue left and follow the main trail, with numerous anglers' trails leading to the lake.

5.8 Cross the outlet of the North Fork of the White River on the well-constructed hiking bridge and grunt up the hill in front of you, angling slightly to the left.

5.9 Back to the main trail, go left.

6.0 You made it.

CARHART TRAIL AROUND TRAPPERS LAKE

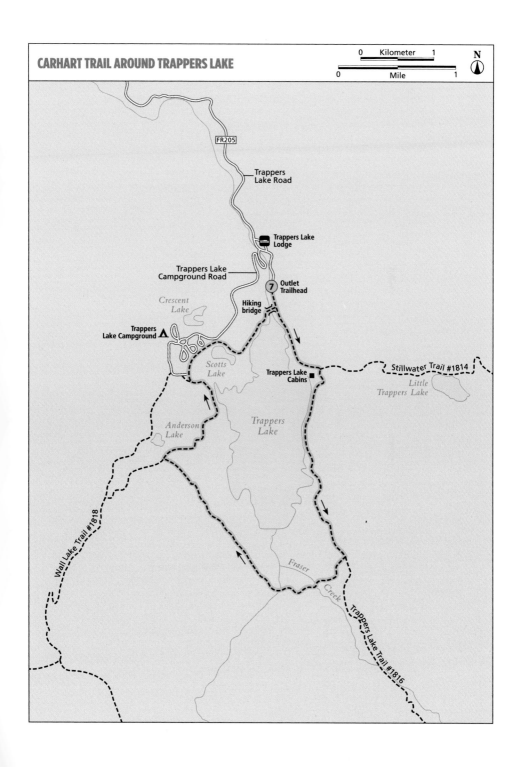

0   Kilometer   1

0   Mile   1

N

FR205

Trappers Lake Road

Trappers Lake Lodge

Trappers Lake Campground Road

7   Outlet Trailhead

Crescent Lake

Hiking bridge

Trappers Lake Campground

Scotts Lake

Trappers Lake Cabins

Stillwater Trail #1814

Little Trappers Lake

Anderson Lake

Trappers Lake

Wall Lake Trail #1818

Fraser Creek

Trappers Lake Trail #1816

THE CRADLE OF WILDERNESS

In 1919, the first full-time landscape architect for the USFS, Arthur Carhart, surveyed the area around Trappers Lake in the White River National Forest near Meeker, Colorado. He was supposed to plot several homesites on the shores of Trappers, the second-largest natural lake in the state.

After weeks of work, Carhart recommended that no development be permitted, insisting that the best use of the area was for wilderness recreation.

That idea—that unprecedented notion—eventually led to The Wilderness Act of 1964.

In 1920, the year following Carhart's suggestion that Trappers Lake remain primitive, the Forest Service designated Trappers Lake as an undeveloped, roadless area. In 1932, the Flat Tops Primitive Area was established.

Carhart went on to work with conservationist Aldo Leopold and lay the foundation of the modern wilderness. Finally, on September 3, 1964, 45 years after Carhart first conceived the idea, the US Congress created The Wilderness Act.

> In order to assure that an increasing population, accompanied by expanding settlement and growing mechanization, does not occupy and modify all areas within the United States . . . leaving no lands designated for preservation and protection in their natural condition, it is hereby declared to be the policy of the Congress to secure for the American people of present and future generations the benefits of an enduring resource of wilderness.

The 235,406-acre Flat Tops Wilderness was established on December 12, 1975, and is the second-largest wilderness area in Colorado. The Carhart Trail travels around the lake where it all began.

> *There are a number of places with scenic values of such great worth that they are rightfully property of all people. Trapper's Lake is unquestionably a candidate for this classification.*
>
> —Arthur Carhart, 1920

HISTORIC CABINS

The historic Trappers Lake cabins have been used to store equipment for the native cutthroat trout spawn-taking operation and to house the crew manning the fish traps since 1914. They were constructed, however, in 1886 to serve as a hunting and fishing lodge for industrialist multimillionaire John Cleveland Osgood, once dubbed "Fuel King of the West" for his vast coal holdings. The cabins have been nominated for inclusion in the National Register of Historic Places because they are one of very few pre-1900 sporting lodges that have survived in good condition to the present day.

Wildflowers abound from spring through fall all along the Carhart Trail in the Flat Tops Wilderness, but scars from the 2002 fire remain.

8 SKINNY FISH TRAIL

This trail leads to a classic "Lake in the Woods," formed in a basin beneath the 600- to 1,000-foot cliffs of the Chinese Wall at the very top of the Flat Tops. While the Carhart Trail (Hike 7) takes you around Trappers Lake and the Cradle of Wilderness, the Skinny Fish Trail allows you to see the Flat Tops as it was prior to the Big Fish Fire of 2002. It winds through aspen, spruce, and fir forest interspersed with broad wildflower-filled meadows where elk and deer thrive and red-tailed hawks soar overhead in search of mice, voles, rabbits, and squirrels.

Start: At the trailhead on the north side of FR 205 (Trappers Lake Road)
Elevation gain: 9,281-10,240 feet (959 feet)
Distance: 5.0 miles out and back
Difficulty: Easy to moderate (most of the elevation gain comes in the first mile or so)
Hiking time: 2.5-3.5 hours
Seasons/schedule: June into Nov (wear blaze orange during fall big game hunting season)
Fees and permits: None
Trail contacts: White River National Forest, Blanco Ranger District, 220 East Market St., Meeker, CO 81641, (970) 878-4039; https://www.fs.usda .gov/recarea/whiteriver/recreation/ recarea/?recid=40411
Canine compatibility: Yes, as long as pets are under strict leash or voice command

Trail surface: Backcountry singletrack dirt and rock trail; expect mud in places
Land status: Flat Tops Wilderness Area, White River National Forest
Nearest town: Meeker
Other trail users: Hiking and horseback only; hunters on foot or horseback during fall big game hunting seasons
Nat Geo TOPO! map (USGS): Devil's Causeway
National Geographic Trails Illustrated map: #150, Flat Tops North
Other maps: White River National Forest map
Special considerations: Want to know more about the geology of the Flat Tops Wilderness? Go to: https://www.fs.usda.gov/ managing-land/natural-resources/ geology/caveskarst/beneath-the -forest/20220716.

FINDING THE TRAILHEAD

From Meeker, take CO 13 east for 1 mile, then turn right (east) on Rio Blanco CR 8. Follow this for 38.5 miles (the first 30 miles is paved). Turn right (south) on Trappers Lake Rd. 205 and cross Ripple Creek. Travel 6.5 miles to the Skinny Fish Trailhead parking area on the left (north) side of the road. (Trappers Lake is another 2 miles up the road.) The Cadillac should have no problem reaching this trailhead on these well-maintained dirt roads.
Trailhead GPS: N40 00.9880' / W107 14.2807'

THE HIKE

While a portion of this hike takes you through an area burned in the Big Fish Fire of 2002 and gives you a sense of its awe and power, most of the trail allows you to view the area as it was prior to the fire.

This short hike begins with a steep 1-mile climb through a lovely aspen forest that sparkles most of the year, especially in the fall when the leaves turn colors.

Walk a few feet from the trailhead, then cross Skinny Fish Creek on its way to join the North Fork of the White River. You'll reach your first switchback in a little more than a tenth of a mile, just past an area that sloughed off the mountainside. These mini landslides continue to shape and form the Flat Tops, as they have for the past 52 million years.

In a half-mile, you'll reach another set of switchbacks that climb to about 9,620 feet. You'll soon cross another tributary that flows into Skinny Fish Creek, and it could be muddy through here.

In a short distance, you'll skirt by a large, burned area. By the time you reach the three-quarter-mile mark, you'll cross a beautiful meadow and can now clearly view portions of the lightning-sparked Big Fish Fire that burned 17,000 acres of Flat Tops forest in 2002.

Once you cross this meadow, you'll enter another beautiful little aspen forest with some spruce and fir that survived the fire. You're now closely following Skinny Fish Creek and the trail will soon rise out of the timber into another grassy meadow filled with corn lily that will display stalks of greenish-white flowers that can reach up to 7 feet tall. Often confused with skunk cabbage, which is not native to Colorado, the corn lily is poisonous to livestock. Its taste is very bitter. As a result, it is rarely eaten by cattle or wildlife.

At 0.9 mile, the Lost Lakes Trail cuts off to the left (north). A trail marker was ripped off the post at this point, but its waypoint is **N40 01.5294' / W107 14.0665'**.

In 1.2 miles, you'll head down a broad valley that was half-burned in the fire. You can see off to the left (northwest) where some stands of spruce and fir escaped. They remain standing along a ridge at about 9,900 feet in elevation. In another tenth of a mile, you'll cross the creek again and then at the 2-mile mark, you'll cross it one more time before reaching the trail split to McGinnis Lake. You could go either way here as it's about a half-mile to either lake. Our track leads to the left here and continues to Skinny Fish Lake, beginning a gentle set of switchbacks up a nearly treeless hillside full of stunning wildflowers.

You'll reach the shores of Skinny Fish Lake at 2.5 miles. There's a great place under the spruce and fir to park your pack in the shade, and soak up the beauty of this idyllic "Lake in the Woods" (not to be confused with the Lake of the Woods Trail on the other side of FSR 209, or the Lake of the Woods Trail on the Grand Mesa, or the Lake of the Woods in Minnesota, or any other Lake of the Woods!). There are numerous quality camping spots around this lake but remember not to camp within 100 feet of a water source or trail.

Skinny Fish in the rain

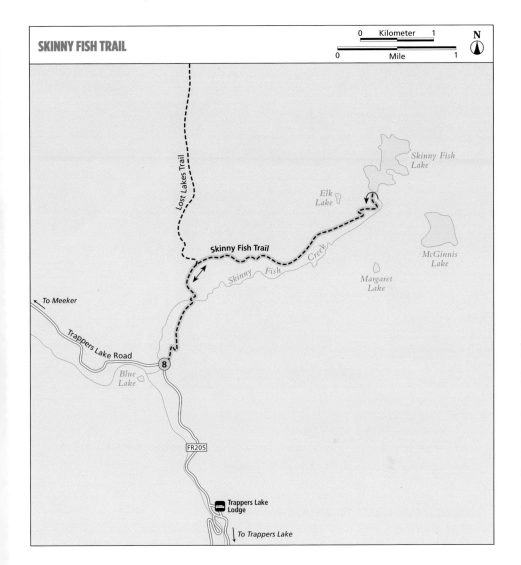

MILES AND DIRECTIONS

0.0 Start from Skinny Fish Trailhead.

0.1 First switchback past slide area that sloughed off.

0.2 Switch back and cruise through the aspen before crossing a wooden footbridge; continue heading southwest.

0.5 Arrive at a second set of switchbacks climbing to 9,620 feet.

0.6 Cross another tributary; the trail is mucky and muddy just above this.

0.7 Cross the meadow and view the burned area.

0.9 Lost Lakes Trail cuts to the left (north). **N40 01.5294' / W107 14.0665'** Stay right.

1.2 Crest the top of the hill and head down into a broad partially burned valley.

Maps may not show it, but this creek crosses the trail in various spots, depending on the year and snowmelt.

2.0   Cross the creek one more time before the trail splits to McGinnis Lake; and then, begin a set of gentle switchbacks.

2.5   Arrive at Skinny Fish Lake at 10,205 feet in elevation. **N40 01.9208' / W107 12.7622'**

5.0   After backtracking, arrive back at the trailhead.

RISK OF FIRE DUE TO DROUGHT

Forests have evolved with and depend on natural cycles of fire, insect outbreaks, disease, and extreme weather. This helps to rejuvenate our forests. The subalpine forests here in northwest Colorado have experienced an unusual sequence of disturbances over the last 125 years. A comprehensive study by University of Colorado researchers analyzed how a century of disturbances interacted with each other to shape this ecosystem. The most surprising result of this study was that "neither bark beetle infestation nor salvage logging had detectable effects on fire severity or extent. Increased risk of fire was attributed to drought." For more, go to: http://digitalcommons.unl.edu/cgi/viewcontent.cgi?article=1053&context=jfspbriefs.

9 STORM KING FOURTEEN MEMORIAL HIKE

This trail was built to honor fourteen men and women who died fighting one of the most explosive wildfires in Colorado history—the South Canyon Fire. It began as a footpath made by families of the firefighters and others as they hiked the mountain to pay their respects to those who had died. Its rough condition is intended as a tribute to firefighters and the challenging conditions under which they work.

Start: From Storm King Fourteen Memorial Trailhead
Elevation gain: 5,672–6,963 feet (1,291 feet)
Distance: 3.3 miles to main memorial and back; 3.9 miles including spur trails
Difficulty: Strenuous
Hiking time: 3–4 hours
Seasons/schedule: Spring, summer, fall
Fees and permits: None
Trail contacts: BLM, Colorado River Valley Field Office, 2300 River Frontage Rd, Silt CO; (970) 876-9000; https://www.blm.gov/documents/colorado/public-room/map/storm-king-memorial-trail-map
Canine compatibility: Dogs permitted on leash
Trail surface: Rugged rock, roots, and dirt on a steep singletrack backcountry path

Land status: BLM
Nearest town: Glenwood Springs
Other trail users: Hunters in the fall
Nat Geo TOPO! map (USGS): Storm King Mountain
National Geographic Trails Illustrated map: #123 Flat Tops SE/Glenwood Canyon
Special considerations: Much of the trail is very rugged and exposed. It can be quite hot in the summer. It is not safe during lightning storms. Be prepared for the weather, wear sturdy footgear, and bring plenty of water.
Other: To learn more about this fire 20 years later, go to National Geographic News at: http://news.nationalgeographic.com/news/2014/07/140704-south-canyon-wildfire-colorado-wildlands-fire.

FINDING THE TRAILHEAD

From Glenwood Springs, travel west on I-70 to the Canyon Creek exit (#109). Turn east on the frontage road that parallels the highway's north side. The road ends in 1 mile at the trailhead.

Trailhead GPS: N39 34.4150 / W107 26.0636'

THE HIKE

On July 2, 1994, "during a year of drought and at a time of low humidity and record high temperatures," according to BLM records, "lightning ignited a fire seven miles west of Glenwood Springs."

In its early stages, the fire burned pinyon and juniper hillsides and was thought to have little potential for spread. Yet it continued to grow. On July 5, a BLM/Forest Service crew hiked 2.5 hours to the fire, cleared a helicopter landing area, and started building a fire

This strenuous hike leads to an inspiring homemade memorial.

line on its southwest side. During the day an air tanker dropped retardant on the fire. In the evening the crew left the fire to repair their chainsaws.

Eight smokejumpers parachuted to the fire and continued constructing the fire line. The fire, however, had crossed the original line, so this crew began a second line on the east side of the ridge. They worked until after midnight, finally abandoning their work due to darkness and the hazards of rolling rocks.

At 4:30 a.m. on July 6, BLM reports showed the original eleven-person BLM/Forest Service crew returned to the fire and worked alongside the smokejumpers to clear a second helicopter landing area. Later that morning eight more smokejumpers parachuted to the fire and were assigned to build a fire line on the west flank. Then, ten hotshot crew members from Prineville, Oregon, arrived, and joined the others.

A stunning view of the rugged terrain

At 3:20 p.m. a dry cold front moved in. The fire made several rapid runs with 100-foot flames leaping into the blackened sky. At 4 p.m. the fire crossed the bottom of the west drainage and spread upward. It soon spotted back across the drainage to the east side beneath the firefighters and moved onto steep slopes and into dense, highly flammable Gambel oak.

Fanned by winds gusting to 45 mph, the fire exploded, racing uphill at 35 feet per second toward the firefighters on the west flank fire line. Failing to outrun the flames, twelve firefighters perished. Two helitack crew members were trapped on the top of the ridge. They also perished as they tried to outrun the fire to the northwest.

The remaining thirty-five firefighters survived by escaping out the east drainage or seeking a safety area and deploying their fire shelters. In 5 hours, the South Canyon fire consumed almost 2,115 acres.

The Storm King Fourteen Memorial Trail was built in memory of those who lost their lives in that fire and as a tribute to those who survived, and to all firefighters everywhere.

The hike from the trailhead to an inspiring homemade memorial site to the twelve perished firefighters is 3.3 miles. A spur trail of 0.3 mile to where the two helitack members lost their lives makes this a hike of closer to 4 miles (including a 0.2-mile backtrack to the spur trail).

The main portion of the trail is about 1 mile long and climbs 700 vertical feet to an observation point. Beyond that, the footpath drops into a steep gully, then climbs to separate memorial sites where the firefighters died. This strenuous up-and-down stretch increases the climb by another 591 vertical feet. The well-worn footpath is marked only with rock cairns and a few well-placed landscape timbers to prevent erosion.

A visitor hikes beneath scarred remains of the South Canyon Fire

MILES AND DIRECTIONS

0.0 Start from Storm King Fourteen Memorial Trailhead, elevation 5,672 feet. Cross gully and immediately start climbing with the heavy noise of I-70 to your right (south) along the Colorado River.

0.1 The trail through private property already becomes so steep that volunteers who built it used treated posts anchored with rebar for steps. Please stay on the trail and respect private property rights.

0.2 Hikers will have already climbed 200 feet, winding upward along several switch-backs through pinyon and juniper, providing some shade on a hot summer day. Within a few hundred yards, a property marker shows the trail has moved onto public (BLM) property and begins climbing north and away from the I-70 corridor.

0.3 A rest bench allows for a breather in front of a small informational sign discussing the Coal Ridge Fire—scars of which can still be seen a hundred years later—from a series of mine explosions between 1896 and 1918 that killed eighty-nine people.

0.5 The trail climbs out of pinyon/juniper and Gambel oak, then up to the ridge where an informational kiosk discusses changing weather patterns. Firefighters must be careful in ridges like these where wind gusts can change quickly.

0.6 As you approach the ridge, notice the thick stands of Gambel oak to your right (southeast); firefighters on Storm King were building a fire line through similar dense stands of oakbrush—an extremely difficult task under the best of conditions. You can now see the South Canyon Fire perimeter. From here, it's an easy hike to the overlook.

1.0 This overlook includes a view of the area where the firefighters were working when they perished. From here, the trail plunges steeply into the deep drainage in front of you and climbs up the other side. Imagine carrying a 100-pound pack and a chain-saw while running up and down these slopes.

1.6 At the ridgetop, the trail splits. Follow the right (south) fork for another 0.1 mile and monuments to the twelve hotshots and smokejumpers who perished here. Follow the left (north) fork for 0.3 mile to monuments for the two helitack crew members who died. This is your turnaround point.

3.3 Arrive back at the trailhead.

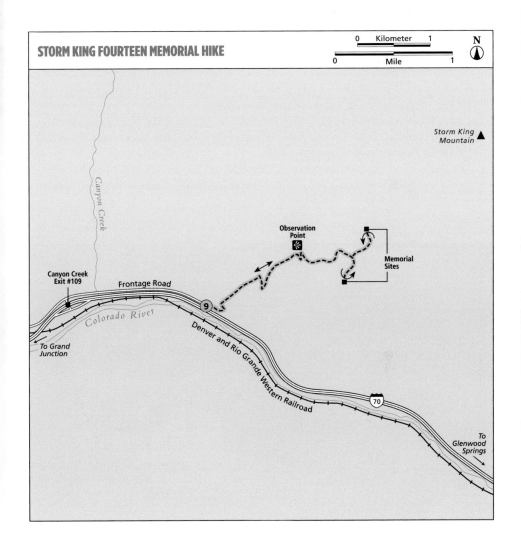

WEST ELKS/ RAGGEDS WILDERNESS

The Elk Mountains cover a large portion of midwestern Colorado. Three wilderness areas are found here: Maroon Bells–Snowmass Wilderness Area, the West Elk Wilderness Area, and the Raggeds Wilderness Area. In total, these mountains contain 423,320 acres of the most majestic wilderness in America.

The most photographed mountains in Colorado are the spectacular Maroon Bells. As noted in the Meet Your Guide section, however, they're now overrun with people. Since

The Raggeds Wilderness boundary on the Oh-Be-Joyful Trail

this book is more about paths less traveled, hikes into the Maroon Bells are not included here. Nonetheless, the West Elks and Raggeds are spectacular themselves.

Throughout the Elk Mountains, past volcanic activity produced lengthy lava flows, creating tall ridges and long valleys. Then, through the action of wind and water erosion, those uplifted ridges have crumbled into impressive turrets and spires, spectacular pinnacles, and long vertical bulwark-type walls. An intricate and intertwined trail network provides endless opportunities to explore this spectacular area.

West Elk Wilderness, within Gunnison National Forest, contains 176,412 acres, the fifth largest wilderness in Colorado. Elevations range from 7,000 to over 13,000 feet.

The 65,393-acre Raggeds Wilderness was established in 1980 and is found in portions of both the White River and Gunnison National Forests. Elevations range from 6,840 feet in Dark Canyon to 13,535 feet at the summit of Treasure Mountain.

10 OH-BE-JOYFUL TRAIL

Some say Oh-Be-Joyful Creek near Crested Butte, Colorado, was named in the 19th century after valuable ore was discovered in the gulch. Other longtime locals, however, insist those stouthearted miners in the late 1800s were "joyful" as they raced down the mountain to visit the brothels in Crested Butte. Today, we're joyful to meander through this wildflower wonderland. A relatively easy hike leads into Oh-Be-Joyful Basin, surrounded by 12,000- to 13,000-foot peaks. It's great for the entire family but expect to see a few more people on this trail than on most other trails listed in this book.

Start: From Oh-Be-Joyful Trailhead (FS Trail #836)
Elevation gain: 8,897 – 10,223 feet (1,326 feet)
Distance: 8.4 miles +/- out-and-back
Difficulty: Moderate (some hefty elevation gain toward the far-end of this route)
Hiking time: 3–5 hours
Seasons/schedule: Best in summer, especially July when wildflowers peak
Fees and permits: None
Trail contacts: USFS, Gunnison Ranger District, 216 N. Colorado St., Gunnison, CO 81230, (970) 641-0471; www.fs.usda.gov/gmug
Canine compatibility: Dogs permitted under leash and/or strict vocal command
Trail surface: Rocky jeep trail to begin, then singletrack dirt backcountry trail and finally some rocky dirt switchbacks with deep roots toward the end of the trail

Land status: USFS, Gunnison Ranger District
Nearest town: Crested Butte
Other trail users: Hiking, horseback only
Nat Geo TOPO! map (USGS): Oh-Be-Joyful and Marcellina Mountain
National Geographic Trails Illustrated map: Kebler Pass/Paonia Reservoir #133 and Crested Butte #131
Other maps: USFS Gunnison Basin Public Lands map
Other: Designated the "Wildflower Capital of Colorado" since 1990, Crested Butte hosts a weeklong Crested Butte Wildflower Festival every July. More than 200 individual events are hosted, including photography and art classes, hikes, garden tours, and cooking seminars. Learn to identify native wildflowers with the experts; www.crestedbutte wildflowerfestival.com.

FINDING THE TRAILHEAD

From the Chamber of Commerce Visitor's Center on CO 317 in Crested Butte, travel north for 0.7 mile on Gunnison CR 317 to the Slate River Road (Gunnison CR 734). Turn left. The road splits at 3.2 miles. Go forward to the right. Continue past the Gunsight Pass Camping Area at 3.9 miles and turn left onto FR 754 (also labeled CR 3220) at 5.4 miles. In .4 miles, this rough road leads to the Oh Be Joyful Campground and trailhead.

A parking area for the trail is located near the two pit toilets adjacent to the campground. The trailhead is located next to the pit toilets and the well-marked trail leads hikers across a new foot bridge over the river.
Trailhead GPS: N38 54.8855' / W107 01.9811'

THE HIKE

Blue Lake sits 11,065 feet above sea level in a bowl at the headwaters of Oh-Be-Joyful Creek, and you can get there from this trail. That is, if the weather cooperates. If you don't get altitude sickness. If you aren't too tired. If the sun's not too hot. If thunderstorms don't drive you off the mountain. If rainstorms don't pelt you into feeling like a wet rat.

I've been here a dozen times and have yet to make it to Blue Lake. A snowstorm stopped me once. Before the footbridge at the trailhead was built, high water on the Slate River stopped me two or three other times. A thunderstorm in July 2024 forced me out of the valley and back to my vehicle. But the nice thing is, you don't have to hike all that way to Blue Lake to enjoy this trek into "the Wildflower Capital of Colorado." This is a great hike in the summer, especially in July when the wildflowers are in full bloom, no matter how far you go.

There's a new footbridge adjacent to the new pit toilets at the trailhead. Once you cross the Slate River, hike up the well-marked Oh-Be-Joyful 4WD Road that's no longer accessible by vehicle. The trail continues on this two-track and into the Raggeds

A relatively easy hike leads to Oh-Be-Joyful Basin near Crested Butte, "The Wildflower Capital of Colorado." Surrounded by 12,000- to 13,000-foot peaks, this hike is great for the entire family.

Silvery lupine, *Lupinus argenteus* (left), and purple fringe, *Phacelia sericea*, are only two of more than 800 plant species found here.

Wilderness Area at 1.7 miles, then gently climbs on a singletrack dirt trail to the end of the valley.

You'll soon discover why this is considered the "Wildflower Capital of Colorado." From late spring, when the last snows melt, into late September, when the first snows fall, you'll find massive fields of wildflowers in this basin (although freak snowstorms can stop you cold in June).

At 1.9 miles, the trail breaks out of dark timber into a wide and lush green basin. On your left (south) is 12,227-foot Peeler Peak. That silvery line of water you see to your southwest flows from the side of 12,000-foot Garfield Peak. Providing a magnificent backdrop at the end of the basin is Mount Owen (13,058 feet) and Afley Peak (12,646 feet).

Soon, you will crest a small hill as the trail enters a broad valley. It meanders on the right side of the stream that pours down through a large meadow of native willows. You'll

Oh-Be-Joyful Creek tumbles down from Blue Lake

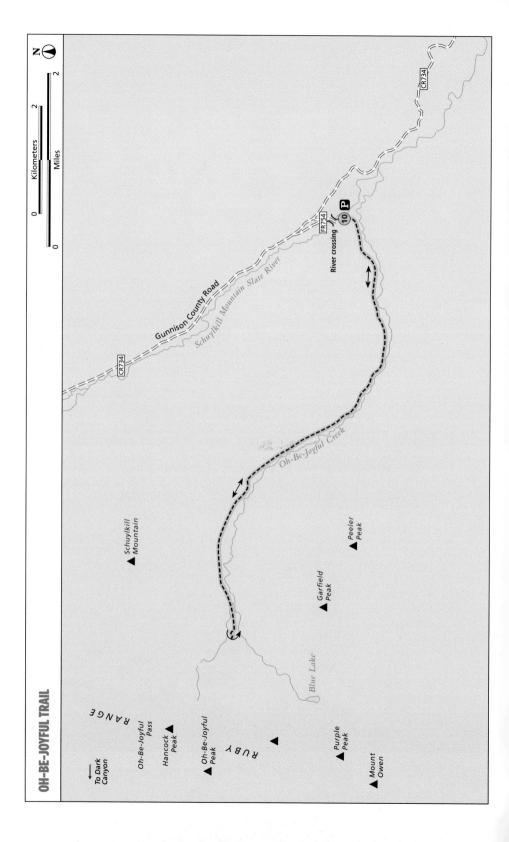

OH-BE-JOYFUL TRAIL

N

Kilometers
0   2

Miles
0   2

To Dark
Canyon

RUBY RANGE

Oh-Be-Joyful
Pass

Hancock
Peak ▲

Oh-Be-Joyful
Peak ▲

▲

Purple
Peak ▲

Mount
Owen ▲

Blue Lake

Schuylkill
Mountain ▲

Garfield
Peak ▲

Peeler
Peak ▲

Oh-Be-Joyful Creek

Gunnison County Road

CR734

Schuylkill Mountain Slate River

FR754

River crossing

10 P

CR734

soon discover this is open range and you share this environment with cattle that have created braided trails here. If you continue upstream with the creek to your left, you'll be fine.

At 2.6 miles, you'll spy a very large beaver dam on the creek. In another 0.4 mile, the trail pops up to a tiny knoll in the pines where you can sit on a rock and marvel at the views both up and down the valley.

You'll come to an open gate across the trail at 3.3 miles. It might have been an old cattle guard, but there's no fence. Then, at the 4-mile mark, you've reached the end of the valley. The trail leads into dark timber and begins climbing to Daisy Pass and Oh-Be-Joyful Pass.

From here, the trail becomes much more strenuous as you rise out of the basin and climb around the northern flank of Garfield Peak. Continue from this point another 0.2 mile to where the trail splits. To the left is Blue Lake. To the right is Daisy Pass, which connects to Silver Basin Trail (FR 834), Ruby/Anthracite Trail #836 (Hike 11), and the Anthracite/Dark Canyon Trail #830 (Hike 12).

Most hikers—like me—never make it this far, preferring to meander in the basin below and photograph wildflowers in one of the most breathtaking settings on earth!

MILES AND DIRECTIONS

0.0 Start at trailhead next to vault toilets and cross footbridge over Slate River.

0.4 Follow signs and continue up the two-track road. **N38 54.5954' / W107 02.2866'**

0.6 Trail veers right around a bog in the middle of the road.

0.8 Trail splits; you can go either way but main trail goes to the right.

1.3 Reach Raggeds Wilderness boundary.

1.5 There's a small footbridge for hikers/horses crossing a seep from the right (northeast).

2.0 Crest a small hill and enter the main valley. Trail meanders on right side of the stream.

3.0 Trail leads onto a tiny knoll in the pines with great views up and down the valley.

3.3 Gate from nowhere.

3.4 Trail crosses the creek—to the right is a beautiful little waterfall.

3.6 A Forest Service sign marks the trail, but meandering cattle mark their own trails through here.

4.0 Most meanders lead to this crossing of the creek and back onto the main trail.

4.1 Trail leads into dark timber with Oh-Be-Joyful Creek on the left (south). It now begins to wind up to the top of the pass.

4.2 This is where we turn around, but if you're going to Blue Lake, keep going!

8.4 Arrive back at the trailhead.

11 RUBY ANTHRACITE TRAIL

This trail leads into the Ruby Anthracite Creek drainage and offers spectacular views of the western side of the Ruby Mountain Range as it drops into one of the largest contiguous aspen forests in North America. The lower Anthracite Creek/Dark Canyon Trail (FS Trail #830) connects to this trail deep inside the Raggeds Wilderness Area. To connect, however, you must cross Ruby Anthracite Creek. That's usually not possible until July due to spring runoff. No matter, an out-and-back trip along this trail is fabulous from early June until the snow flies in the fall.

Start: From Ruby Anthracite Creek Trailhead (FS Trail #836) on Kebler Pass
Elevation loss: 8,663–7,341 feet (1,322-foot descent)
Distance: 6.4 miles out and back to Ruby Anthracite Creek
Difficulty: Moderate to strenuous due to elevation gain—especially on the way back!
Hiking time: 4–5 hours
Seasons/schedule: June to Oct
Fees and permits: None
Trail contacts: Gunnison National Forest, Paonia Ranger District, 403 Rio Grande Ave., Paonia, CO 81428; (970) 527-4131; www.fs.fed.us/r2/gmug
Canine compatibility: Dogs permitted on leash or under strict voice command

Trail surface: Backcountry singletrack rock and dirt trail
Land status: USFS, Gunnison National Forest, Raggeds Wilderness Area
Nearest towns: Paonia, Crested Butte
Other trail users: Some limited horseback use, mostly during fall big game hunting seasons
Nat Geo TOPO! map (USGS): Marcellina Mtn, CO
National Geographic Trails Illustrated map: Kebler Pass/Paonia Reservoir
Other maps: USFS Gunnison Basin Public Lands map
Other: While there is plenty of water here, giardia is present. It's a microscopic parasite that causes intense diarrheal discomfort! Therefore, carry lots of water with you or be prepared to treat stream water.

FINDING THE TRAILHEAD

From US 50 in Delta, turn east on CO 92 and travel 20 miles to Hotchkiss where the highway splits. Veer left onto CO 133 and travel 23 miles past Paonia to the Kebler Pass Road, CR 12, leading to Crested Butte. Turn right (southeast) and travel 19 miles on this well-maintained dirt road to the trailhead, located on the left (east) side of the road. If you reach the Lost Lake turn, you've gone about 2.5 miles too far. That's the turnoff for the Beckwith Pass Trail.

From Crested Butte, take CR 12 west for 19 miles to the trailhead, which will be on your right, heading northeast. **Special Note:** Both CO 133 and Kebler Pass Road / CR 12 were washed out following the heavy snow winter of 2023. They have since been repaired but check road conditions before traveling here.
Trailhead GPS: N38 54.6928' / W107 13.9573'

This trail offers great views of the Ruby Range with Ruby Anthracite Creek flowing beneath the base of these impressive mountains.

THE HIKE

The Ruby Range is a subrange of the Elk Mountains. It's located between Crested Butte and Paonia, along one of the most beautiful and accessible mountain passes in Colorado—Kebler Pass (CR 12). A hike down the Ruby Anthracite Trail leads you to the foot of this range and offers solitude, adventure, and stunning scenery.

This trail system also connects to Horse Ranch Park on top of Kebler Pass, to Oh-Be-Joyful Trail (Hike 10) via Daisy Pass and the Silver Basin Trail on the east side of the Ruby Mountains, and to the lower Anthracite Creek/Dark Canyon Trail (Hike 12). You could spend weeks on these trails and cross paths with few other hikers or backpackers during that time—unless you're here in the fall during big game hunting season. Then, you'll see quite a bit of activity, especially on horseback.

While this rugged range seems like a climber's paradise, it is largely overlooked because only one peak in the range reaches a height more than 13,000 feet above sea level—Mt. Owen at 13,008 feet.

In fact, the ridge crest along the Ruby Range crosses the summits of nine peaks (five ranked 12,000-footers, three unranked 12,000-footers, and Mt. Owen). The ridge never drops below 11,700 feet in elevation, according to www.14ers.com, a site that keeps close track of that type of stuff.

This trail leads down into the Ruby Anthracite drainage, well below that ridge. With names like Purple Mountain, Ruby Peak, and Oh-Be-Joyful Peak, they shine like colorful sentinels in the evening sun, with thousands of acres of aspen forest dancing at their feet. During fall, just prior to big game hunting season, this is one of the most spectacular displays of aspen splendor in the Rocky Mountain West.

To find the trailhead, follow Kebler Pass east from Paonia Reservoir (or west from Crested Butte). There are no signs marking this spot, only an old jeep road on the northeast side of the pass at a big turn in the road. Pull as far off the road as possible to park. If you have a four-wheel-drive vehicle, you could drive up that old jeep road for a quarter-mile to a small parking area near the actual trailhead. (Our hike begins on Kebler Pass Road.)

From the trailhead, the trail leads between a handful of old beaver dams on Trout Creek. Make sure you have proper footwear. You may get your feet wet, and this trail is a bit steep—probably not appropriate for tennis shoes anyway.

You'll travel downhill through a mixture of willows and aspen, and around a couple more beaver dams for 2.7 miles before a switchback begins a major climb down to Ruby Anthracite Creek. In another 0.2 mile, you'll get a great view of the entire Ruby Range to the east as the trail continues its plunge toward the creek bottom. Soon, you'll be able to see the Ragged Mountains ranging off to the north.

Once you reach the creek bottom, travel a short distance upstream to the creek crossing. From here, it's 7 miles to Erickson Springs to the northwest, and 10 miles to Horse Ranch Park, to the southwest and at the top of Kebler Pass. From July to the first snowfall, this is a relatively easy crossing. In the spring, however, this creek rages and crossing is too dangerous. It's time to take a break and prepare for the 1,322-foot climb hike out.

Ruby Anthracite Creek

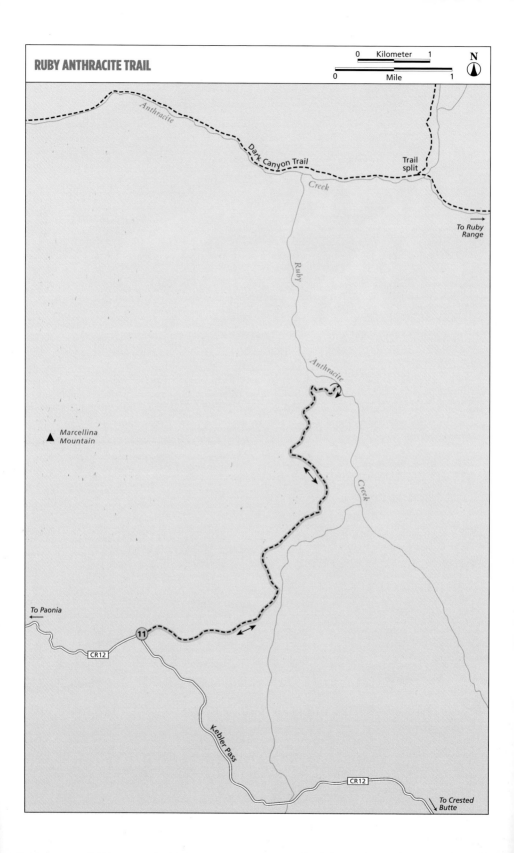

MILES AND DIRECTIONS

0.0   Start from Kebler Pass (CR 12) and Ruby Anthracite Trail signpost, hike up the old four-wheel-drive road on the northeast side of the road.

0.3   You'll reach the actual trailhead at **N38 54.7290' / W107 13.9419'**. The trail leads across a small tributary of Trout Creek and between three or four beaver dams.

2.7   A switchback starts the major climb DOWN to Ruby Anthracite Creek.

2.9   Another switchback to the right offers great views of Ruby Mountain Range.

3.2   You'll reach the creek at **N38 56.0720' W107 12.5302'**. Travel upstream for a short distance to the creek crossing at **N38 56.0731' / W107 12.4945'.**

6.4   After backtracking, arrive back at the trailhead.

Don't miss the Paonia Cherry Days Festival, July 4, Paonia, CO, 70+ years running; www.paoniacherrydays.com, or the Mountain Harvest Festival, also in Paonia. It's an annual 4-day celebration of local music, art, farms, food, and spirits the last full weekend in September; www.mountainharvestfestival.com.

12 DARK CANYON TRAIL TO ANTHRACITE CREEK

The Raggeds Wilderness covers 65,443 acres in the Gunnison and White River National Forests and preserves two ranges in the Elk Mountains: the Raggeds, jutting skyward to serrated ridgetops; and the Ruby Range, white capped through much of the year. This trail leads right to the middle of it, following Anthracite Creek beneath the towering rock walls of Dark Canyon. Elevations range from 6,800 feet to about 13,000 feet, but this trail is lower—from 6,855 feet to 7,347 feet in elevation—so hiking is relatively easy on the stretch described here.

Start: From Dark Canyon Trailhead at Erickson Springs Campground
Elevation gain: 6,855–7,347 feet (492 feet)
Distance: 7.8 miles out and back
Difficulty: Easy to moderate due to some short climbs and quick descents
Hiking time: 3–4 hours
Seasons/schedule: May to Oct
Fees and permits: None
Trail contacts: Paonia Ranger District, 403 N. Rio Grande Ave., Paonia, CO 81428, (970) 527-4131; www.r2 _gmug_visitor_information@fs.fed.us
Canine compatibility: Dogs permitted but must be always under leash control. It's illegal for dogs to chase wildlife.
Trail surface: Dirt and rock singletrack backcountry trail, muddy in spots

Land status: USFS, Gunnison National Forest, Raggeds Wilderness Area
Nearest town: Paonia
Other trail users: Some horseback use, especially during fall big game hunting seasons
Nat Geo TOPO! map (USGS): Paonia Reservoir, Marcellina Mountain and Anthracite Range
National Geographic Trails Illustrated map: #133, Kebler Pass/Paonia Reservoir
Other maps: Gunnison Basin Public Lands map
Other: Wilderness.net is a national organization that connects federal employees, scientists, educators, and the public with their wilderness heritage: www.wilderness.net/NWPS/wildView?WID=479.

FINDING THE TRAILHEAD

From Paonia, travel northeast for approximately 14 miles on CO 133 to CR 12 (Kebler Pass Road). Turn east and travel approximately 6 miles, then turn left to Erickson Springs Campground just after crossing the bridge. Travel 0.2 mile to the end of the road and a parking area near the vaulted toilet and Dark Canyon Trailhead. **Special Note:** Both CO 133 and Kebler Pass Road / CR 12 were washed out following the heavy snow winter of 2023. They have since been repaired but check road conditions before traveling here.
Trailhead GPS: N38 57.5446' / W107 15.7498'

THE HIKE

The Maroon Bells–Snowmass Wilderness Area is the most famous—and most visited—wilderness within the Elk Mountains. Yet, the West Elk Wilderness Area and the Raggeds Wilderness Area are spectacular in their own right, and far less traveled.

The Raggeds derives its well-deserved name from the rocky slopes and serrated ridges that make up this range. The Ruby Range joins the Raggeds along this trail. You'll soon see why it's called Dark Canyon, as the trail winds beneath 600-foot-tall cliffs to the north along the rushing Anthracite Creek, and the backside of the 11,348-foot Marcellina Mountain on the south.

Beginning at the east end of the Erickson Springs campground past the vault toilet, the trail leads east through the aspen/pine forest to a well-constructed footbridge across Anthracite Creek. Once across the bridge, you'll go right, continuing east along a reconstructed section of trail that used to be a muddy mess. Good job, Forest Service. Trail crews must continually maintain stretches of this trail as it becomes overgrown. Bracken fern line the trail through here and soon it leaves the spruce, fir, aspen, and a few ponderosa pines, for a deciduous forest of box elder, narrow-leafed cottonwood, willow, and low-elevation juniper. Box elder is actually a maple, in the genus *Acer*. The leaf looks quite similar to the leaf of poison ivy.

In about a third of a mile, you'll reach the Raggeds Wilderness boundary and in 0.7 mile, you'll be following Anthracite Creek upstream through a rich riparian zone full of raspberry, thimbleberry, serviceberry, and elderberry. As you enjoy the soothing sound of moving water, you'll notice that Gambel oak thrives here at this relatively low elevation of 6,900 feet. The acorns from those oak and other foods high in fat, sugar, and

This trail takes you beneath the towering rock walls of Dark Canyon, deep within the Raggeds Wilderness Area.

Anthracite Creek offers excellent scenery—and really good fishing, too!

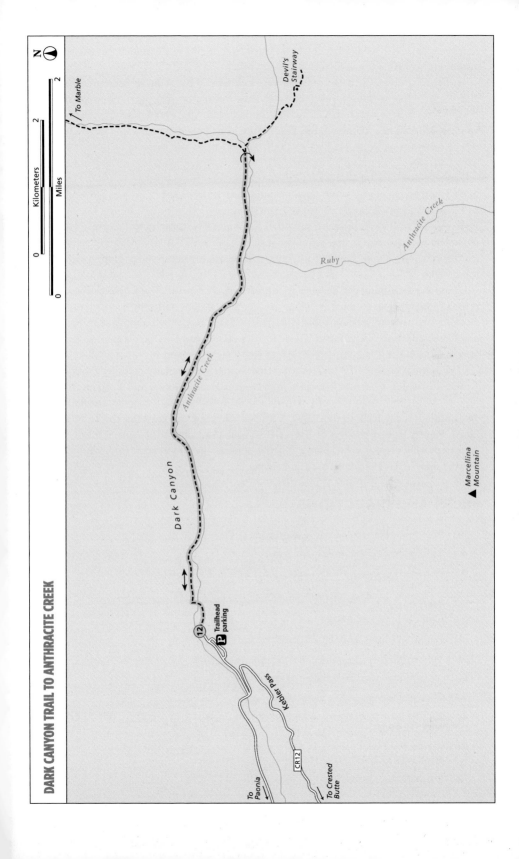

DARK CANYON TRAIL TO ANTHRACITE CREEK

N

To Marble

Devil's
Stairway

Kilometers

Miles

0   2

0   2

Ruby

Anthracite Creek

Anthracite Creek

Dark Canyon

Marcellina
Mountain

12

Trailhead
parking

P

Kebler Pass

CR12

To Paonia

To Crested
Butte

starch—such as the wild berries—attract black bears in the late summer and fall as they gorge on them to fatten up before the long winter.

By the way, a black bear encounter is very rare here. They're pretty secretive animals. They'll stay close to rough topography or dense vegetation that provides escape cover. If you make a little noise, they'll be long gone before you ever know they are in the vicinity. (If you'd like to know more about black bears, mountain lions, and other critters whose territory we've entered, go to the Colorado Parks and Wildlife website at www .cpw.state.co.us.)

The trail now goes up and away from the creek, then back down again. At the 2-mile mark you may encounter some shoe-sucking mud. Be prepared. The trail is overgrown and lush with thimbleberries, a native bramble shrub with thornless stems. They grow rapidly and form dense thickets from 4 to 6 feet high. The large leaves (between 4 and 8 inches across) have five points, reminiscent of a maple leaf. Between May and early July, clusters of showy white flowers form, after which the berries develop. Hope you catch it just right!

In another half-mile, you'll come to a great rest area in the shade next to the creek prior to climbing up to a rocky bench 50 feet above. The trail rises quickly, and then descends just as rapidly on a couple switchbacks. You'll reach the confluence of Anthracite Creek and Ruby Anthracite Creek at 3.1 miles. If you look across both streams to your southeast, you'll see Prospect Point, at 8,645 feet.

Continue for another 0.8 mile to the marked trail crossing: Go north (left) up North Anthracite Creek to Anthracite Pass and eventually Marble, on the backside of the Maroon Bells–Snowmass Wilderness Area; or, head south (right) over the Devil's Stairway, and eventually back to the Ruby Anthracite Trail (if you cross the creek), or up to Horse Ranch Park at the top of Kebler Pass. Your third option, of course, is to retrace your steps back to your vehicle for a 7.8-mile out-and-back excursion through this lush, botanic oasis in the bottom of a Dark Canyon.

MILES AND DIRECTIONS

0.0 Start from the trailhead at Erickson Springs Campground.

0.2 A stout footbridge crosses the creek.

0.3 Trail winds in and out of box elder and willow at the wilderness boundary at 0.34 mile.

0.7 Raspberries and thimbleberries next to creek are colorful and tasty.

0.8 Gambel oak at 6,900 feet.

1.4 Following a climb, the trail descends to creek level.

2.0 Shoe sucking mud. Be prepared.

2.4 Cross a small seep that flows into Anthracite.

2.5 Great rest area prior to a short climb.

3.1 Ruby Anthracite Creek flows into Anthracite Creek at GPS waypoint: **N38 57.2798′ / W107 12.8507′.**

3.9 Trail crossing with trails to Marble and Horse Ranch Park—7,349 feet at GPS waypoint: **N38 57.2527′ W107 11.9508′.** Turn around here.

7.8 Arrive back at the trailhead.

HUNTER-FRYINGPAN/ HOLY CROSS/EAGLES NEST WILDERNESS AREAS

This stretch of the southern Rockies dramatically displays the ancestral rocks that formed them. You'll find extensive amounts of granite dating back to what is generally considered the first of three major uplifts 1.7 billion years ago. It's a reminder of the awesome forces of nature that have shaped the Rockies, from northern Canada to New Mexico.

The 2.3 million-acre White River National Forest is the most visited national forest in the nation. With eleven ski resorts, eight wilderness areas, ten mountain peaks above 14,000 feet, and 2,500 miles of trails, there's lots to explore.

Just from the paved road past Chapman Campground on the Fryingpan Road (Hike 13), for example, you'll catch marvelous views of the Sawatch Mountain Range in the Holy Cross Wilderness to the east and the Williams Mountain Range in the Hunter-Fryingpan Wilderness to the southeast. The Eagles Nest Wilderness, a little farther to the northeast, features the rugged mountains of the Gore Range.

All three areas are more vertical than horizontal. Jagged peaks, sharp-edged ridges, turquoise-colored alpine lakes, and deep valleys were created millions of years ago as volcanic activity lifted the youthful Rocky Mountains. Wind and water erosion did the rest.

Hikers climb the saddle beyond Independence Lake on Lost Man Trail.

13 FRYINGPAN LAKES TRAIL

Total ascent: 1,708 feet. Total descent: 1,476. There's a lot of up and down to this Fryingpan Lakes Trail, but your rewards are well worth it. The scenery, the lakes, and the jagged peaks of the Hunter-Fryingpan Wilderness all help make this a fabulous hike. The river was named for a frying pan hung in a tree to mark the spot of a wounded trapper in a fight with Native American Utes. This area has a proud history of trapping, mining, and life on the Colorado frontier, where legends of wealth continue to grow.

Start: From Fryingpan Lakes Trailhead at the end of FR 505
Elevation gain: 9,815–11,021 feet (although total ascent and descent is much greater)
Distance: 9.1 miles out and back
Difficulty: Moderate to strenuous due to length and elevation
Hiking time: +/- 4 hours
Seasons/schedule: As soon as snow melts in late May or June until snow flies again, usually Oct
Fees and permits: None
Trail contacts: White River National Forest Service, Sopris Ranger District, 620 Main St., Carbondale, CO 81623, (970) 963-2266; www.fs.usda.gov/recarea/whiteriver/recarea/?recid=41606
Canine compatibility: Dogs must be on leash at all times.
Trail surface: Rocky, backcountry singletrack path
Land status: USFS White River National Forest / Hunter-Fryingpan Wilderness Area

Nearest town: Basalt
Other trail users: Minimal horseback use
Nat Geo TOPO! map (USGS): Mt. Champion, Nast
National Geographic Trails Illustrated maps: #127, Aspen/Independence Pass
Other maps: White River National Forest Service map
Special considerations: Watch the weather and be prepared for afternoon thunderstorms!
Other: The Wilderness Workshop is the conservation watchdog of the White River National Forest and adjacent federal public lands. It provides "free guided hikes with a purpose," and its goal is "to keep our beloved backcountry more or less 'as is' and, where possible, to restore wildness to this nationally important landscape." www.wildernessworkshop.org

FINDING THE TRAILHEAD

From Basalt, take the Fryingpan River Road (CR 4, that turns into CR 104) for approximately 31 miles to FR 505 (it is 0.5 mile past the 32 mile marker on the county road.) This is the Fryingpan Lakes Road. Turn right (south) and continue on this somewhat rough, yet well-maintained two-wheel-drive dirt road for 5.6 miles to its end near the gauging station and water diversion structure for the Boustead Tunnel. The trailhead is to the left (east) of the water diversion structure.
Trailhead GPS: N39 14.6611' / W106 31.8155'

THE HIKE

The first thing you see at the Fryingpan Lakes Trailhead is a gauging station and cement diversion dam to the Charles H. Boustead Tunnel. This structure diverts water from the west slope and transports it 5.5 miles to the other side of the Continental Divide, where it spills into Turquoise Lake near Leadville. From there, the water flows east to a thirsty front range (see "The Fry-Ark").

Once you get past that initial visual shock, you'll certainly enjoy this trail as it traverses through a wonderland of high-mountain woodlands and meadows full of wildflowers. It follows the world-famous Fryingpan River to its headwaters beneath the serrated ridge of the Continental Divide to Fryingpan Lakes.

You're led across the west side of 14,421-foot Mount Massive, the second tallest peak in Colorado, to two small lakes nestled in a high alpine valley beneath this immense mountain.

Wild columbines, the state's flower, are found all along the trail throughout the summer, but this is so high up the drainage, it's usually covered in snow until June.

There are actually two trailheads at this spot. The trail for Lily Pad Lake, FS Trail #1907, leads to the left (east) while the Fryingpan Lakes Trail #1921 leads to the right, or south.

Upper Fryingpan Lake, at 10,970 feet in elevation, is the headwaters of the world-famous Fryingpan River.

Start on the Fryingpan Lakes Trail just above the water diversion project and immediately cross a stout footbridge over the Fryingpan River. There's an information kiosk just across the river and adjacent to Marten Creek, which flows into the Fryingpan from the south.

After one quick switchback, you'll travel 0.4 mile south to the Hunter-Fryingpan Wilderness boundary. You'll cross a lovely meadow, then return into the dark timber and wind your way upstream. The trail is overgrown but easy to follow as it skirts a rockslide between the creek and hillside to the right (west).

You'll continue to gain and lose elevation all along this stretch of trail for another 1.5 miles, when the trail leads into another beautiful columbine-filled meadow that flows down to the river—again from the west. The imposing ridge all along that west side of this drainage towers between 13,000 and 13,300 feet in elevation. The other side is even more impressive, as a long bare granite ridge on your left (east) side leads to Mount Massive, which soon comes into view.

At 2.4 miles, you'll cross from the west side of the river to the east side on a sturdy footbridge. The trail leads into the dark timber and then continues upstream to the south. From this side of the valley, you get to see a different perspective of that 13,000-foot ridge of unnamed peaks on your right (west).

You'll have to maneuver through a large boulder field, the bottom of a massive rockslide off the western flank of Mt. Massive, at 2.8 miles. You'll catch your first glimpse of the lower lake at 3.6 miles. It's still another 0.3 mile ahead. There are plenty of spots to stop for a break at this lake before continuing on a trail that's much less well defined from this point. However, you can see where you're heading as you continue into the upper basin.

Before reaching the upper lake, you'll pass by a small, yet scenic pond lined with wild marsh marigolds and white alyssum. The trail then leads through a boulder field on the east side of this pond and up to the main lake at just past 4.5 miles. It's surrounded by tall willows, colorful columbines, and massive granite peaks—and it's breathtaking!

MILES AND DIRECTIONS

0.0 Start from the Fryingpan Lakes trailhead above and to the left (east) of the water structure.

0.4 Wilderness boundary.

1.9 Another beautiful meadow full of columbines flowing down from the right (west).

2.4 Cross on a footbridge over the Fryingpan River. **N39 13.2538' / W106 30.6568'**

2.8 Trail traverses through a massive rockslide that flows down the western flank of Mt. Massive.

3.6 Here's your first view of the lower Fryingpan Lake.

3.9 Arrive at lower Fryingpan Lake. **N39 12.1467' / W106 30.9129'**

4.4 This is a small pond just below the upper lake.

4.55 You've reached the upper Fryingpan Lake at 10,970 feet in elevation. **N39 11.6866' / W106 31.0333'**

9.1 After backtracking, arrive back at the trailhead.

Mount Massive, 14,421 feet, towers over the small pond between the Upper and Lower Fryingpan Lakes.

THE FRY-ARK

The Fryingpan-Arkansas Project—Fry-Ark—is a water diversion project. It takes water from the less populated West Slope of Colorado and diverts it through an elaborate network of twenty-two tunnels and conduits for 87 miles—including 5.5 miles beneath the Continental Divide—to fill Turquoise Reservoir, south of Leadville.

Authorized in 1962 by President Kennedy, the project diverts water from the Fryingpan River basin and delivers an average of 52,000 acre-feet of water a year for irrigation and municipal use to Colorado Springs, Pueblo, La Junta, Lamar, and other southeastern Colorado municipalities. (An acre-foot of water equals about 326,000 gallons, or enough water to cover a football field a foot deep.)

This series of interconnected tunnels carries water from sixteen small diversion dams, all at an elevation of more than 10,000 feet. Using gravity, they collect snowmelt and run it to the Charles H. Boustead Tunnel, located at this trailhead. The Boustead Tunnel then conveys that water underneath the Continental Divide 5.5 miles before discharging it into Turquoise Lake just west of Leadville.

A sister project, the Colorado-Big Thompson Project, was authorized by President Franklin Roosevelt in 1937 near the headwaters of the once mighty Colorado River at Grand Lake. Likewise, it takes water from the west and transports it to the thirsty metropolitan areas of the East Slope. Originally built for agricultural purposes, its main demands have now shifted to municipal and industrial supply.

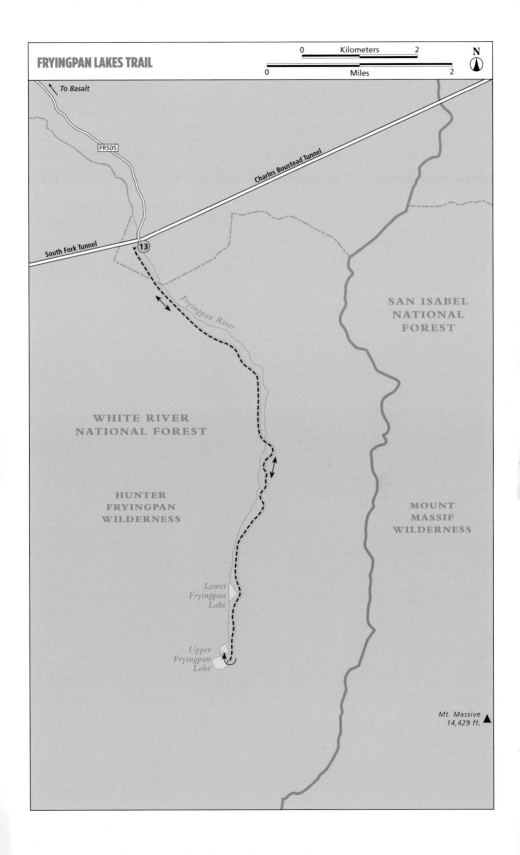

FRYINGPAN LAKES TRAIL

0 Kilometers 2
0 Miles 2

N

To Basalt

FR505

Charles Boustead Tunnel

South Fork Tunnel

13

Fryingpan River

SAN ISABEL
NATIONAL
FOREST

WHITE RIVER
NATIONAL FOREST

HUNTER
FRYINGPAN
WILDERNESS

MOUNT
MASSIF
WILDERNESS

Lower
Fryingpan
Lake

Upper
Fryingpan
Lake

Mt. Massive
14,429 ft.

14 LOST MAN TRAIL

A trek along Lost Man Trail #1996 off Independence Pass above Aspen offers stunning views with access to pristine lakes and jagged peaks along the very spine of the Continental Divide. Leading from the headwaters of the world-famous Roaring Fork River, much of your time is spent above timberline enjoying the sounds of silence and the exhilaration of hiking to what seems like the top of the world. This is not a complete loop hike, so a shuttle vehicle is recommended. You could, however, easily hitchhike back up the road. Everyone parked here is doing the same thing you are.

Start: From Upper Trailhead off Independence Pass near mile marker 59.1

Elevation gain: Beginning elevation; 11,506 feet; highest elevation: 12,791 feet; ending elevation: 10,507 feet

Distance: 8.8 miles point to point

Difficulty: Moderate to strenuous up to Lost Man Pass because of elevation gain; moderate the rest of the way

Hiking time: 5+ hours

Seasons/schedule: Summer (see Other below)

Fees and permits: None

Trail contacts: Aspen Ranger District, 199 Prospector Rd, Aspen, CO 81611, (970) 925-3445; https://www.fs.usda.gov/recarea/whiteriver/recarea/?recid=40407

Canine compatibility: Dogs must be on leash at all times.

Trail surface: Rocky, backcountry singletrack path

Land status: White River National Forest / Hunter-Fryingpan Wilderness Area

Nearest town: Aspen

Other trail users: Some horseback use from lower trailhead to Midway Trail

Nat Geo TOPO! map (USGS): Independence Pass, Mt. Champion

National Geographic Trails Illustrated map: # 127, Aspen/Independence Pass

Other maps: White River National Forest map

Special considerations: The time to recreate here is limited to when Independence Pass is open. It typically closes on or near Nov 7 and almost always reopens on the Thurs before Memorial Day each May. However, just because the pass is open doesn't mean you can hike here. There may be too much snow. You may, however, ski here—usually beginning in Oct and often through May and into June. This is some of the finest backcountry skiing and snowboarding in the Rockies. You just have to climb up a couple thousand feet to get to it!

Other: This is Aspen and it's summer. Give yourself plenty of time to get through town. Also, NO VEHICLE AND/OR TRAILER COMBINATION MORE THAN 35-FEET LONG IS ALLOWED ON THIS PASS. If you travel here with such a vehicle, every other person on the road will curse you, and you will incur a $1,500 fine. You will also have to pay for being towed off the mountain and back to the most expensive town in Colorado!

FINDING THE TRAILHEAD

From Aspen, drive east on CO 82 up Independence Pass for approximately 17 miles, just past mile marker 55, to Lost Man Trailhead and Lost Man Campground. The campground will be on your right (south); turn left into the trailhead parking area and leave one vehicle here. Continue up Independence Pass for another 3.9 miles to the upper Lost Man Trailhead on the left-hand side of the road, just before the last major switchback leading to the top of Independence Pass and the Continental Divide.

Trailhead GPS: N39 07.4809' / W106 34.9127'

THE HIKE

Rugged, pristine and largely forgotten between its more famous neighbors the Collegiate Peaks and Maroon Bells–Snowmass Wilderness Areas, the Hunter-Fryingpan Wilderness is seldom seen. Yet, located just outside Aspen, Colorado, it's easily accessible—once you get through the crowded, glitzy tourist town and billionaire mecca.

Located on the north side of Independence Pass, Lost Man Trail #1996 takes you to the headwaters of the Roaring Fork River, which travels from here for 61 miles before it spills into the Colorado River at Glenwood Springs. In that short distance, it drops more in elevation (from 13,000 feet to 5,761 feet) than the entire Mississippi River drainage from Canada to the Gulf of Mexico.

The hike described here takes you from the upper Lost Man Trailhead to the lower Lost Man Trailhead. That doesn't mean, however, that your entire trek is downhill. On the contrary, this hike begins at 11,506 feet in elevation, and immediately climbs to Lost Man Pass at 12,791 feet in elevation. On the way, you'll pass Independence Lake—the headwaters of the Roaring Fork River.

The trail begins at timberline and soon splits with the Linkins Lake Trail. Keep right. In 0.5 mile, it crosses the Roaring Fork and continues up the east side of the newly formed river between 13,711-foot Twinning Peak to the east (your right) and 13,301-foot Geissler Mountain to the west.

From here, the trail travels northeast until you reach the banks of Independence Lake at 12,513 feet in elevation (**N39 08.5531' / W106 34.1910'**). It will, however, eventually travel to the northwest, and then south to circumnavigate Geissler Mountain.

First, you'll follow the bank of the lake around its left (northwest) side, then begin your climb up Lost Man Pass. Take your time. It's a steep grade. The pass tops at 12,791 feet in elevation (**N39 08.9136' / W106 34.0343'**).

From here, you'll enjoy spectacular views back (south) over Independence Lake, and forward (north) over Lost Man Lake on the other side of the pass. Both are surrounded by the jagged peaks of the Hunter-Fryingpan.

Be careful on your way down the steep switchbacks and sections of talus (slopes formed by an accumulation of broken rock debris). In 0.2 mile, you'll reach the eastern bank of Lost Lake, which is much larger than Independence Lake. Expect snow on this stretch of trail well into July. This is the headwaters of Lost Man Creek, which spills into the Roaring Fork downstream from the Lower Lost Man Trailhead and campground.

The trail continues past the lake and heads up the next bench to the northeast, before eventually veering to the northwest. Two miles from the lake, you'll head downhill—finally—and enter a large drainage from the north (your right). In another 0.1 mile, you'll

Lost Man Lake, at the top of the world

come to the South Fork Trail leading to South Fork Pass. You're still at 11,642 feet in elevation. Take a hard left here, and head downhill.

In another 1.2 miles, you should find a nice place in the shade for lunch, before continuing your trek downhill to Lost Man Reservoir, a manmade lake that gets a fair amount of fishing pressure in July and August. Continue past the reservoir on its west side, still heading south, to the lower trailhead and parking area—and relax. You've just climbed from 11,506 feet, up to 12,791 feet, then back down to 10,507 feet. Give your knees a break!

MILES AND DIRECTIONS

0.0   Start from upper Lost Man Trail #1996 trailhead, 11,506 feet.

0.1   Cross the headwaters of the Roaring Fork River on the sturdy footbridge. The trail then splits; go right (north) to Lost Man Lake Trail and enter Hunter-Fryingpan Wilderness Area.

1.0   Climb over a grassy, flower-filled knob to expose a wide alpine bench with great views.

1.7   Reach the banks of Independence Lake, 12,513 feet; **N39 08.5531′ / W106 34.1910′.**

2.2   Lost Man Pass, 12,791 feet; **N39 08.9136′ / W106 34.0343′.**

2.6   Lost Man Lake, 12,466 feet; **N39 09.1280′ / W106 34.0394′.**

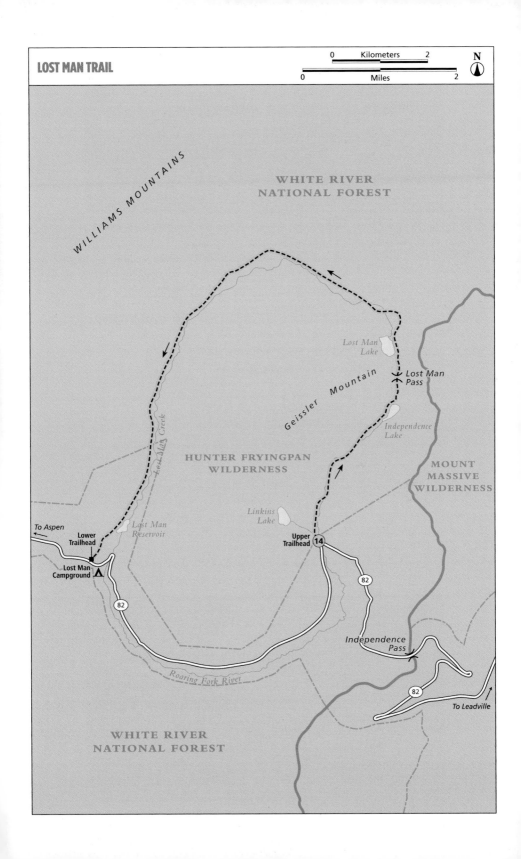

Lost Man Lake, from the saddle between Lost Man and Independence Lakes

2.8 Trail moves to the right (northeast) and away from the lake, up to the next bench before veering toward the northwest.

4.7 Head down a little as you enter a large drainage that enters Lost Man Creek from the north (right).

4.8 Trail crossing for South Fork Trail and Lost Man Trail; **N39 10.0403' / W106 35.5485'.** Take a hard left and head downhill (southwest)

5.6 Good spot for lunch! **N39 09.5181' / W106 36.3057'**

6.2 Nice view spot. **N39 09.0484' / W106 36.6261'**

6.8 Head into dark timber.

7.1 Major creek crossing **N39 08.6426' / W106 36.8751'** at 10,784 feet.

7.3 Double-wide trail through dark timber.

7.6 Back into the wide open out of dark timber and still on wide trail.

8.2 As you head down toward Lost Man Reservoir, the dark timber comes closer to the trail.

8.4 Reach Lost Man Reservoir dam and dam structure.

8.6 Trail splits with Midway Trail with numerous switchbacks; go left.

8.7 Foot trail goes left, horse route goes right; cross the footbridge over Lost Man Creek.

8.8 Reach lower trailhead and parking area. **N39 07.3065' / W106 37.4672'**

At 12,466 feet in elevation, Lost Man Lake remains frozen for much of the year.

15 NOLAN LAKE TRAIL

Who can resist the temptation of following a sparkling stream to its origin from a high-mountain lake surrounded by jagged peaks? This trail takes you to the southeast base of 12,550-foot New York Mountain, but the harsh granite ridges of 11,902-foot Craig Peak, directly to the north of the lake dominate the skyline. Aspen, fir, and spruce woods line this trail as it climbs around the east side of Craig Peak and into the 123,000-acre Holy Cross Wilderness Area, before dropping to Nolan Lake from the southeast.

Start: At Nolan Lake Trailhead #1898
Elevation gain: 2,020 feet (9,220 feet at trailhead to 11,240 feet at Nolan Lake)
Distance: 6.0 miles out and back
Difficulty: Moderate due to elevation gain—it's all uphill to the lake!
Hiking time: About 3 hours
Seasons/schedule: Late June to Oct
Fees and permits: None
Trail contacts: White River National Forest, Eagle Ranger District, 125 West 5th St., Eagle, CO 81631-0720; (970) 328-6388; www.fs.usda.gov/whiteriver
Canine compatibility: Dogs are allowed under leash or strict voice control. It is illegal for dogs to chase wildlife!

Trail surface: Backcountry dirt, rock, and roots on a singletrack path after starting on a rugged jeep road now closed to motorized traffic.
Land status: Holy Cross Wilderness Area in the White River National Forest
Nearest town: Eagle
Other trail users: Foot and horse travel only
Nat Geo TOPO! map (USGS): Fulford, Crooked Creek Pass, Mt. Jackson
National Geographic Trails Illustrated map: #149, Eagles Nest and Holy Cross Wilderness Areas
Other maps: White River National Forest map

FINDING THE TRAILHEAD

From the I-70 Eagle interchange, turn south on Eby Creek Road to the US 6 roundabout. Turn right (west) on US 6/Grand Avenue and travel 0.8 mile to the next roundabout. Here, take the third right onto Sylvan Lake Road. Continue 1.6 miles to Brush Creek Road and turn right (east). Follow this for 9 miles. You'll pass the Sylvan Lake State Park Visitor Center where the pavement ends. Continue on this well-maintained dirt road to the fork of East and West Brush Creek. Take the left (east) fork, now FR 415, and follow this for 6.7 miles past the Yeoman Park Campground. Turn left on FR 418 and continue for 3.6 miles to the town of Fulford. Go past Old Fulford Road which will be on your left and park at the trailhead parking on the right-hand side of FR 418. (If you get confused going through Eagle, just head south as most roads through town lead to either the Sylvan Lake Road or Brush Creek Road. Once you're on the Brush Creek Road, it's clear sailing!)
Trailhead GPS: N39 30.8406' / W106 39.1170'

THE HIKE

Rushing streams, fields of wildflowers, an old ghost town, aspen, spruce, fir, waterfalls, chipmunks, golden eagles and a high-mountain lake—there's plenty to see on a 3-mile hike to Nolan Lake, at the base of New York Mountain south of Eagle, Colorado. Of course, that's 3 miles up! But look at it this way. It's 3 miles back down, too.

Lying in a glacier-carved depression in what some consider the "Water Wilderness," Nolan Lake is surrounded by soaring ridges and peaks of the Sawatch Range. Holy Cross is called the Water Wilderness because of its numerous cascading streams emanating from dozens of high alpine lakes, and its tremendous valleys beneath more than twenty-five peaks above 13,000 feet in elevation that become inundated by spring snowmelt. This water caused one of Colorado's most contentious "wilderness vs. water development" battles before the area was designated as wilderness in 1980.

While neither New York Mountain nor Craig Peak is a 13,000-foot peak, they nonetheless dominate the skyline and are clearly visible 25 miles away from the I-70 corridor near Eagle.

The start of the trail is on an old mining road that leads up through aspen, fir, and spruce to the upper town of Fulford. During the late 1800s, Fulford was a booming gold mine town with an assay office, saloons, stores, cabins, and hotels. Today, all that remains of the upper town are a few remnants of old cabins. The lower town (where you parked

Not much remains of the old mining town of Fulford.

Some enjoy Nolan Lake for its wild fighting brook trout, others for its scenery, still others for its serenity.

your vehicle) experienced a sort of renaissance in the late 1960s and early 1970s when a handful of families began building summer cabins.

In 0.2 mile, the trail crosses Nolan Creek and begins a climb up White Quail Gulch. Parts of the old ghost town can be seen upstream from here. In another 0.1 mile, the trail splits and leaves the old mining road. Go left and uphill on the well-marked Nolan Lake Trail. You'll only travel along White Quail Gulch for a short way before heading south toward Nolan Creek.

You'll huff and puff for another 0.4 mile or so until the trail levels off a little. By a mile, you'll have reached 10,400 feet in elevation (the trailhead was at 9,220 feet!). The trail now descends for a short distance through a fair amount of downed timber, eaten and killed by the mountain spruce beetle (see the sidebar for Hike 1: North Lake Trail).

About a half-mile farther, you'll cross through the lower end of a rockslide—or more accurately an alluvial fan. This "debris flow" was caused by glaciers eons ago. These alluvial fans are where the action of water and glaciers finally lost their force.

At the 2-mile mark, you'll be hiking up a 9 percent grade hill. Watch your footing as some of the gravel is loose. Don't look down too much, though, or you'll miss a pretty little waterfall at 2.1 miles as the trail angles back to Nolan Creek.

The trail soon cuts through an open meadow heading east before retreating into the dark timber. It then circles around to the west, arriving on the picturesque lake's southeastern shoreline. You can easily hike around this 7.2-acre pond that's loaded with brook trout, before heading downhill and back to your vehicle.

MILES AND DIRECTIONS

0.0   Start from Nolan Lake Trailhead #1898.

0.2   Cross Nolan Creek and head up White Quail Gulch.

0.3   Trail splits; go left and uphill on Nolan Lake Trail.

0.7   The trail levels off a little as you cut across a sidehill in dark timber.

1.0   At 10,400 feet in elevation.

1.5   The trail travels through the rockslide/debris flow left from ancient glaciers.

2.0   You're climbing up a 9 percent grade now.

2.1   Watch for a waterfall to your right.

2.3   The trail cuts through an open meadow before returning to dark timber at 11,158 feet.

3.0   Reach the shores of Nolan Lake. This is your turnaround point.

6.0   Arrive back at the trailhead.

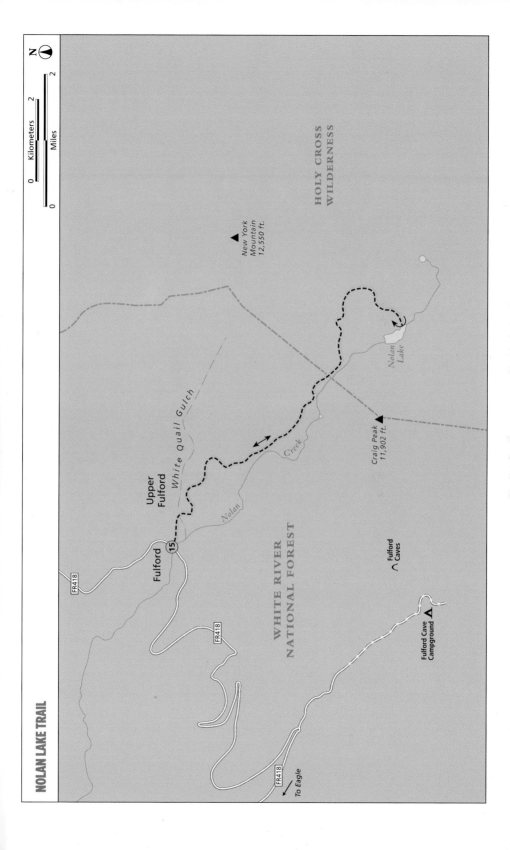

NOLAN LAKE TRAIL

N

Kilometers
0   2

Miles
0   2

HOLY CROSS
WILDERNESS

New York
Mountain
12,550 ft.

White Quail Gulch

Upper
Fulford

Fulford

FR418

15

Nolan

Creek

Craig Peak
11,902 ft.

Nolan
Lake

WHITE RIVER
NATIONAL FOREST

Fulford
Caves

FR418

FR418

To Eagle

Fulford Cave
Campground

Larry and Marj McKenna of Grand Junction navigate the rough trail of roots, rocks, and dirt on a return trip from Nolan Lake.

CENTRAL COLORADO PLATEAU/ COLORADO RIVER DRAINAGE

The Colorado Plateau, as the name implies, is broad, open, mostly flat and elevated land. This plateau is a physiographic region characterized by a dramatic range in the ages and colors of the sedimentary rocks—exposed in deep canyons eroded by the powerful tributaries feeding the Colorado River. We can easily recognize this process as we hike through these brightly colored and exposed layers, deep canyons, and stark walls of mesas and buttes.

Colorado National Monument, on the northeast edge of the Colorado Plateau, towers over Grand Junction and the Grand Valley below.

In some places we get a peek at Precambrian crystalline and metamorphic rocks that were formed between 1 and 2 billion years ago.

The vegetation can be sparse and characterized by cactus, sage, rabbit brush, native grasses, and other hardy plants that can wait as long as it takes for the next rainfall.

Higher elevations are covered by juniper and pinyon pine, forming some of the highest and most isolated forests in the West.

16 RATTLESNAKE CANYON ARCHES TRAIL

Seven major sandstone arches display their age, majesty, and delicacy on this great hike into Black Ridge Wilderness Area. The 75,550-acre wilderness forms the core of the BLM's 123,000-acre McInnis Canyons National Conservation Area, which was designated as a "nationally significant area" by Congress in 2000. Located near Grand Junction and Fruita, Colorado, it extends from the western border of the Colorado National Monument, into Utah. This area includes the second-largest collection of arches in the country outside Arches National Park, only 90 miles to the west.

Start: Upper Rattlesnake Arches Trailhead at the end of Black Ridge Road
Elevation loss: 5,868–5,390 feet (478 feet)
Distance: 6.0 miles round-trip
Difficulty: Moderately strenuous; a 0.2-mile section connecting the top of the mesa to the bench below is rocky and steep
Hiking time: About 3–5 hours
Seasons/schedule: Late Apr until the first snow flies. (Note: Motorized travel is prohibited from Feb 15 to Apr 15. Rattlesnake Arches Trail can be accessed from the Pollock Bench trailhead during those months.)
Fees and permits: None
Trail contacts: BLM, Grand Junction Field Office, 2815 H Rd., Grand Junction, CO 81506; (970) 244-3000; www.blm.gov/visit/rattlesnakemee -canyons.
Canine compatibility: Allowed under control
Trail surface: The trail follows an old jeep road for the first half-mile, before descending a rocky, steep 0.2-mile stretch. It then follows an easy, sandy backcountry trail to its terminus.
Land status: BLM McInnis Canyons National Conservation Area
Nearest towns: Fruita, Grand Junction

Other trail users: Horseback riders (rarely seen but horse access may be found at the lower Pollock Bench Trail).
Nat Geo TOPO! map (USGS): Mack, Ruby Canyon and Battleship Rock
National Geographic Trails Illustrated map: CO National Monument/McInnis Canyons NCA
Special considerations: While this area is only 36 miles from downtown Grand Junction and 23 miles from Fruita, the last 2 miles of the 10-mile Black Ridge dirt road is mean, nasty, and impassable when wet. A high-clearance four-wheel-drive vehicle is required. The drive takes 1 hour, 40 minutes from Grand Junction.

You can reach Rattlesnake Canyon Arches via a 15.5 mile out-and-back hike from the Pollock Bench Trail, but it's not an "easy" hike. It's long and hot.
Other: The Colorado Canyons Association fosters community stewardship of National Conservation Lands with a focus on Dominguez-Escalante, Gunnison Gorge, and McInnis Canyons National Conservation Areas in western Colorado. This nonpartisan, nonprofit volunteer organization encourages cooperation among all NCA users and interests. 543 Main St. #4, Grand Junction, CO 81501; (970) 263-7902; www.coloradocanyonsassociation.org.

FINDING THE TRAILHEAD

From Grand Junction, take I-70 west to the Fruita exit (#19), turn left onto CO 340, and follow the signs to the Colorado National Monument (south). Travel 2.5 miles to the national monument west entrance. Turn right and travel 0.2 mile to the entrance gate, and continue on Rim Rock Road another 13.6 miles to the Glade Park Store Cutoff and Black Ridge Road turnoff. Turn right and travel a short distance to Black Ridge Road. Turn right again. A seasonal closure dictates which road you take from here (there's an upper and lower road), but follow directions and stay on the main dirt road for 10.1 mile. The last 2 miles are very rugged. A high-clearance four-wheel-drive vehicle is required. (Remember: the road is closed completely from Feb 15 through Apr 15.)

Trailhead GPS: N39 08.2309' / W108 50.0051'

THE HIKE

Black Ridge, south of the Colorado River and on the eastern edge of the Colorado Plateau, is situated on an east-west plain and is dissected by seven red rock canyons varying in length. Rattlesnake Canyon is one of the longer canyons dissecting the ridge, eventually spilling into the Colorado River near the Colorado/Utah state line. Rattlesnake Canyon Arches Trail is certainly one of the most adventurous and fascinating trails here.

A trip through Rattlesnake Canyon is a kaleidoscopic journey through time and earth—from the upper ends of Black Ridge along the green, gray, and purple Morrison formation, down through rust-colored Entrada sandstone and beneath the spectacular Wingate formations with their towering stone walls. Its colorful geological features include spires, windows, gorgeous giant alcoves, and at least seven fabulous arches (although some literature notes there are eleven arches along this trail).

Pinyon, juniper, sagebrush, and riparian vegetation in this area provide habitat for mule deer, mountain lion, and a herd of bighorn sheep as well as peregrine falcons, and bald and golden eagles.

From the trailhead at the west end of the parking area, the trail follows an old, closed jeep road winding down from the top bench for 0.5 mile to a trail junction. For those not willing to take the 0.2-mile downward plunge to the next bench below this, go left to the First Arch overlook, half a mile away. For everyone else, turn right and travel 0.2 mile down a steep, rocky set of switchbacks to the next junction with the Pollock Canyon Trail.

Here, go left and follow a narrow, sandy backcountry path around the northwest tip of this mesa. As you round the turn, notice the tall, rust and red sandstone walls and watch for windows into the sky on your left. There are seven major arches from here to the end of the trail, along with numerous spires, giant alcoves, and contrasting desert patina. Notice how these canyons and their pinyon-juniper-covered mesas all slope downward toward the Colorado River in the distance.

Waterfalls can be found here during spring runoff and after summer thunderstorms. Many visitors attempt to climb through First Arch. This route is very steep and requires some climbing skills. The BLM notes, "This is not part of the designated trail."

No camping or fires are allowed in this area. Hiking off trails can be dangerous and destroys cryptobiotic soils (see "Cryptobiotic Soils."). From this spot, it's wise to retrace your steps back to the vehicle instead of climbing up through First Arch. Smile, and say, "Well, I could have done that, but BLM doesn't want me to break my neck!"

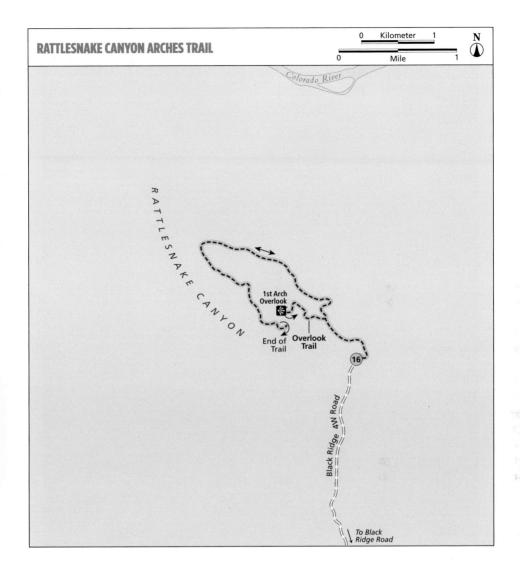

MILES AND DIRECTIONS

0.0   Sign in at trailhead. **N39 08.2309' / W108 50.0051'**

0.5   Trail junction. Go left for 0.5 mile to First Arch overlook; go right to follow path to Rattlesnake Canyon Arches Trail.

0.7   Trail junction with Pollock Bench Trail. Go left to lower Rattlesnake Arches Trail.

3.0   End of trail beneath First Arch. Retrace steps.

6.0   Arrive back at trailhead.

Rattlesnake Canyon, inside the 75,550-acre Black Ridge Wilderness Area, has more arches than any canyon outside Arches National Park near Moab, Utah, about 90 miles west of here.

CRYPTOBIOTIC SOILS

According to Jayne Belnap, a soil ecologist with the National Geological Survey, "Cryptobiotic soil crusts, consisting of soil cyanobacteria, lichens and mosses, play an important ecological roles in the arid Southwest. In the cold deserts of the Colorado Plateau region (parts of Utah, Arizona, Colorado, and New Mexico), these crusts are extraordinarily well-developed, often representing over 70 percent of the living ground cover. Cryptobiotic crusts increase the stability of otherwise easily eroded soils, increase water infiltration in regions that receive little precipitation, and increase fertility in soils often limited in essential nutrients such as nitrogen and carbon."

They're really important here in the Desert Southwest. Don't tread on them!

The First Arch on the Rattlesnake Canyon Arches Trail, seen from above

17 MEE CANYON

With arches, windows, spires, and alcoves, Mee Canyon offers one of the most exciting hikes in this high-desert country. This route is not recommended for inexperienced hikers as it steeply descends both Entrada and Wingate sandstone layers with exposed cliffs and very limited access. Also, directional signs and other evidence of human imprints are limited. If you think you're up for it, though, you'll crawl through a small window arch, shinny down an old "Navajo-style" ladder, inch your way across a sandstone ledge, and finally enter into one of the largest natural alcoves on the Colorado Plateau.

Start: From Mee Canyon Trailhead
Elevation loss: 6,742 feet–5,343 feet (1,399 feet)
Distance: 5.5 miles out and back
Difficulty: Moderately strenuous to strenuous because of elevation loss/gain; some scary sections along rock ledges, through a window and down a ladder built into the side of a rock wall.
Hiking time: 3–5 hours
Seasons/schedule: Late Apr until the first snow flies. (Note: Motorized travel is prohibited from Feb 15 to Apr 15.)
Fees and permits: None
Trail contacts: BLM, Grand Junction Field Office, 2815 H Rd., Grand Junction, CO 81506; (970) 244-3000; https://www.blm.gov/visit/rattlesnakemee-canyons
Canine compatibility: Allowed under control.
Trail surface: Primitive singletrack backcountry trail marked intermittently with rock cairns. Some path-finding skills are necessary.
Land status: BLM McInnis Canyons National Conservation Area

Nearest towns: Fruita, Grand Junction
Other trail users: Foot traffic only
Nat Geo TOPO! map (USGS): Mack, Ruby Canyon and Battleship Rock
National Geographic Trails Illustrated map: CO National Monument/McInnis Canyons NCA
Special considerations: Moisture of any kind can make these roads impassable. Summer daytime temperatures can exceed 100 degrees F; this hike is best done early in the morning at this time of year. Water sources are limited and unreliable, so pack your own water. Biting gnats can be nasty from May through Aug; pack insect repellent.
Other: Don't miss the Mike the Headless Chicken Festival, usually held the first or second weekend in June in Fruita, dedicated to the amazing story of one chicken's will to live. Events include a 5K run, disc golf tournament, wing and peep eating contests, live music, delicious food, and artisan booths. (970) 858-3894; www.miketheheadlesschicken.org

FINDING THE TRAILHEAD

Take I-70 west to the Fruita exit (#19). Turn left on CO 340 and follow signs for 2.5 miles to Colorado National Monument. Turn right and travel 0.2 mile into the West Entrance of the national monument. Visitors headed to Glade Park or the McInnis Canyons National Conservation Area do not have to pay the entrance fee.

Travel 13.6 miles from the monument entrance station to the Glade Park Store turn-off sign, located just past Upper Liberty Cap trailhead. (Turn right and travel 0.2 mile to the Black Ridge Hunter Access Road. Turn right and stay on this road for 7.2 miles to the Mee Canyon Access Road. Turn left and travel 0.2 mile to the trailhead.)

There are two roads leading to this trailhead. Use of these roads is seasonally rotated for motorized travel. The upper road is open from mid-Apr to mid-Aug and the lower road from mid-Aug to mid-Feb. No motorized travel is allowed on either road from mid-Feb to mid-Apr. A high-clearance vehicle or four-wheel-drive vehicle is highly recommended.

Trailhead GPS: N39 05.8405' / W108 50.6435'

THE HIKE

There are parts of this hike that are scary—like the part where hikers inch their way across a narrow ledge of sandstone high above the canyon floor, or the part where they crawl through a tiny, narrow window arch on the edge of a massive alcove, then shinny down a Navajo-type ladder to the next narrow ledge leading to the bottom of this steep, yet fascinating gorge.

For adventurous hikers, however, this is one of the finest hikes on the upper Colorado River Plateau.

It's located in the heart of the Black Ridge Wilderness Area, so motorized and mechanized activities are limited. (Read: No ATVs, motorcycles or mountain bikes.) That's no big deal, though, since you couldn't ride or drive into this rugged canyon anyway.

The trail begins with a gentle 1.3-mile decline across the top of the cap rock Kayenta Sandstone to the rim of Mee Canyon. This may bore some of those thrill-seekers racing to the edge of the canyon, but in the spring, the desert is in bloom with desert primrose,

A lone hiker is seen as a speck inside the Mee Canyon Alcove, one of the largest in the United States, situated in the heart of the Black Ridge Wilderness Area in west-central Colorado.

Indian paintbrush, yellow and purple daisies, orange globe mallow, crimson red barrel cactus, as well as pink and yellow prickly pear cactus.

From this point, you'll rapidly descend through the Entrada and Wingate sandstone layers to the bottom of the canyon. At 1.8 miles, you'll be grinning—or swearing—as you crawl through a window arch on your hands and knees, then down a Navajo-style ladder, providing a great photo opportunity. Use caution here. This is a wilderness area and as such, don't expect any "improvements" to the ladder.

The trail then crawls down and along the base of this large alcove, before traversing farther down a couple more benches in the sandstone layers. Just prior to reaching the bottom of the canyon, you'll scoot across a narrow 30-foot-long ledge of sandstone—with your back against the wall. It looks scarier than it is.

Once at the bottom of the canyon at 2.5 miles, turn upstream and hike for another quarter mile to one of the largest alcoves in these canyon lands. You can explore the alcove or bushwhack upstream a little farther, but the trail ends here. It's a good place for lunch in the shade before hiking back up and out.

The best time to be in this canyon is the spring, when the desert is in full bloom and the gnats haven't made their presence known. During the summertime, temperatures can

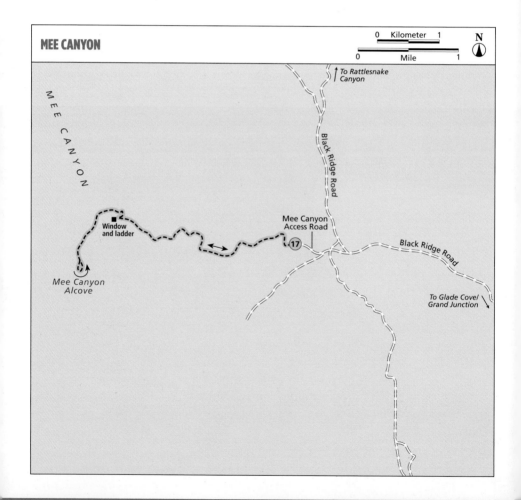

Climbing a Navajo-style ladder through a small window-arch

Colorful collared lizards are found throughout this high-desert country. They chew on twigs, eat grasshoppers, crickets, and even other lizards!

exceed 100 degrees, and the biting gnats in those pinyon and juniper trees at the start of the trail may drive you off the edge, even before you get there. Take plenty of bug juice, sunscreen, and water. Fall is also a great time to be here, because no one else is! You just miss those springtime desert wildflowers.

MILES AND DIRECTIONS

0.0 Sign in at trailhead then follow gentle decline to rim of Mee Canyon.

1.3 Drop down one bench into the canyon.

1.6 Drop down to the next bench.

1.7 Drop onto the third bench.

1.8 Crawl through a window-arch, then climb down Navajo-style ladder. Follow curve of alcove to next bench down.

2.2 Drop around the corner of this alcove, then up, following rock cairns. Continue another 50 yards, and then drop again. Careful. Loose rock.

2.5 Cross side creek and hike into bottom of canyon, then continue upstream past first alcove.

2.75 Take right fork out of creek bottom and hike into Mee Canyon Alcove.

5.5 Follow your tracks and arrive back at the vehicle.

18 MONUMENT CANYON TRAIL

The Colorado National Monument is one of the least visited monuments in the United States, yet it's only minutes from the largest population center in western Colorado, Grand Junction.

Operated by the National Park Service, it rises from the Colorado River on the eastern edge of the Colorado Plateau, preserving 20,000 acres of incredible, steep-walled red rock canyons.

Monument Canyon Trail winds its way beneath many of the park's major rock sculptures, such as Independence Monument, Kissing Couple, and the Coke Ovens, which tower overhead. It's best to leave a vehicle at each end of this hike, and shuttle one vehicle back after the 6-mile trek downhill.

Start: Upper Monument Canyon Trailhead on Rimrock Drive
Elevation loss: 6,140–4,700 feet from top to bottom (1,440 feet)
Distance: 6 miles one way, top to bottom
Difficulty: Easy to moderate if going downhill – and you have good knees!
Hiking time: 2.5–4 hours
Seasons/schedule: Year-round, although HOT in the middle of a summer day. Guided walks available spring, summer, fall. Contact National Monument for further details. (970) 858-2800
Fees and permits: $15 individual hikers/bicycle riders (7-day permit); $25 per car (7-day permit); $45 yearly Colorado National Monument Pass; $80 Yearly National Parks Service Pass
Trail contacts: Colorado National Monument, Fruita, CO 81521; (970) 858-3616; www.nps.gov/colm.
Canine compatibility: No dogs allowed within national monument boundaries
Trail surface: Relatively smooth rock and dirt backcountry trail
Land status: National Park Service, Colorado National Monument

Nearest towns: Grand Junction, Fruita
Other trail users: Foot traffic only
Nat Geo TOPO! map (USGS): Colorado National Monument
National Geographic Trails Illustrated map: Colorado National Monument/McInnis Canyons NCA
Other: The Palisade Peach Festival is one of the original agricultural festivals in Colorado. Held in mid-August—just as the area's peaches reach their peak—it's Peach Mania: Satisfy your hunger for "local and authentic" with delicious peach products: from pies to ice cream, preserves to salsas, peach brandy and wine to virgin peach daiquiris, not to mention bushels of just-picked fresh peaches . . . all in a very scenic setting. http://palisadepeachfest.com

Colorado Mountain Winefest, mid-September, the granddaddy of Colorado wine festivals, the Winefest features fifty wineries from across Colorado. Events include wine tasting, chefs, artisans, live music, seminars, food, special VIP tickets, bottle sales, winery tours, and more. https://coloradowinefest.com

FINDING THE TRAILHEAD

UPPER TRAILHEAD

From Grand Junction, travel through the east entrance of the National Monument on Monument Road. The upper trailhead is on the right-hand side of the road, 15 miles from the east entrance.

From Fruita, take CO 340 to the West Entrance of the National Monument and travel past the Visitor Center 3.8 miles to the trailhead on the left. This is also the trailhead for the Coke Ovens Trail.

Upper Trailhead GPS: N39 04.6602' / W108 43.6873'

LOWER TRAILHEAD

From Grand Junction, take Grand Avenue over the Colorado River Bridge, where it becomes CO 340 (Broadway). Stay on this until you reach the Monument Canyon trailhead turn, approximately 7.5 miles. The turn is located just past (northwest of) Deer Park subdivision on the left. (It appears as if you're turning into someone's private driveway, but follow the signs and continue 0.1 mile to the trailhead parking.)

From Fruita, take CO 340 past the west entrance of the national monument and proceed 2.1 miles, then turn right just beyond mile marker #5 onto a dirt road that appears to be a driveway, then continue 0.1 mile to the parking area and trailhead.

Lower Trailhead GPS: N39 06.5231' / W108 42.0876'

THE HIKE

A one-way hike of 6 miles from the top of Monument Canyon to its mouth in the valley below allows hikers to descend through a sequence of sedimentary rock layers that span 50 million years—from the Upper Jurassic to the Upper Triassic Periods of the Mesozoic Era.

This easy hiking trail descends 1,440 feet, from 6,140 feet above sea level to 4,700 feet. (It's easy, that is, if you have the knees for a 1,400-foot descent! Take hiking poles and ibuprofen if you're worried.) Much of the descent comes within the first mile as you'll view the massive rounded "Coke Ovens" across the canyon to the south. This series of beehive-shaped rock domes resembles the ovens in the 19th century that processed coke, a fuel with few impurities and a high carbon content, made from coal.

After that, the route follows a gentle course and in very short order makes a sweeping left turn, traveling north around the base of a sheer cliff to reveal a number of tall, freestanding monoliths. The first is Kissing Couple—two sandstone towers that appear entwined in a lover's embrace. Next to this is "Praying Hands."

Farther into the canyon, you'll encounter the iconic and impressive Independence Monument. This structure was once part of a massive rock wall that separated Monument and Wedding Canyons. Slowly, as the forces of erosion enlarged these canyons millions of years ago, the dividing wall was narrowed and weakened. Eventually the wall was breached and parts of it collapsed. Independence Monument survived as a freestanding monolith.

For the next 2 miles, the trail descends on the right (south) side of "the Island," what's left of that wall between Monument and Wedding Canyons. This large and colorful canyon wall is actually a monocline (downward-sloping rock layers). Soon, you will travel through the harder and darker 1.7-billion-year-old Precambrian rock that lies beneath the reddish Chinle Formation. This is the base rock here and among the oldest rocks on the Colorado Plateau.

Independence Monument, left, was once part of a massive rock wall that separated Monument and Wedding Canyons. Over millions of years, the dividing wall was narrowed and weakened. Eventually the wall was breached and parts of it collapsed. Independence Monument survived as a freestanding monolith.

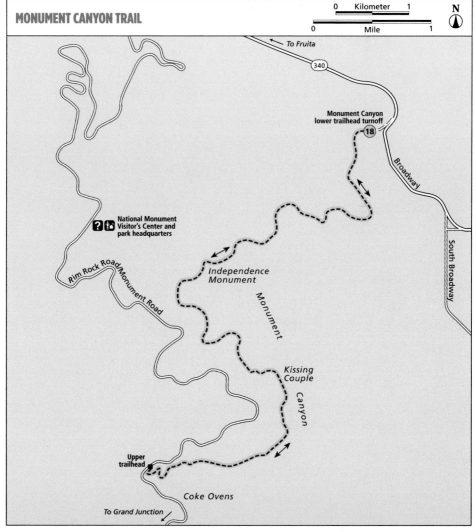

MONUMENT CANYON TRAIL

0 — Kilometer — 1

0 — Mile — 1

N

To Fruita

340

Monument Canyon
lower trailhead turnoff

18

Broadway

South Broadway

National Monument
Visitor's Center and
park headquarters

Rim Rock Road/Monument Road

Independence
Monument

Monument

Kissing
Couple

Canyon

Upper
trailhead

Coke Ovens

To Grand Junction

Independence Monument soars 450 feet above the canyon floor.

In 5 miles, you'll reach the mouth of the canyon, filled with 150-year-old Fremont cottonwoods. The trail here takes a sharp left turn and follows a very tall fence along the west side of the Deer Park subdivision and back to the lower trailhead and parking area. This fence was built to keep buffalo from wandering out of the park (see "Buffalo in the Desert?").

This is a great area to watch for desert bighorn sheep, which are found in this area year-round.

MILES AND DIRECTIONS

0.0 Start at trailhead at southwest end of parking area.

0.16 Go left (to the right is Coke Ovens Trail).

0.19 Sign in for this backcountry trail.

0.62 Cross creekbed at elevation 5,521 feet.

3.38 Elevation 5,281 feet at base of Independence Monument; go right to continue on Monument Canyon Trail.

5.0 Arrive at mouth of canyon beneath 150-year-old Fremont cottonwoods; go left and follow tall fence line adjacent to subdivision.

5.37 Wedding Canyon trail leads to the left; go right to Monument Canyon trailhead parking.

6.0 Arrive at lower Monument Canyon trailhead.

BUFFALO IN THE DESERT?

It's true. There used to be buffalo (American bison) here, though with sparse vegetation and limited water sources, it simply was not suitable habitat for them.

Some historical evidence suggests that Navajo butchered buffalo near here, but it wasn't until the 1920s when a man named John Otto got the idea that the monument should include a herd of buffalo. They were to be purchased by donations of buffalo-head nickels from schoolchildren and by contributions from the Odd Fellows and others.

Fifteen years earlier, Otto had single-handedly built many of the trails within the monument. He collected signatures, penned newspaper editorials, and wrote endless letters to Washington politicians in support of national recognition for the ancient canyons and towering monoliths of this area. On May 24, 1911, President Taft signed the proclamation that established Colorado National Monument, and Otto became its first full-time caretaker.

Otto eventually raised enough money to purchase two cows and one bull bison. His efforts produced a small herd that grew to forty-five animals. Generally, the herd was kept at about 20–25 head until the 1970s. Although the last animal allowed to remain there died in the early 1980s in Wedding Canyon, most of the herd was quarantined and relocated to other areas in the northwest United States before then.

As for Otto, after 16 years as the monument's custodian, he retired to Yreka, California, and died a pauper on June 19, 1952, at the age of 81.

19 MT. GARFIELD TRAIL

"I'm tired." "My knees hurt." "I'm really hot."

We hadn't even started hiking yet, but the Mt. Garfield Trailhead sign read:

"2 miles, 2,000 feet elevation gain!"

We looked up, realizing we'd have to come down the same way. On loose dirt.

Why is this one of the best hikes in western Colorado? Because it takes you to the top of the colorful Book Cliffs, one of the most recognizable landforms in western Colorado. Views from here are spectacular, and it's so much more than a huge, steep pile of dirt, as it may appear from the trailhead.

Start: From Mt Garfield Trailhead
Elevation gain: 4,842–6,777 feet (1,935 feet)
Distance: 3.4 miles round-trip (the sign says it's only 1.7 miles to the top! Huh! It feels a lot longer!)
Difficulty: Strenuous because of its steepness and trail surface
Hiking time: About 3 hours
Seasons/schedule: Year-round
Fees and permits: None
Trail contacts: BLM, Grand Junction Field Office, 2815 H Rd., Grand Junction, CO 81506; (970) 244-3000; https://www.blm.gov/visit/mount-garfield
Canine compatibility: Dogs permitted, but most humans should be put in the shelter if they attempt to bring a dog here, especially in the heat of the day!
Trail surface: Very loose gravel, dirt and rock
Land status: BLM
Nearest towns: Palisade, Grand Junction, Fruita
Other trail users: None
Nat Geo TOPO! map (USGS): Clifton, CO and Round Mountain, CO

National Geographic Trails Illustrated map: #208, Colorado National Monument/McInnis Canyons NCA
Other maps: BLM Mt. Garfield Trail map, available from BLM Grand Junction office
Special considerations: This is a steep hike—especially the first half-mile up and last half-mile down. Footing is unstable and slippery. The use of hiking poles is advised. Do not attempt this hike in the middle of the day in the middle of the summer. You can't drink enough water and even if you could, the gnats would eat you alive!
Other: Mt. Garfield lies just outside the Little Bookcliffs Wild Horse Area boundary, but the horses don't know that. Friends of the Mustangs (FOM) is a local nonprofit organization established to assist with the management of wild horses. It works alongside the BLM to keep water holes and tanks flowing and clean, mountain trails clear and marked, help with gathers and adoptions, and even provide birth control to mares. www.friendsofthemustangs.org

FINDING THE TRAILHEAD

From Grand Junction, take I-70 east to Palisade exit #42. Turn right off the exit and travel 0.1 mile, cross the Grand Canal and turn right (west) on G.7 Rd., the first paved road. Travel 1.5 miles to the end of G.7 Road. The pavement ends here. Turn right onto 35.8 Road. Drive 0.2 mile through the narrow cement underpass of I-70 to the parking area. The trailhead is located toward the north end of the parking area.

Trailhead GPS: N39 07.1476' / W108 23.3168'

THE HIKE

Yes, it's steep and slippery. But it's so cool to stand on the top of Mt. Garfield and survey the Grand Valley. You'll certainly feel like you've accomplished something!

The Book Cliffs are a unique series of desert mountains and cliffs that extend for 200 miles from DeBeque Canyon on the Colorado River near Palisade, to Price, Utah. It's one of the few mountain ranges in the world that orients from east to west instead of north to south. Because of that orientation, the sun and shadows dance and shimmer across the steep-sided slopes of the Book Cliffs, changing color, shape, and shade from dawn to dusk.

A trip to the top of Mt. Garfield not only offers great views, but you may also encounter some of the wild mustangs that live here on the top southern edge of the Little Book Cliffs Wild Horse Range.

The trail leads northwest (left) from the trailhead for less than 0.1 mile to an unmarked 6×6 post. Here, you'll head to your right and begin climbing up the steep spine of a Mancos Shale ridge. This shale is soft and claylike. It swells when wet and shrinks when dry.

Hikers navigate the first—and steepest—stretch of this hike.

Mount Garfield, at 6,777 feet, is an imposing sight for travelers along the I-70 corridor as they enter or exit the Grand Valley.

There is very little plant life on this section of trail because of the swelling and shrinking soils. This lack of plant life increases erosion that continues to reshape these desert mountains.

After huffing and puffing up 0.4 mile, you'll see a small trail split. Go left here, but if you miss it, don't worry. All trails lead UP and to the same point from here.

Soon, you'll top a rise to find a painted yellow brick marked "1/2" next to the trail. You've made it up the steepest and slickest half-mile stretch. The trail flattens out across a broad grassy field before climbing again in 0.1 mile.

Vegetation increases dramatically and you should begin to see signs of wild horses. The lead stallion will defecate on the same spot, creating large "stud piles" as territorial markings.

Now, you'll begin climbing through a boulder field of Mesa Verde sandstone, deposited along a shoreline of an ancient sea 145.5 to 65.5 million years ago. Coal seams can be seen in this section of the trail, created as shallow lagoons with exotic plants built up into peat bogs and later hardened into thick layers of coal.

In 0.75 mile, you'll climb into the pinyon/juniper zone and relish the shade. The trail reaches another grassy shelf that's not visible from below and at 0.9 mile, it winds its way up again.

At the 1-mile mark, the trail cuts west at the base of the last cliffs to the top of Mt. Garfield. In 1.2 miles, the trail climbs a saddle on the backside of Mt. Garfield and in another 0.2 mile, you'll find a smooth trail that gradually leads you to the pinnacle, where you'll find an American flag at 1.7 miles and the end of the trail.

The summit provides a breathtaking 360-degree view. The Mancos Shale you just climbed contrasts sharply with irrigated fields as the Colorado River courses through the valley below. The Uncompahgre Plateau and Colorado National Monument are set on the horizon beyond. The Grand Mesa rises impressively to the east and the Roan Cliffs and Roan Plateau rise to the northeast. The steep canyon between Mt. Garfield and the

The ledge on the top of Mt. Garfield offers spectacular views of the Grand Valley below.

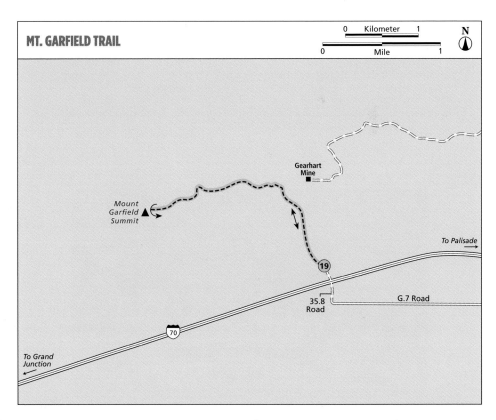

MT. GARFIELD TRAIL

Kilometer 0 1

Mile 0 1

N

Mount Garfield Summit ▲

Gearhart Mine ■

To Palisade

19

35.8 Road

G.7 Road

70

To Grand Junction

Roan Cliffs is Coal Canyon, which is where the major portion of the 30,261-acre Little Book Cliffs Wild Horse Area lies.

Bring lots of water for this hike and take your time on the return trip to your vehicle. You don't want to tumble down.

MILES AND DIRECTIONS

0.0 Start from Mt. Garfield Trailhead.

0.06 Turn right at the 6X6 post and start climbing.

0.4 The trail splits; go left.

0.5 A brightly painted yellow brick reads "1/2" and the trail flattens out briefly.

0.6 Start climbing again!

0.75 Reach the pinyon and juniper—and shade!

0.9 Following a flat bench, the trail begins to climb once more.

1.0 The trail cuts west at base of the last red cliffs on the top of Mt. Garfield.

1.2 The trail leads behind the back (northeast) side of Mt. Garfield.

1.4 Climb up the rock before hitting a smooth trail that leads you to the top.

1.7 Reach the American flag marking the top of Mt. Garfield at 6,777 feet in elevation. Head back down but be careful. It's slick. You may need to slide down on your butt.

3.4 Arrive back at the trailhead.

The Book Cliffs were so named because the cliffs of sandstone that cap many of the south-facing buttes resembled "books on a shelf." At least that's what they looked like to E. G. Beckwith, who chronicled Captain John Gunnison's 1853 expedition through the Grand Valley. By 1882 settlers began moving to the Grand Valley and dedicated the promontory of Mt. Garfield to President James Garfield, who was assassinated in 1881.

The Little Book Cliffs Wild Horse Area is one of only three areas in the United States set aside specifically for wild horses.

The Dominguez Canyon Wilderness is a 66,280-acre maze of incredibly picturesque canyons located in the heart of the 210,000-acre Dominguez-Escalante National Conservation Area. Both were created by an act of Congress in 2009. Here, red-rock canyons and sandstone bluffs provide breathtaking scenery and hold geological and paleontological resources spanning 600 million years.

This area contains many well-preserved cultural and historic sites from the past 10,000 years and offers quiet solitude and outstanding wildlife viewing opportunities. You can find incredible pictographs and petroglyphs and take photos of nimble desert bighorn sheep, all clinging to the sides of canyon walls.

Start: Dominguez Canyon Trailhead at the end of the Bridgeport Road
Elevation gain: 4,684–5,112 feet (428 feet)
Distance: 6.6 miles to Newspaper Rock, out and back
Difficulty: Easy
Hiking time: 2.5–4 hours
Seasons/schedule: Year-round, but very hot during the summer
Fees and permits: None
Trail contacts: BLM Grand Junction Field Office, 2815 H Rd., Grand Junction, CO 81506; (970) 244-3000; https://www.blm.gov/programs/national-conservation-lands/colorado/dominguez-escalante-nca
Canine compatibility: Dogs allowed under control and on leash around other users and during spring (lambing season for desert bighorn sheep)
Trail surface: Road base for first mile, then wide, smooth dirt path to Newspaper Rock
Land status: BLM Dominguez-Escalante National Conservation Area

Nearest towns: Grand Junction, Delta
Other trail users: Foot and horseback travel only (horseback travel has been restricted because of flash flooding. Check with BLM prior to saddling up!) No motorized vehicles, equipment, bicycles, or hang gliders within the wilderness area.
Nat Geo TOPO! map (USGS): Triangle Mesa
Other maps: Uncompahgre National Forest map; BLM Delta Resource Area map
Other: The Palisade Bluegrass and Roots Music Festival, early to mid-June, featuring notable bluegrass and roots musicians, on-site camping, band scramble jam sessions, workshops, food, artisans, and activities for children. Held along the Colorado River in Riverbend Park, a stunning venue with 110 acres of riverfront scenery, complete with pavilions, playground, boat launch, fishing ponds, bike paths, and disc golf course. Sponsored by the Town of Palisade. www.palisademusic.com

FINDING THE TRAILHEAD

From Grand Junction, take US 50 south, approximately 17 miles past the Mesa County Fairgrounds to Bridgeport Road at highway mile marker 52. Slow down as you approach the road at the top of the hill, as there is no exit lane. Turn right on Bridgeport Road and travel down this narrow, yet well-maintained gravel road for 3 miles to its terminus at the Gunnison River.
Trailhead GPS: N38 50.9614' / W108 22.3554'

Evidence throughout the canyon details several distinctive prehistoric and early European American cultures.

THE HIKE

Frankly, the first mile of this hike following the Denver/Rio Grande Western Railroad tracks and the Gunnison River used to be quite boring. The river itself is beautiful, but it was hidden behind tall stands of tamarisk, rabbit brush, and greasewood. Recently, a species of leaf beetle that eats only tamarisk, an invasive nonnative species, has been slowly munching away at the woody plant and opening up views of the river. The rest of this hike, of course, is fabulous! (Please note: The BLM built a new parking area with a vault toilet about 0.2 miles from the old one, so add that distance to this trip if you park here.)

After that first mile, and a few hundred feet past an old, closed private bridge, you'll reach a newer pedestrian/horse bridge spanning the river. Cross this bridge and turn left (south), continuing upstream.

In 0.3 mile, you'll pass the first of a handful of group camping sites for boaters floating down the Gunnison River from Delta. Continue past the camping areas along the river for another 0.4 mile until you reach the mouth of Dominguez Canyon. The trail then turns to the right (west) and away from the river. There is a large BLM kiosk and fence marking the wilderness boundary.

Just inside the boundary, there's a good spot to take a quick break, have a sip of water, and check out the short waterfall coming from Dominguez Creek before it flows into the Gunnison.

The trail here is wide and easy to follow in a southerly direction. In another 0.7 mile, the main trail bends toward the west (right) again as the canyon splits. To the right (west) is Big Dominguez Canyon; to the left (farther south) is Little Dominguez Canyon, also within the wilderness area. (Interestingly, Little Dominguez Canyon is much larger than Big Dominguez. Go figure.)

Continue right for another 0.4 mile and cross through an old livestock fence. About a half-mile from here, on your right-hand side (north of the trail), you'll hike past a not-so-ancient rock shelter. It's obviously been put to good use during infrequent yet sudden storms that can occur in this region at any time of year. Not far from here, there's an interesting side-canyon waterfall to the south, your left, at least when there's water in the creek. Watch for rock cairns that lead to the water.

In another tenth of a mile, Newspaper Rock, a freestanding sandstone rock about the size of a trailer, squats in the center of the trail. Here are fine examples of Native American petroglyphs, featuring pecked outlines of desert bighorn sheep, bear, deer, lizards, snakes, and human figures. (Pictographs are painted figures on stone.) The native American Utes who once roamed this area still consider this a sacred place.

Look up and to your right (north) from Newspaper Rock and you should be able to spy petroglyphs on the canyon walls high above you. You may need binoculars or a high-power camera lens. There are also many other petroglyphs and pictographs, along with Native American artifacts like wickiups and arrowheads throughout this area.

The trail continues from here for another 6.3 miles to the top of the Uncompahgre Plateau at about 7,500 feet in elevation. (Elevation at the Bridgeport trailhead is 4,682 feet.) A waterfall can be found another quarter-mile up the trail, but to continue much farther would turn this into an overnighter.

Archaeologists believe that Dominguez Canyon has been sporadically inhabited for the past 1,500 years.

A breathtaking view of the Dominguez Canyon Wilderness

Please remember, take only pictures and leave only footprints, then trace your footsteps back to your vehicle.

MILES AND DIRECTIONS

- **0.0** Start from trailhead along the railroad tracks.
- **0.3** Road/trail crosses railroad tracks.
- **0.9** Hike past old, private black bridge over Gunnison River.
- **1.0** Cross pedestrian/horse bridge over river.
- **1.3** First group campground used for river runners.
- **1.7** Mouth of Dominguez Canyon. Stay right and travel into wilderness area.
- **2.4** Canyon forks; to the left is Little Dominguez Canyon, to the right is Big Dominguez Canyon. Stay right.
- **2.8** Pass old cattle fence.
- **3.2** There's an interesting side-canyon waterfall here; watch for rock cairns leading to the water.
- **3.3** Arrive at Newspaper Rock.
- **6.6** Arrive back at the trailhead.

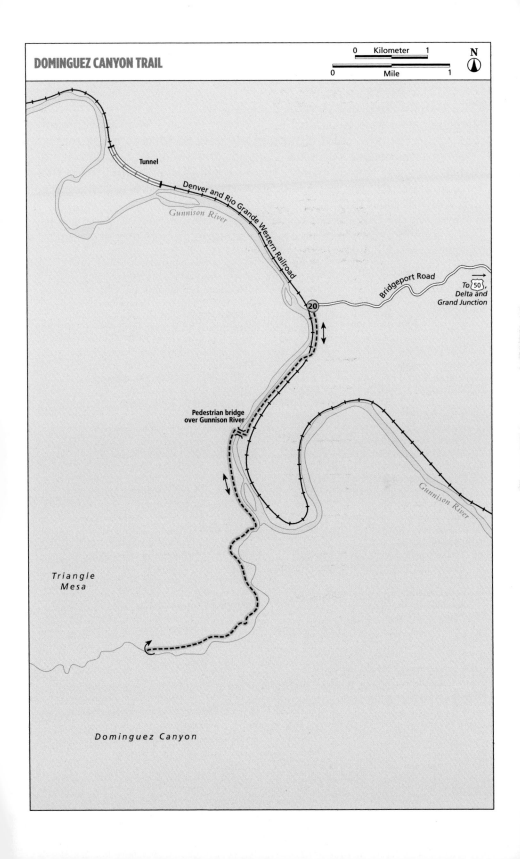

DOMINGUEZ CANYON TRAIL

0   Kilometer   1

0   Mile   1

N

Tunnel

Denver and Rio Grande Western Railroad

Gunnison River

Bridgeport Road

To 50,
Delta and
Grand Junction

20

Pedestrian bridge
over Gunnison River

Triangle
Mesa

Gunnison River

Dominguez Canyon

21 JUANITA ARCH

The Natural Arch and Bridge Society says Juanita Arch is the real deal! Located south of Gateway, Colorado, Juanita "is an adult meander natural bridge" carved through Wingate Sandstone in the meandering creekbed of Maverick Canyon. The society considers it an adult "because the abutments have retreated significantly from the stream bed that runs between them. The result is a very respectable span of 100 plus feet."

Crossing the Dolores River and hiking through Maverick Canyon to view Juanita's span and gaze at her abutments presents an enticing backcountry adventure.

Start: From mile marker 101 on CO 141, head down the bank toward the Dolores River, and find a crossing. Maverick Canyon is directly across the river to the northeast.
Elevation gain: 4,600–5,156 feet (556 feet)
Distance: 4.2 miles out and back
Difficulty: Moderate to strenuous, especially if you miss the primitive trail and are forced to bushwhack along the canyon bottom
Hiking time: 2–2.5 hours
Seasons/schedule: Early spring, late summer, fall, winter
Fees and permits: None
Trail contacts: BLM, 2815 H Rd., Grand Junction, CO 81506; (970) 244-3000
Canine compatibility: Dogs allowed under control
Trail surface: Primitive, rocky, dirt, backcountry path, sandy and slippery in spots
Land status: BLM
Nearest town: Gateway
Other trail users: None

Nat Geo TOPO! map (USGS): Juanita Arch
Other maps: BLM Grand Junction Resource Area map
Special considerations: You must cross the river to hike this canyon. The river is raging in the spring and often into the summer. You cannot cross at this time of year. (You could, however, rent a raft or kayak from the Gateway Canyons Resort in Gateway and float down from above.) You can wade across the river during the late fall and early winter, then again in the early spring before the runoff. Use extreme caution, however. It's not too deep—about 2.5–3 feet deep—but the river bottom is very slick. Use a wading stick! After crossing, leave your wading gear on the opposite shore and change footwear. You'll need sturdy boots or hiking shoes to continue to Juanita Arch.
Other: If you want to know what's happening locally, stop at the Gateway General Store, 43228 CO 141, Gateway, CO 81522, (970) 931-2831.

FINDING THE TRAILHEAD

From Grand Junction, drive approximately 9 miles south of Grand Junction on US 50 to Whitewater and the turnoff to CO 141, Uniweep Canyon. Turn right (west) and continue on this scenic byway for 43 miles to Gateway. Continue on CO 141 through Gateway and past Gateway Canyons Resort for about 11 miles to Z6 Road on your right. This is Salt Creek. Find a place to park here, and then walk a little farther south along the highway until you reach mile marker 101. Here, scramble down the bank to the Dolores River, and find a crossing that you can manage. Once you cross, you're in Maverick Canyon.

Trailhead GPS: N38 33.4863' / W108 54.9644'

THE HIKE

The hike into Juanita Arch through Maverick Canyon is almost as exciting as finding the arch itself. It's challenging, changing, rugged, and remote. Some path-finding skills may be required, although if you miss the primitive trail along the north edge of Maverick Canyon, you can simply follow the drainage. The difficulty here is that several rockslides through the centuries have created numerous obstacles, extending this trip by an hour or more.

The hike begins with a bushwhack down to the river from mile marker 101 on the highway. Social paths lead up and down the bank, but if you head directly down the gully at this point, you should find a property marker to the left of an old juniper tree just above the river. Scramble down the bank here, then wade upstream for a dozen yards or so until you feel there's enough solid rock underfoot to cross. The stream bottom is covered with muddy silt and is always slippery.

The Dolores River flows in a rough U-shape from its headwaters near Lizard Head Pass in the San Juan Mountains all the way to the Colorado River in Utah—some 246 miles. It is an important piece of a Colorado River system that provides water for millions of people and agricultural acres in the Southwest.

Take your time and, facing upstream at all times, cross the river. On the opposite bank, you'll see where Maverick Canyon flows into the Dolores River at this point. Shed your wet wading gear, then follow the sandy bottom of Maverick Canyon to the northeast until you leave the river delta and begin heading up the canyon. As soon as you can, climb the left (north) bank and find an old primitive backcountry trail. Continue to the northeast into the canyon and you will eventually stumble onto an old trail that's sparsely marked with rock cairns.

As the trail winds into the inner depths of the canyon, Little Maverick Canyon will enter the main stem from the southeast (to your right) at approximately 1.4 miles. Continue following the main canyon around the rim to the left. At the 2-mile mark, you may wish to cross over to the right side of the canyon and climb the blackened sandstone before you. Shortly, you'll veer to the right again. Look up to see Juanita Arch spanning the creekbed!

On your way back—at 3.2 miles—where Little Maverick and Maverick Canyons converge, look up and to your right for the Dinosaur Rock at waypoint **N38 33.9943' / W108 54.1860'**. A smaller set of dinosaur footprints can easily be seen from the trail. Larger tracks, however, can only be investigated from above. This involves climbing around the back and to the top of the rock. Loose rock, gravel, cactus, and other desert hindrances keep most people on the main trail. The land managers from BLM are grateful for that.

The hike into and out of Maverick Canyon to view Juanita Arch is remote and challenging, but well worth the trip.

MILES AND DIRECTIONS

0.0 Start from mile marker 101 on CO 141, head directly down the bank of the Dolores River and cross where it's safe.

0.4 Climb out of canyon bottom and find primitive trail on the north (left) side.

0.7 Drop back into main canyon wash.

0.9 Watch for cairns on left side of canyon and again climb out of canyon bottom to the north side.

1.26 Watch your step, real loose dirt on north slope.

1.4 Trail turns left and north into main Maverick Canyon and away from Little Maverick Canyon.

2.0 Cross over to the right and climb face of blackened sandstone rock.

2.1 Veer to the right around this wash and you should be facing Juanita Arch. **N38 34.4981 W108 53.6225**

3.2 Backtrack and return on the same trail. Little Maverick and Maverick Canyon converge at this point. Look up to your right to find the Dinosaur Rock at waypoint **N38 33.9943' / W108 54.1860'.**

4.2 Arrive back at trailhead.

Juanita Arch was carved through Wingate Sandstone in the meandering creekbed of Maverick Canyon.

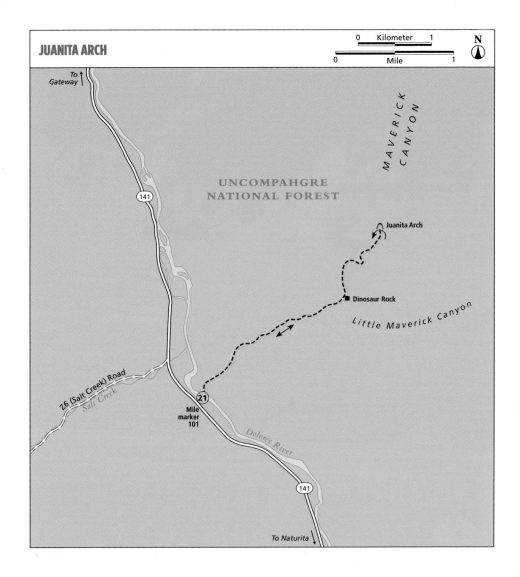

JUANITA ARCH

0 — Kilometer — 1

0 — Mile — 1

N

To Gateway

141

MAVERICK CANYON

UNCOMPAHGRE NATIONAL FOREST

Juanita Arch

Dinosaur Rock

Little Maverick Canyon

Z6 (Salt Creek) Road

Salt Creek

21

Mile marker 101

Dolores River

141

To Naturita

Discovery Channel founder John Hendricks created Gateway Canyons Resort, a luxury, world-class destination dedicated to nurturing guests' curiosity "through intellectual stimulation and adventure within a naturally intriguing environment." Hendricks is no longer connected, yet Gateway Canyons Resort remains one of the top resorts in the Rocky Mountain West, with a great restaurant open to the public.

22 DOLORES RIVER CANYON TRAIL

The Dolores River drains the western side of the Uncompahgre Plateau and San Juan Mountains. It flows southwest from 12,500-foot Hermosa Peak before making a U-turn and flowing north from Durango, for 241 miles to meet the Colorado River near Cisco, Utah. It is considered one of the most endangered rivers in the United States because of McPhee Dam near Durango, low water flows, high salt content, diversions, invasive plant species such as tamarisk, and a number of other issues. Nonetheless, this trail offers a unique hiking opportunity in a remote and beautiful canyon where the solitude is engulfing.

Start: From Dolores River Canyon Trailhead
Elevation gain: 4,911–5,126 feet (215 feet)
Distance: 7.1 miles out and back
Difficulty: Easy to moderate
Hiking time: 3.5–4.5 hours
Seasons/schedule: Year-round, although accessibility could be limited in winter
Fees and permits: None
Trail contacts: BLM Uncompahgre Field Office, 2465 South Townsend Ave., Montrose, CO 81401; (970) 240-5300; www.cec.org/north-american -partnership-for-environmental -community-action/napeca-grants/ dolores-river-restoration-partnership -drrp-a-collaborative-community -based-approach-to-watershed -restoration; BLM Tres Rios Field Office, 29211 Hwy. 184, Dolores, CO 81323; (970) 882-1120.
Canine compatibility: Dogs allowed under control
Trail surface: Relatively even dirt and rock backcountry path
Land status: BLM Wilderness Study Area

Nearest towns: Gateway, Naturita, Norwood
Other trail users: No one, really, but mountain biking and horseback riding are allowed
Nat Geo TOPO! map (USGS): Paradox, CO; La Sal, UT
Special considerations: This is canyon country. It gets hot in the summer. Carry and drink plenty of water. Wear a hat, sunglasses and sunscreen, and don't forget insect repellent as gnats can get nasty, especially in late spring and early summer. Also, cellphone coverage is minimal to nonexistent here.
Other: The Dolores River Restoration Partnership (DRRP) is a public-private collaboration of local, state, and federal agencies, universities, not-for-profit organizations, landowners, foundations, and citizen volunteers. The goal of the partnership is to restore riparian habitat along the Dolores River. https://waterinfo.org/ resources/dolores-river-restoration -partnership/

FINDING THE TRAILHEAD

From Montrose, drive 27 miles south to Ridgway on US 550. Turn right (west) onto CO 62 and continue 23 miles over Dallas Divide to Placerville. Turn right (west) onto CO 145. Drive 37 miles west through the towns of Norwood, Redvale, and Naturita to the intersection with CO 90. Turn left on CO 90 and continue west for 21 miles to the small town of Bedrock. Just after crossing the river bridge (west side) as you approach Bedrock, look for a BLM Boat Ramp sign on your left (southwest) at the historic Bedrock Store and gas station. Turn onto this road and follow it 0.8 mile to a BLM parking/camping area near the boat ramp. From here, you could drive south another 0.2 mile to the end of the road in a high-clearance four-wheel-drive vehicle. Otherwise, park here and walk. (**Note:** There are numerous dirt roads and trails leading into the canyon, but they all end at the same spot in 0.2 mile where no motor vehicles are allowed to proceed.)

Trailhead GPS: N38 18.0679' / W108 53.7778'

THE HIKE

The Dolores River is one of the most significant tributaries of the Colorado River Basin, not just because of the water it carries, but also because of the salt.

The Dolores River Canyon is located along the Colorado/Utah border. Few hikers ever find their way into the canyon because it's so far from anywhere. Yet, this phenomenal canyon is so expansive, so large, it will take a mile or two of easy hiking for your senses to adjust.

The trail follows the river to its confluence with La Sal Creek. Along the way, you'll hike beneath red rock canyon walls that tower 2,000 feet above, through open meadows filled with Indian rice grass and broad sagebrush flats where mule deer graze. Ravens, red-tailed hawks, and golden eagles fly high in the thermals created by the canyon winds. Don't be surprised to see desert bighorn sheep or hear the melodious cries of canyon wrens as you pass numerous boulders with ancient, weathered petroglyphs.

From the trailhead the route leads into the canyon on the west side of the river and away from Bedrock. You'll immediately notice a small industrial site on the opposite (east) side of the river. That's a major part of the Paradox Valley Desalination Project (see sidebar).

You'll also notice large amounts of dead vegetation in the river bottom. Most of it is tamarisk, an intensely invasive, water-sucking plant with roots hundreds of feet long. The BLM, along with the Dolores River Restoration Partnership (DRRP), is trying to get a handle on this nonnative plant that has wreaked havoc throughout the Colorado River Basin (see "Other" in The Rundown).

According to former BLM biologist John Toolen, a species of leaf beetle that eats only tamarisk has been slowly munching away at the woody plant in this drainage. The beetle was developed by the Colorado Dept. of Agriculture at its Palisade, Colorado Insectary. After the beetle did its job, members and volunteers from BLM and DRRP, "went in there in 2015, opened up some corridors and wide spots and re-planted native grasses and shrubs," Toolen said. "The idea is to use the cover of the dead tamarisk and shade things a bit to help get the native plants established."

As you continue south into the canyon, you'll see a tremendous wall of red sandstone towering 1,500 feet above you to your right (west), covered with dark desert patina. (The canyon walls to the southeast are even taller, about 2,000 feet above the river.) Also called desert varnish, patina is a dark red to black coating of iron and manganese oxides and silica deposited on sandstone. As dew and moisture are drawn to the surface by capillary evaporation, these dissolved minerals are deposited on the surface. Over a couple of thousand years, the wind then polishes it to a fine sheen, creating the magnificent colors you see today.

A lone hiker treks into Dolores River Canyon beneath towering red sandstone walls covered with desert patina. This dark red to black coating of iron and manganese has been polished to a fine sheen by wind and weather over thousands of years.

Faded petroglyphs, pecked or carved into rock, remain from the Archaic period, 1,500 to 4,000 years ago.

Before you reach the 3-mile mark, you'll begin to notice boulders near the trail with very old, very faded petroglyphs. Please don't touch, as the oils from your skin will deteriorate the sandstone even faster than normal. Many figures have been vandalized over the years, but many remain from the Fremont Period (2,000 to 700 years ago), as well as the Archaic Period (1,500 to 4,000 years ago).

In another half-mile, you'll reach La Sal Creek. You can bushwhack up this side of the canyon for another 0.2 mile before native box elder, sagebrush, Mormon tea, goldenrod, reeds, and willows make the trail impassable. The wide sandstone ledge above the river at the confluence of La Sal Creek is a great place to lunch before retracing your steps to your vehicle.

MILES AND DIRECTIONS

- 0.0 Start from the end of road past the BLM picnic/camping area at "No Vehicles" sign; head south on the old jeep trail.
- 0.2 Trail veers toward the river and you're looking beyond treated tamarisk to the desalination plant.
- 1.2 Trail drops toward river again, following a big bend to the west (your right).

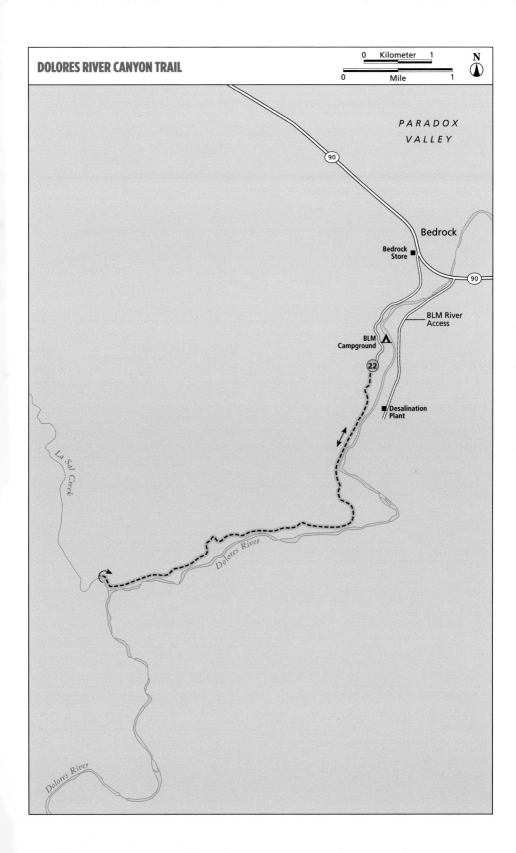

0   Kilometer   1

0   Mile   1

N

PARADOX
VALLEY

Bedrock

Bedrock
Store

90

90

BLM River
Access

BLM
Campground

22

Desalination
Plant

La Sal Creek

Dolores River

Dolores River

2.4 Trail leads into significant side canyon along an old built-up mining road.

2.5 Trail splits. Stay on the main trail to the left (although the cool side canyon to the right is worth a short visit).

2.9 Watch for petroglyphs. They're all around. (**N38 16.8507′ / W108 55.3624′.**) Most are very faded. Some have been vandalized.

3.4 Trail leads to a wide red sandstone ledge above the river at the confluence with La Sal Creek. The trail leads to the right and up into La Sal Creek.

3.6 Tired of bushwhacking? Turn around here.

7.1 After backtracking, arrive back at the trailhead.

Bureau of Reclamation studies show the Dolores River picks up more than 205,000 tons of salt annually as it passes through the Paradox Valley—the heaviest salt load in the entire Colorado River Basin. That's because the valley was formed about 250 million years ago when a huge salt dome collapsed. The river now bisects the valley instead of flowing through it, thus the name Paradox.

Across the river from this trailhead is a small Bureau of Reclamation desalination plant. Since it began operation in 1991, it has taken about 3 million tons of salt out of the river. It is the most productive of dozens of projects in the Colorado River Basin Salinity Control Program, created by Congress in 1974.

The Colorado River is very saline by the time it reaches Mexico. In 1974 it was so bad, the United States risked violating its treaty with Mexico. That salty water also reduced crop yields on the 5 million acres of farmland along the Colorado River, messed with water treatment plants in urban areas like Phoenix and Los Angeles, and adversely affected fish and other aquatic life on the river.

This project has mined nearly 200 gallons of brine per minute since 1991 from throughout the Paradox Valley to prevent it from leaching into the river. The brine is seven times saltier than ocean water. After being pumped up to the surface, that brine is piped to this facility where it is reinjected into the earth, only much deeper—about 2.5 miles down into the Mississippian Leadville formation.

Now, however, experts say that space will fill in about 10 years. Then, there's the problem of earthquakes. Since injection began, approximately 6,000 earthquakes have shaken this valley, some large enough to be felt as far away as Grand Junction, 120 miles to the north. Previous seismic activity had been virtually unknown here.

Scientists generally agree this activity is caused by the deep injection at the facility, just as wastewater injection wells are causing quakes in oil and gas fields in eastern Colorado, Oklahoma, and elsewhere.

What to do? A second well could be drilled, risking more earthquakes, or the salt could be deposited in vast evaporation ponds, but that's expensive and there's no place to do it nearby.

An environmental impact study is now underway to review alternatives.

With all the problems the Dolores River has borne, it is only prophetic that its name derives from the Spanish *El Rio de Nuestra Señora de Dolores*, River of Our Lady of Sorrows.

The Dolores River is one of the most
endangered rivers in the United States
because of low water flows, high salt
content, diversions, invasive plant
species, and a myriad of other issues.

23 WILDCAT TRAIL

Unaweep Canyon slashes dramatically from east to west across the northern section of the Uncompahgre Plateau, exposing a geologically unique landscape that's as spectacular as it is distinctive.

This trail takes hikers from the "divide" in the canyon floor at 6,955 feet in elevation, to the upper reaches of the plateau at 8,433 feet—in 3 miles. It's a stout climb, but well worth the effort!

The native American Utes' name "U-na-weep," means "canyon with two mouths." This canyon is unique in that one mouth (East Creek) drains eastward to the Gunnison River and the other mouth (West Creek) drains westward to the Dolores River.

Start: Lower Trailhead along CO 141 on canyon floor: N38 47.0537' / W108 40.5252'
Upper Trailhead adjacent to Thimble Point Rd. #417: N38 45.6006' / W108 39.5860'
Elevation gain: 6,955–8,433 feet (1,428 feet)
Distance: 3.0 miles one way; 6.0 miles round-trip
Difficulty: Strenuous
Hiking time: 1.5–2 hours one way; 3–4 hours round-trip
Seasons/schedule: Late spring through early fall
Fees and permits: None
Trail contacts: USFS 2250 S. Main St., Delta, CO 81416, (970) 874-6600; https://www.fs.usda.gov/main/gmug
Canine compatibility: Dogs allowed under control (Numerous elk and deer in this area. Don't allow your dog to chase wildlife!)
Trail surface: Dirt singletrack across lower valley, rocky but wide path up the side of the plateau with some slippery gravel stretches; easy, though little-used doubletrack on top.
Land status: USFS Uncompahgre National Forest
Nearest towns: Grand Junction, Gateway
Other trail users: Some horseback use; big game hunters in the fall
Nat Geo TOPO! map (USGS): Snyder Flats
Other maps: Uncompahgre National Forest map
Special considerations: For a shorter hike, shuttling vehicles would be appropriate. Leave one vehicle at the lower trailhead and the other at the upper trailhead. Hike up, or down depending upon your knees.
Other: FOND, Friends of the Northern Dolores seeks permanent protection for the landscape, wildlife, and way of life found in the Northern Dolores River area. (Follow Friends of Northern Dolores on Facebook.)

FINDING THE TRAILHEAD

From Grand Junction, travel south on US 50 for approximately 10 miles to Whitewater. Turn right (west) on CO 141, the Unaweep/Tabeguache Scenic and Historic Byway. In another 14.5 miles you'll see the Divide Road cut to the south.

To reach the lower trailhead, continue past the Divide Road on CO 141 for another 7 miles. On the left, or south side of the road just before you reach mile marker 133, you'll see a dirt road cut through the fence. Turn here and park near the Forest Service–issue picnic table adjacent to the trailhead.
Lower Trailhead GPS: N38 47.0537' / W108 40.5252'

To reach the upper trailhead, turn left (south) onto the Divide Road and travel to the top of the plateau and the northern forest boundary. From the Uncompahgre National Forest boundary sign, travel another 2.3 miles south on the Divide Road (now FR 402) to the Thimble Point Road, FR 417. Turn right (west) onto the Thimble Point Road and travel another 2.5 miles to the upper Wildcat Trailhead. It is located at the intersection of FR 417 and Hungry Gulch ATV Trail 665 just behind the gate. **Upper Trailhead GPS: N38 45.6006' / W108 39.5860'**

THE HIKE

Technical climbers come from all over the world to "practice" here in Unaweep Canyon. Its vast granite walls are filled with fabulous climbing routes. Not only are these granite walls incredible for climbing, according to the experts at www.coloradomountaineering .com, "the boulder fields of Dakota and Burro Canyon Sandstone that you pass through en route to the granite offer an almost endless supply of boulders."

You don't have to be a technical climber to enjoy this canyon, however. Sightseers enjoy the trip from the Grand Junction to Gateway along CO 141, the Unaweep/ Tabeguache Scenic and Historic Byway. Geology buffs are fascinated with this unique canyon. Its towering granite walls and almost imperceptible "divide" forces streams to flow in opposite directions.

The Wildcat Trail itself is really for hikers, as most of the technical climbing in Unaweep Canyon is located on the north side of the canyon while this trail heads across the valley floor and up through a cut on the south side of the canyon.

This description (and the Miles and Directions below) start from the lower trailhead, located just west of the "divide" near mile marker 133, so reverse these instructions if you start from the upper trailhead. From the trailhead, you'll travel southeast across the

Looking east from the canyon floor of what the native Ute people called Unaweep, or "canyon with two mouths"

The granite walls on the north side of Unaweep Canyon draw technical climbers from all over the world. The rest of us climb up the south side of this canyon to the top of the Uncompahgre Plateau.

sagebrush- and grass-covered valley floor where elk tracks abound. Watch for the first of seven or eight wooden 4×4 inch posts marking the trail across the valley.

Within a half-mile, the trail veers to the east and into a mixed growth of pinyon, juniper, and Gambel oak. It climbs steeply, from 7,000 feet in elevation at the valley floor to about 8,200 feet on top of the Uncompahgre Plateau. The Wildcat Trail is designed for foot and horseback travel only, but very few horseback riders will take their steeds up this steep, rocky slope.

The trail widens through a rock-strewn gully and in eight-tenths of a mile, the trail begins to switch back up and to the south. And up. Then up. And then, up a little more. At 1.2 miles, you'll reach another switchback to the right at the base of a huge granite outcropping. There's a great view of the valley floor from here. (Could I capture that view on my digital camera? No way. The sun was in my eyes, someone kicked dirt on my lens, I was out of breath. Pick one of those excuses. You'll have to take your own photo here!)

The trail winds UP through the Gambel oak and into a lovely aspen stand along Gill Creek; to the left are the rocky crags of Unaweep Canyon that you could see from the bottom of the valley. From here, the trail climbs a little more while paralleling the intermittent Gill Creek lined with wild roses.

After about 2 miles of hiking, the trail eventually travels beneath a handful of very large, very old, very proud ponderosa pine in a long meadow lined on the east with more Gambel oak.

Most of the steep climb is over now, as the trail meanders to the top of the plateau through sagebrush, ponderosa pine, and along an old ATV road. There's a sign that reads "Wildcat Trail," carved and painted. The trail now gently winds along the left side of the sage, between two large rock cairns that mark the trail through a wide former ATV track.

This is open range, and you'll also pick up a few meandering cattle trails. In 2.8 miles, you should be able to see a fence to your left (east). Continue on your path to where that fence line meets the top of the trail, 20 yards from the dirt intersection of FR 417 and Hungry Gulch Trail #665. (Those roads/trails are open to hiking, horses, mountain bikes, motorcycles, and ATVs less than 50 inches wide.)

After such a quiet trek, most hikers will take a short break here, then hightail it back down the hill to escape the motorized traffic.

MILES AND DIRECTIONS

0.0 From the lower trailhead, travel 40 paces forward, then veer to the right.

0.7 The trail begins to climb into Gambel oak with a few small pines and the trail soon widens through a rock-strewn gully.

0.9 The rubble picks up in the bed of the gully with lots of granite, quartz, etc.

1.0 You'll reach the first real switchback. It's pretty slick with loose gravel.

1.3 The trail opens a bit. To the right is an aspen grove.

1.4 As the trail enter the aspen grove, the sage have disappeared and the trail isn't quite as steep as it reverts back to a narrower single path.

Hikers climb beneath and around huge slabs of granite on the south side of the canyon.

1.6 A major talus slope flows down from left side to the trail.

1.9 Trail climbs to a sagebrush flat lined with giant ponderosa pines.

2.2 Lots of meandering cattle trails appear. Look for the wide path that was a former ATV trail, but don't panic as most trails lead in the same direction.

2.4 There's a stock pond to the right. If you've wandered that far, wander back toward the left.

2.6 Two sets of rock cairns mark the passage on doubletrack.

2.8 You should be able to see a fence line to your left.

3.0 Reach the intersection of FR 417 and Hungry Gulch Trail #665.

6.0 Arrive back at the trailhead if doing the round-trip hike.

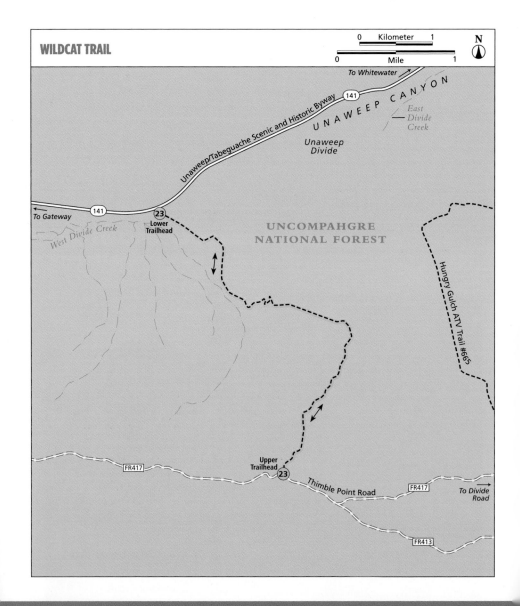

GRAND MESA

The Grand Mesa is the largest flattop mountain in the world. With an area of 500 square miles, it stretches for 40 miles east from Grand Junction while rising 6,000 feet above the surrounding Colorado and Gunnison river valleys.

The Grand Mesa National Forest covers most of the mesa. Dedicated by President Benjamin Harrison on December 24, 1892, it became the third forest reserve in the United States. The mesa is topped with hard volcanic basalt formed by dozens of small volcanic eruptions that occurred about 10 million years ago. The Gunnison and Colorado Rivers then eroded soft rock, leaving a high flattop mesa.

While the mesa is flat in some areas, it's quite rugged across most of it. About 250 lakes and reservoirs, most of them loaded with wild fighting trout, are scattered across the top of the formation and on benches below its rim.

The top of the mesa is 2 miles above sea level. That means daytime temperatures in the summer are mild and drop quickly after sunset. During the winter, the mesa is covered in 60-plus inches of snow, often more. A small family-oriented alpine ski area—Powderhorn—is located on its northern flank, and the Nordic (cross-country) skiing is world class. In cooperation with the US Forest Service, the Grand Mesa Nordic Council, a not-for-profit volunteer organization, provides 54 kilometers (32.4 miles) of groomed ski trails for free.

If you get the opportunity, check out these wildlife-related events held each year:

—Eckert Crane Days, early March to Late April, watch greater sandhill cranes in small and large flocks glide into Hart's Basin and land at Fruitgrowers Reservoir on the south side of the Grand Mesa near the town of Cedaredge. This is a major stopover for migrating cranes moving from their wintering area at Bosque del Apache National Wildlife Refuge in New Mexico to their breeding grounds in the northern United States and southern Canada. www.blackcanyonaudubon.org

—Moose Day on the Grand Mesa, last Saturday in July, join the USFS and Colorado Division of Parks and Wildlife for a day of moose activities including presentations on moose biology, moose reintroductions, and radio tracking. Kids will love the moose nature hike. www.fs.usda.gov/detail/gmug/home/?cid=stelprdb5298584

Considered a "typical" trail on the Grand Mesa, the Lake of The Woods Trail flows through thick meadows of tall grass and wildflowers, dense stands of aspen, Douglas fir, and Engelmann spruce. It bobs up, down, and over intermittent streams and around several small ponds.

24 CRAG CREST TRAIL

The Grand Mesa is the largest flattop mountain in the Northern Hemisphere, rising abruptly above the Grand Valley and its communities of Palisade, Grand Junction, and Fruita. The valley floor lies around 4,700 feet in elevation. The top of the mesa varies from 10,000 to 11,000 feet above sea level, with the "Crag Crest" at its peak.

Crag Crest Trail is a designated National Recreation Trail and is considered "the signature hike" on the Grand Mesa. While you will encounter other hikers, this out-of-the-way gem receives minimal impact compared to most other nationally renowned hikes.

Start: From the east trailhead at Crag Crest Campground

Elevation: East trailhead, 10,087 feet; West trailhead, 10,447 feet; peak elevation on top of the crest, 11,189 feet

Distance: 10.4 mile round-trip (6.2 mile upper trail from east to west trailhead; 4.2 mile return trip on lower trail)

Difficulty: Moderate to strenuous

Hiking time: 5+ hours

Seasons/schedule: Late spring to early fall

Fees and permits: None

Trail contacts: US Forest Service Office, 1010 Kimbell Ave., Grand Junction, CO 81501; (970) 242-8211

Canine compatibility: Dogs allowed under control

Trail surface: Backcountry trail through wet wildflower meadows and dark subalpine fir and Engelmann spruce forest; portions of the trail cut through massive volcanic rock fields; upper section consists of hard volcanic rock, dirt

Land status: US Forest Service, Grand Mesa National Forest

Nearest towns: Mesa, Palisade, Grand Junction, Fruita, Collbran, Cedaredge, Delta

Other trail users: No motorized traffic allowed; some horseback/mountain bike use allowed on short stretches of trail

Nat Geo TOPO! map (USGS): Skyway and Grand Mesa, CO

Other maps: Grand Mesa National Forest map available from US Forest Service Office, 1010 Kimbell Ave., Grand Junction, CO 81501; (970) 242-8211, or Grand Mesa Visitor Center, Intersection of CO 65 and FR 121, (970) 856-4153.

Special considerations: This is a great trail to shuttle vehicles, with one vehicle parked at each trailhead. This shortens the hiking distance considerably, but please be conscious of your carbon footprint! Take plenty of insect repellent, especially in the middle of the summer when mosquitoes can get nasty. This trail crests at 2 miles above sea level. If you feel lightheaded or acquire a nasty headache, get to a lower elevation immediately. Carry extra water and hydrate often to help prevent altitude sickness. Always remember you're in the Rockies and weather can change rapidly. Be prepared and dress appropriately.

FINDING THE TRAILHEAD

Take I-70 east to exit 49 (Powderhorn/Grand Mesa exit). This is CO 65, a National Scenic Byway. Stay on it for 34 miles, through the town of Mesa, past Powderhorn Ski Area, and past Mesa Lakes Resort. About 0.3 mile past Grand Mesa Lakes Lodge, turn left into the West Crag Crest Trailhead parking area near mile marker 28.

The east trailhead is located at the Crag Crest Campground on FSR 121 (Trickle Park Road). Continue on CO 65 past the west trailhead for approximately 1 mile. Turn left on FR 121 at the Grand Mesa Forest Service Visitor Center, a good place to check on current trail conditions—if it's open (lack of funding closed the center in 2024). Follow this paved road for 1.9 miles and continue on FR 121 when the road turns to gravel. Turn left in 0.5 mile and continue 0.9 mile to Eggleston Reservoir. The Crag Crest Trail parking area is on the right (south) side of the road. The trailhead is located past the campground on the left (northeast).

West Trailhead GPS: N39 02.9297' / W107 56.2005'
East Trailhead GPS: N39 02.5624' / W107 59.8577'

THE HIKE

This route follows the loop from the east on the upper trail, returning west on the lower trail because it's best to hike the higher trail early in the day and avoid afternoon thunderstorms. Most of the elevation gain occurs within the first 2 miles, where hikers are blessed with spectacular views in all directions.

The "Crag" crest is a long ridge left behind by two parallel glaciers in the last ice age. While the trail is not terribly difficult, other than an ascent on one end or the other, it is not suitable for hikers who fear heights. Along the crest, this trail narrows to about 3 feet wide with steep drops on both sides.

The upper trail is well marked. The lower Crag Crest Trail is relatively well marked, although you must pay attention. (**Note:** This hike is shortened considerably by shuttling two vehicles, leaving one at each trailhead, and then skipping the lower Crag Crest Trail. Don't skip the upper stretch—it's just too scenic!)

Watch your footing as jagged rocks grab ankles and stub toes along this trail. Good footgear is required. The upper trail traverses across numerous black volcanic rock fields colored with green lichen and mosses, and dotted with raspberry, red elderberry, blue gentian, and Colorado columbine. Scurrying about in these rock fields are busy populations of pikas and yellow-bellied marmots, enjoying the sun and eating wildflowers (see "Pikas and Marmots").

At the 2-mile mark, hikers trek along the crest for another 1.5 miles before descending toward the lower trailhead. Great panoramic views are found all along this stretch. The San Juan Mountain range is visible to the south. The West Elk Range spreads to the east. The Bookcliffs Range can be seen to the north. On most clear days, the LaSal Range in Utah can be seen to the west.

At the 5.5-mile mark, about a half-mile before reaching the West End trailhead, the trail splits. The West trailhead is located to the right in 0.5 mile. (If you've shuttled vehicles, this is where you turn right.) The lower trail proceeds to the left and returns to your vehicle at the east trailhead parking area.

This lower trail flows through a lush forest with thick tall grass and wildflowers amid dense stands of aspen, Douglas fir, and Engelmann spruce. You'll cross large swaths of blowdown where the dark timber was knocked down in a tremendous windstorm dozens of years ago. Pay close attention to the trail through here. Also, in the late 1990s, an irreverent and illegal bulldozer driver demolished portions of this lower trail when he drove his machine up the drainage on the northeast side of Hotel Twin Lake, then headed east for about a mile before being stopped by the US Forest Service.

No motorized traffic is allowed on these trails, while some horseback/mountain bike use is allowed on short well-marked stretches.

You'll hike for 2 miles before you reach the crest, then hike 2 miles along it with magnificent views in all directions. The crest peaks at 11,189 feet in elevation.

Red squirrels are just one of the dozens of species of wildlife you might encounter.

This trail crests 2 miles above sea level. If you feel lightheaded or acquire a nasty head-ache, get to a lower elevation immediately. Carry extra water and hydrate often to help prevent altitude sickness.

Remember, you're in the Rockies and the weather can change quickly, so be prepared for this "signature hike" and you won't be disappointed.

MILES AND DIRECTIONS

0.0 Cross road from parking area to trailhead, 0.1 mile east, below the Crag Crest campground.

0.1 Upper and lower trail splits. Go right to the upper trail.

1.1 Pass Bullfiinch Reservoir #1; begin climb through volcanic rock field.

1.6 Pop out of dark timber and enjoy the views of the San Juan Mountains and Lone Cone Mountain, 125 miles to the south.

2.8 Ascend to 11,162 feet, the highest point along the crest.

3.5 Begin winding down the switchbacks from top of the ridge.

5.0 Junction with Cottonwood Trail #712. Bicycles and horses allowed along this stretch of trail.

6.2 Junction of lower and upper trails. West trailhead is 0.5 mile to the right. Go forward and to the left along lower Crag Crest Trail.

6.3 Another trail intersection; go left via lower loop trail to east Crag Crest Trailhead.

7.7 Enjoy views from above Alexander Lakes Lodge and vicinity.

8.2 Cross creek, go right; climb through deadfall and continue back toward east trailhead.

10.2 Junction of upper/lower trails; go right to trailhead and parking area.

10.4 Arrive at parking area.

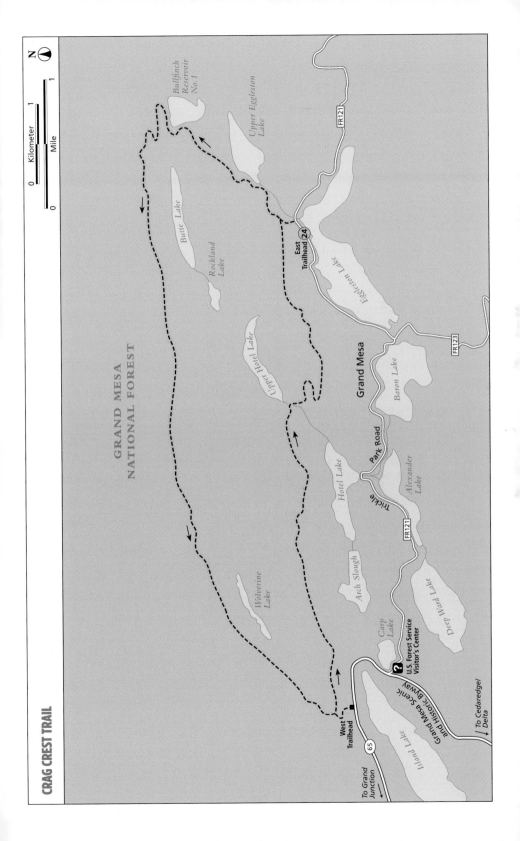

CRAG CREST TRAIL

GRAND MESA
NATIONAL FOREST

Bullfinch
Reservoir
No. 1

Upper Eggleston
Lake

East
Trailhead 24

Butte
Lake

Rockland
Lake

Eggleston Lake

Upper Hotel Lake

FR121

Grand Mesa

Baron
Lake

FR123

Hotel Lake

Park Road

Trickle

Alexander
Lake

FR121

Wolverine
Lake

Arch Slough

Deep Ward Lake

Carp
Lake

U.S. Forest Service
Visitor's Center

West
Trailhead

65

Island Lake

Grand Mesa Scenic
and Historic Byway

To Grand
Junction

To Cedaredge/
Delta

N

Kilometer
0   1

Mile
0   1

PIKAS AND MARMOTS

American pikas (*Ochotona princeps*) have been called little rodents or squirrels, which they're not, being more closely related to rabbits and hares. Yellow-bellied marmots (*Marmota flaviventris*), on the other hand, have been mistaken for eastern woodchucks, although they're bulky, stout-bodied ground squirrels.

American pikas are the small, short-eared mammals you'll see and hear scurrying about the talus slopes of Crag Crest Trail, as well as many talus slopes in western Colorado above 10,000 feet in elevation.

The grayish-brown pikas are 7–8 inches long with hindlimbs only slightly longer than forelimbs. They have stout bodies, big round ears, and no visible tail.

The busy little pikas are herbivores. They eat grasses, weeds, and tall wildflowers that grow in their rocky, high-mountain habitat. To prepare for winter, pikas collect piles of wildflowers and grasses in the summer and fall and lay them in the sun to dry. The plants are then stored—mold free—in "haypiles" until winter.

American pikas are heard before they are seen. Their calls define and protect territory, alert others pikas to the presence of dangers, and attract mates. Some say the call sounds like the bleat of a lamb, but more high-pitched and squeakier.

Climate change has had a dramatic effect on the American pika by increasing the average air temperature and the frequency of high-temperature events, which can cause pika mortality from overheating.

Yellow-bellied marmots, also known locally as "whistle-pigs," have short bushy tails and their pelage consists of long, coarse outer hairs and shorter, woolly underfur. Individuals vary in color, from yellow-brown to tawny. There's usually a whitish band across the nose, and the sides of the neck are typically buffy.

Larger than squirrels, marmots weigh from 3.5 to 11.5 pounds. Marmots occupy various habitats but are most common above 8,000 feet in alpine tundra and subalpine and montane meadows. They love wildflowers as much as pikas but eat a variety of forbs.

Unlike pikas, marmots hibernate throughout the winter. Eighty percent of a marmot's life is spent in its burrow and 60 percent of that time is spent in hibernation.

A variety of whistles function as alert, alarm, or threat signals. An undulating scream is a response to fear or excitement, and a tooth chatter signals aggression.

Source: Mammals of Colorado
by James P. Fitzgerald, Carron A. Meaney, et al.
Published by Denver Museum of Natural History
and University Press of Colorado 1994

Hiking the crest

25 WEST BENCH TRAIL

The benches along the terraced Grand Mesa, the largest flattop mountain in the world, provide cool shaded hikes during the heat of the summer in the valley below. At 10,000 to 11,000 feet in elevation, temperatures here are 10 to 20 degrees F cooler from May through September. The benches are lower in elevation than the top of the mesa, making them slightly easier for those not acclimated to altitude.

West Bench is the classic Grand Mesa bench hike, traversing through dark timber and aspen forests, with abundant wildflowers from spring through fall. This trail becomes a great backcountry Nordic ski track in the winter.

Start: From West Bench Trailhead at Sunset Reservoir
Elevation loss: 9,926–9,850 feet (76 feet)
Distance: 6.0 miles out and back to Powderhorn Ski Area Lift #1
Difficulty: Easy to moderate
Hiking time: 2.5+ hours
Seasons/schedule: Late spring to early fall
Fees and permits: $6 day-use fee. Pay at self-serve fee station adjacent to Jumbo Campground, Fishermen's parking area. (If you have a National Parks and Federal Recreational Lands Pass, place it on your dashboard. Or, park for free on CO 65 at the Jumbo Lake parking area, and take the trail across Jumbo Lake to the trailhead at Sunset Lake. It adds a half-mile one way to the trip.)
Trail contacts: US Forest Service Office, 1010 Kimbell Ave., Grand Junction, CO 81501; (970) 242-8211
Canine compatibility: Dogs allowed under control
Trail surface: Wide, easy dirt trail into the forest, then singletrack backcountry trail through aspen/subalpine fir/Engelmann spruce; portions of the trail cut through volcanic rock fields but most of the trail is relatively smooth and level
Land status: USFS, Grand Mesa National Forest
Nearest towns: Mesa, Cedaredge
Other trail users: No motorized traffic allowed; some horseback/mountain bike use

Nat Geo TOPO! map (USGS): Skyway and Grand Mesa, CO
Other maps: Grand Mesa National Forest map available from US Forest Service Office, 1010 Kimbell Ave., Grand Junction, CO 81501; (970) 242-8211, or Grand Mesa Visitor Center, Intersection of CO 65 and FR 121, (970) 856-4153.
Special considerations: Remember insect repellent; mosquitoes can get nasty here. While this trail is lower in elevation than the top of the mesa, altitude sickness can still be a problem if visitors are not acclimated; if you feel lightheaded or acquire a nasty headache, get to a lower elevation immediately. Carry extra water and hydrate often to help prevent altitude sickness. (See "Three Deadly Killers" in the "Before You Hit The Trail" section!) Always remember you're in the Rockies and weather can change rapidly. Be prepared and dress appropriately.
Other: The Volunteers for GMUG (Grand Mesa/Uncompahgre) assist the Forest Service by helping maintain recreation sites and trails, reduce hazardous fuels, restore watersheds, monitor wildlife populations, inventory and monitor archaeological and historic sites, provide input to proposed management activities, conduct conservation education programs, and respond to emergency incidents. http://www.fs.usda.gov/main/gmug/workingtogether

FINDING THE TRAILHEAD

Take I-70 east to exit 49 (Powderhorn/Grand Mesa exit). This is CO 65, a National Scenic Byway. Stay on it through the town of Mesa and past Powderhorn Ski Area. You may park for free at the Jumbo Reservoir parking area on CO 65. The trail starts near the restroom facility and takes the new bridge over the Spillway running through to another bridge over Sunset Reservoir and along Mesa Creek. Or, drive just a little farther and turn right toward the old ranger station sign after passing Jumbo Reservoir. If you reach Mesa Lakes Resort, you've gone about a tenth of a mile too far. Follow Forest Service signs toward the old ranger station (now a Forest Service residence) through the Mesa Lakes group. Pay a $6 day-use fee at the self-serve fee station, and then continue to the right toward the anglers' parking area and trailhead. (If you have a National Parks and Federal Recreational Lands Pass, place it on your dashboard.)

Trailhead GPS: N39 03.1308' / W108 05.7072'

THE HIKE

Lying between the converging Gunnison and Colorado Rivers, the Grand Mesa National Forest covers 360,960 acres, about a third the size of Rhode Island. Established by President Benjamin Harrison in 1892, it was the second national forest to be created in Colorado and the third in the United States. (Harrison, a Republican, had defeated Grover Cleveland for the presidency in 1888 and facilitated the creation of the National Forests through an amendment to the Land Revision Act of 1891 creating "forest reserves" (see "Forest Reserve Act").

This is an enjoyable, easy hike through aspen glades and Engelmann spruce/subalpine fir forests, with wildflowers sprinkled along the way from late spring following snowmelt, well into the fall. In winter, it's transformed into a cool, backcountry cross-country ski trail.

The hike begins by crossing a footbridge over the dam to Sunset Lake, one of the small ponds in the "Mesa Lakes Group" that also includes Jumbo Reservoir, Mesa Lake, and Glacier Spring. The trail follows the top of the dike on the northwest end of Sunset Lake for 0.2 mile before entering the forest. Private cabins have stood here as long as the old ranger station on the north side of the creek, built by the Civilian Conservation Corps in 1941. Please respect this property. Part of the trail is on a private dirt road used to access these cabins.

The small lakes here are representative of the 250 or so lakes found on the mesa. None are too large and most are easily accessible by vehicle. Some, however, are accessible only by foot or horseback (for example, Lake of the Woods Trail, Hike #26).

Most of these small impoundments hold catchable trout and combined, they comprise one of the most unique—and clean—water storage systems in the United States.

In 0.3-mile, West Bench Trail crosses Rim View Trail #533. Continue forward and to the right. At 0.4 mile, West Bench trail crosses Mesa Creek Trail #505. Go left and follow the signs along West Bench Trail, traveling between the final two cabins in this area and down the hill.

You'll then wind your way along a bench of the mesa that lies in the transition zone between aspen and dark timber. It crosses a few ancient volcanic rock fields as it continues slightly north and west until it winds into a lovely aspen forest with open meadows and lots of wildflowers at 1.3 miles.

Columbines grow wild through the boulder fields of volcanic rock covered in lichens and mosses.

A colony of aspen, a clonal organism representing an individual male quaking aspen, *Populus tremuloides*

At 2.25 miles, you'll cross a small, muddy creek where close observation will show elk and deer prints in the mud. At 2.4 miles, dark timber on the left and a thick aspen grove on the right frame a beautiful wildflower meadow frequented by numerous wildlife species: deer, elk, bear, porcupine, yellow-bellied marmots, thirteen-lined squirrels, golden eagles, hawks, bats—and mosquitoes (because of all the water on the mesa). Take bug juice. It's been known to get bad.

In another half-mile, the trail splits. To the right, you can see a hut and picnic table used by the Ski Patrol at the top of the Powderhorn Ski Area Lift 1. To the left, you can continue another 2.5 miles to Powderhorn Ski Area Lift 2. That, however, adds another 5 miles to this 6-mile out-and-back trek. The trail is relatively easy to follow from here, and continues in that same flowing pattern of aspen, dark timber, meadow, small boulder field, wet spring, aspen, dark timber, meadow. It's mesmerizing. So much so, it'll take you all day! The true end of the trail is on the private ski area property which is well signed.

If you don't feel up to increasing your hike by 5 miles, take a right and use the Ski Patrol picnic table. It's a good spot for lunch, and you can easily retrace your steps back from here.

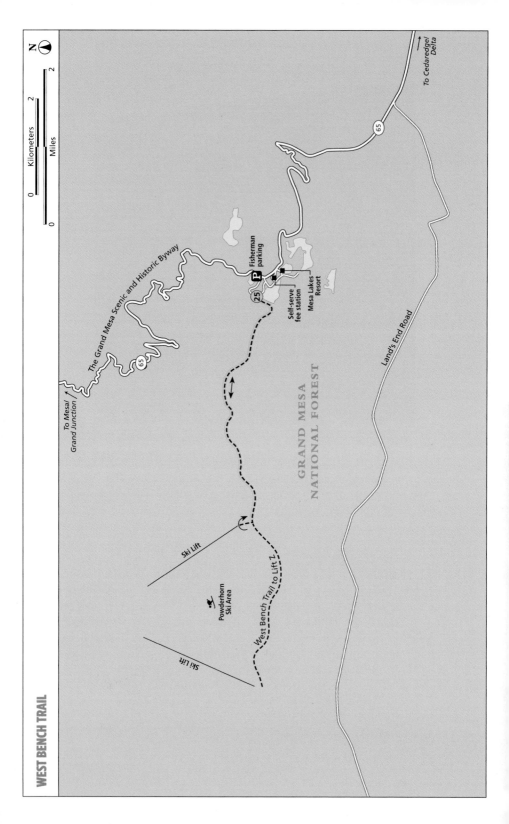

WEST BENCH TRAIL

N

Kilometers
0   2

Miles
0   2

To Mesa/
Grand Junction

The Grand Mesa Scenic and Historic Byway

65

25

Fisherman
parking

P

Self-serve
fee station

Mesa Lakes
Resort

GRAND MESA
NATIONAL FOREST

Land's End Road

65

To Cedaredge/
Delta

Ski Lift

Powderhorn
Ski Area

Ski Lift

West Bench Trail to Lift 2

MILES AND DIRECTIONS

0.0 From the anglers' parking area and trailhead, cross footbridge over Sunset Lake dam.

0.2 Go right, follow signs to West Bench Trail, Powderhorn Ski Area Lifts 1 and 2.

0.3 Rim View Trail #533 crosses West Bench Trail. Continue forward (right).

0.4 Trail connects to private road and cabins. In a few feet, it crosses Mesa Creek Trail #505. Continue left and follow signs to West Bench Trail.

0.5 Cross between last two cabins, leaving the private property behind.

1.3 Trail peeks out of dark timber into aspen and open meadows.

1.4 Original Mesa Creek Ski Area used to top out in this area. Excellent expert cross-country ski runs exist from here to the lower bench, approximately 1,000 feet below.

2.25 Cross muddy creek and look for signs of wildlife.

2.4 Large wildflower meadow framed with dark timber on the left and aspen on the right.

2.8 Trail splits. Go right to top of Lift 1; go left for 2.5 miles to top of Lift 2.

3.0 Arrive at picnic table/Ski Patrol hut and top of Powderhorn Ski Area Lift 1. This is your turnaround point.

6.0 Arrive back at the trailhead.

Sunset Lake

FOREST RESERVE ACT

Using the Forest Reserve Act of March 3, 1891, President Harrison created the nation's first forest reserve on March 30—the Yellowstone Park Timberland Reserve (now part of the Shoshone and Bridger-Teton National Forests in Wyoming). Shortly thereafter, he created fifteen forest reserves containing 13 million acres across the United States. They included reserves on the White River Plateau and Grand Mesa in western Colorado and the Grand Canyon in Arizona.

ASPEN COLORS

In early autumn, in response to the shortening days and declining intensity of sunlight, leaves begin to turn colors. There are three types of color pigments involved that produce the spectacular autumn colors you see in aspen trees: chlorophyll, which gives leaves their basic green color; carotenoids, which produce yellow, orange, and brown colors; and anthocyanins, which produce the reds. These anthocyanins are usually produced only in the fall.

According to Forest Service scientists, this is how it occurs: "The veins that carry fluids into and out of the leaf gradually close off as a layer of cells forms at the base of each leaf. These clogged veins trap sugars in the leaf and promote production of anthocyanins. Once this separation layer is complete and the connecting tissues are sealed off, the leaf is ready to fall." Source: https://www.fs.usda.gov/visit/fall-colors/science-of-fall-colors

26 LAKE OF THE WOODS TRAIL TO BULL BASIN

A complex road and trail system provides numerous options for exploring the Grand Mesa in general, and Bull Basin, in particular. Situated on a large bench on the northern flank of the Grand Mesa, the Lake of the Woods Trail to Bull Basin, however, isn't too complicated. This trail is considered a "typical" trail on the mesa. It flows through a lush forest with thick tall grass and wildflowers, patches of low-growing Oregon grape, with dense stands of aspen, subalpine fir, and Engelmann spruce. It eventually arrives at a crystal-clear high-mountain lake full of native Colorado River cutthroat trout.

Start: Lake of the Woods Trailhead at the end of FR 250
Elevation gain: 9,971–10,176 feet (205 feet)
Distance: 5.3 miles, round-trip to Bull Basin Reservoir #2
Difficulty: Easy to moderate; slippery when wet
Hiking time: 2.5–3 hours
Seasons/schedule: Late spring to early fall
Fees and permits: None
Trail contacts: US Forest Service Office, 1010 Kimbell Ave., Grand Junction, CO 81501; (970) 242-8211
Canine compatibility: Dogs allowed
Trail surface: Backcountry trail through wet meadows, hard rock, dirt
Land status: USFS, Grand Mesa National Forest
Nearest towns: Mesa, Cedaredge
Other trail users: No motorized traffic allowed; some horseback/mountain bike use, but this trail is mostly used by backpackers, backcountry anglers, and hunters during big game seasons in the fall, generally mid-Oct to mid-Nov.
Nat Geo TOPO! map (USGS): Skyway and Grand Mesa, CO
Other maps: Grand Mesa National Forest map available from USFS Office, 1010 Kimbell Ave., Grand Junction, CO 81501; (970) 242-8211, or Grand Mesa Visitor Center, Intersection of CO 65 and FR 121; (970) 856-4153 (Note: Lack of funding closed the Visitor Center in 2024, with plans to reopen "in the future.")
Special considerations: Take plenty of insect repellent, especially in the middle of the summer, when the mosquitoes can get nasty. This trail is nearly 2 miles above sea level; if you feel lightheaded or acquire a gripping headache, get to a lower elevation immediately. Always carry extra water and hydrate often to help prevent altitude sickness. Always remember you're in the Rockies and weather can change rapidly; be prepared and dress appropriately.

FINDING THE TRAILHEAD

Travel east from Grand Junction on I-70 for 20 miles to the Grand Mesa/Powderhorn exit (#49). That's CO 65, a National Scenic and Historic Byway. Go through the town of Mesa, past Powderhorn Ski Area and into the Grand Mesa National Forest. About 2 miles past the Mesa Lakes Resort area, on the last long curve before heading up the final stretch to the top of the Grand Mesa, you'll come to mile marker 38. Beyond the mile marker is a long, cabled guardrail. Just past the cabled guardrail, turn left on graveled FR 250. (This Forest Service road is not marked.) Travel 0.4 mile to a parking area large enough for horse trailers. The road ends here.

Trailhead GPS: N39 03.733'/ W108 02.800'

THE HIKE

The trailhead for Lake of the Woods is at about 10,200 feet. (Lake of the Woods Trail actually gives up a couple hundred feet of elevation from the trailhead before climbing again.)

This particular trail is designed for foot and horseback traffic. Motorized vehicles are not allowed, unless you work for the Bull Creek Reservoir Company, which owns the reservoirs on this bench and uses ATVs to monitor the reservoirs.

Hikers skirt a bog shortly after starting on this trail, before winding past a mixture of aspen, fir, and pine. About 1.5 miles from the trailhead, you'll come to the misspelled junction of Lake of the Woods Trail 506, and Bull Creek "Cutofe" Trail 506-1A. If you take the Bull Creek Cutoff, you'll wind your way over to Bull Creek Reservoir #4, and eventually to a road that leads past Waterdog Reservoir and back to CO 65 across from Jumbo Reservoir in the Mesa Lakes group.

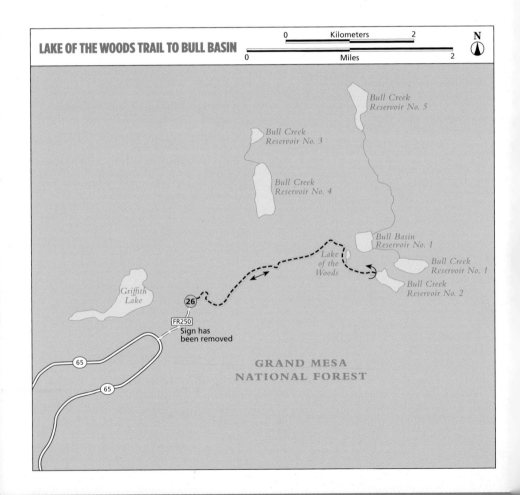

Cutthroat and rainbow trout congregate at the outlet of Bull Basin Reservoir #2. Fishing pressure here is considered moderate with flies and lures only and a bag and possession limit of two fish, 16 inches or longer. And, yes, there are rainbow trout here longer than 16 inches!

Lake of the Woods itself is just an overgrown bog that sometimes fills with water. Hundreds of these bogs on the Grand Mesa are nursery basins for mosquitoes—don't forget your bug juice!

If you stick to the Lake of the Woods trail, however, you'll generally follow the high ridge of the Crag Crest to Bull Basin. Crag Crest is the famous top ridgeline of the Grand Mesa that runs parallel to this trail. This "Crag" crest is a long rocky ridge left behind by two parallel glaciers in the last ice age. It's about 6 miles long and reaches an elevation of 11,160 feet (see Hike 24: Crag Crest Trail.] In about 10 minutes, you'll discover a few other trail junctions, but stick to the right, or toward the ridgeline, and you'll pop up to Lake of the Woods. It's really just a tiny pond, again mislabeled.

Continue on the trail to the north and east of this pond and you'll come to Bull Creek running between reservoirs #1 and #2. In another few hundred yards, you'll arrive at Bull Creek Reservoir #1. #1 and #2 are almost identical in size, about 10 acres and 10–12 feet deep, although the water level fluctuates greatly with irrigation demand.

No developed campsites exist at these reservoirs, so you must pack out what you pack in. (Note to anglers: Fishing here is by artificial flies only. The bag, possession, and size limit for trout is two fish, 16 inches or longer.)

The trail gets a little more rugged from here, but you can continue on Lake of the Woods Trail #506 all the way to Cottonwood Lake #1, about 2 miles farther to the northeast. This stretch of trail is seldom used. Keep in mind, however, that there are about seven lakes in the Cottonwood Lakes area, with four-wheel-drive roads everywhere. That access brings lots of anglers and lots of motorized vehicles. If you want to maintain your peace and tranquility, turn around at the Bull Creek reservoirs.

MILES AND DIRECTIONS

0.0 Start from trailhead and parking area.

0.3 Veer to your left around the marshy meadow in front of you.

1.5 Intersection with Bull Creek Cutoff.

2.6 Arrive at Bull Creek Reservoir #2.

5.3 Arrive back at the trailhead.

Drop off the edge of the largest flattop mountain in the world for great views of the San Juan Mountains 100 miles to the south, the Uncompahgre Plateau 30 miles to the west, and the West Elk Mountains 25 miles to the east. This easy trail across the top of the Grand Mesa traverses aspen, spruce, and fir forests adjacent to Flowing Park—a 2-mile-long high-mountain meadow! In the summer, it glows with wildflowers. In the fall, the aspen surrounding the park show their splendor with stunning colors of lime-green, yellow-gold, and crimson red.

Start: Drop off Trailhead #726 at the end of Flowing Park Road (FR 109)
Elevation loss: 10,163–9,310 feet (853 feet)
Distance: 5.0-mile lollipop loop
Difficulty: Easy (moderate from the dropoff to Porter Reservoir #4)
Hiking time: 2–3 hours
Seasons/schedule: May to Oct
Fees and permits: None
Trail contacts: Grand Mesa Visitor Center (located on top of Grand Mesa), (970) 856-4153. Summer hours 9 a.m. to 5 p.m. The visitor center closes after the last Sun in Sept (Color Sunday); or contact Grand Mesa, Uncompahgre and Gunnison National Forest, 2250 S. Main St., Delta, CO 81416; (970) 874-6600.
Canine compatibility: Dogs allowed under strict voice control or on a leash; it is illegal for dogs to chase wildlife!

Trail surface: Easy singletrack dirt path across the top; steep and rocky with some loose gravel following the dropoff.
Land status: Grand Mesa National Forest
Nearest town: Cedaredge, Mesa
Other trail users: Open to hiking, horseback, mountain bikes, and motorbikes (but not ATVs as the trail is too narrow), although it's rarely used by anyone but hikers.
Nat Geo TOPO! map (USGS): Hells Kitchen, CO
National Geographic Trails Illustrated map: #136, Grand Mesa
Other maps: Grand Mesa National Forest map
Special considerations: Mosquitoes! Sometimes they're bad. Be prepared!
Other: This is open range. Expect to see cattle here in the summer. The Point Cow Camp near the end of this hike at Porter Reservoir #4 is active in the fall.

FINDING THE TRAILHEAD

From CO 65 (the Grand Mesa Scenic Byway) and the intersection of Lands End Road (FR 100), travel southwest on Lands End Road for 1.2 miles to FR 109, the Flowing Park Road. It's the first major road to the left (south). Turn onto Flowing Park Road and continue on this well-maintained dirt road for 5.6 miles to its end on the south side of Flowing Park Reservoir. The road is closed at this point to motorized access by a metal, road-closure gate. Indian Point Trail #715 continues on the closed road. Drop Off Trailhead #726 is to the left (south) of the gate.
Trailhead GPS: N38 57.3175' / W108 06.2090'

The Drop Off Trail ends at Porter Reservoir #4. Don't forget your fishing rod on this hike. The reservoir is loaded with hungry brook trout.

THE HIKE

There's a great mountain bike trail that leads from an adjacent trailhead—Indian Point Trail #715—so the mountain bikers go that way. There are hundreds of miles of ATV/motorbike access on the mesa, so most motorized activity generally occurs in other spots. That's one good reason to hike along the Drop Off Trail. You'll have it all to yourself . . . well, you and the elk and deer and red-tailed hawks, and the cattle. This is open range, so expect to see cattle. Nonetheless, this is an easy, enjoyable hike for the entire family.

It begins at the end of the Flowing Park Road (FR 109). You can park next to Flowing Park Reservoir, but don't expect to see water in this reservoir every year. In some years, it's a dry marsh since it has no real inlet, only seeps and snowmelt, and there are no fish in the lake.

Drop Off Trail leads to the south (left) of the Indian Point Trail and heads immediately into spruce/fir forest. Soon, however, you'll find yourself in a lovely meadow lined with aspen. At 0.3 mile, you'll see why this is literally a walk in the park as you enter Flowing Park, a 2-mile-long high-mountain meadow surrounded by dark timber where hundreds of elk sleep in the day. They venture into the open park at daybreak and dusk for a healthy meal. Watch closely and walk quietly to catch a sight of elk, mule deer, or even moose.

In 0.7 mile as you wander in and out of the timber and open meadows, watch for a series of three wooden posts that mark the trail.

At the 1-mile mark, you'll again pop out of the woods and into an extension of Flowing Park that will make you gasp at its vastness. In another half-mile, you'll reach the edge of the Grand Mesa, but your best views will come in another 0.3 mile as you get out of the trees. The North Fork Valley unfolds beneath you and the rim of the Black Canyon of the Gunnison River is just beyond that. Far to the south, nearly 100 miles away, are the mighty San Juan Mountains, with 14,157-foot Mt. Sneffels the tallest point.

To the west (your right) you can see the length of the Uncompahgre Plateau, a huge uplift averaging 9,500 feet in elevation and extending from Grand Junction to the San Juans. To your left (northeast) are the West Elk and Ragged Mountains (see Hikes #10: Oh-Be-Joyful Trail, #11: Ruby Anthracite Trail, and #12: Anthracite Creek/Dark Canyon Trail). You can also see Porter Reservoirs #1 and #4 below you.

The easy part of the hike is now complete. From here, the trail gets rocky and steep, with some slick sections of loose dirt and gravel. You may need some path-finding skills as you get closer to the reservoirs. Cattle meander in and out of this area and you must look for the most used trail. (Following the trail through here is much easier after the Forest Service completed trail maintenance on this stretch in 2015.)

You'll soon descend quickly through a massive field of mule's ears (*Wyethia amplexicaulis*), larkspur, silvery lupine, and black-eyed Susans. At 2.2 miles, the trail leads to the southeast before heading into a wooded area. At 2.4 miles, you'll find an old cabin at the Point Cow Camp. Travel just past the cabin and take a right (west) on a jeep road leading between the cabin and an older outhouse. In a tenth of a mile, you'll come to the reservoir. Have lunch and fish a little for one of those feisty brook trout before retracing your steps back to your vehicle.

The hike out is steep, but you'll be shouldering your way through wild mountain lupine, giant corn lilies, and yellow composite sunflowers on a path seldom used by humans.

MILES AND DIRECTIONS

0.0 Start from Drop Off Trailhead #726 to the left (south) of Indian Point Trailhead #715.

0.1 Trail opens into a nice meadow lined with aspen.

0.3 Hike above the lower meadow and into Flowing Park.

0.7 Look for a series of three posts marking the trail.

0.9 Pass another post trail marker; continue southeast into the woods.

1.0 Trail leads out of the woods and into an extension of Flowing Park.

1.5 From 10,100 feet in elevation, you'll descend into mixed aspen/fir/spruce forest—with more aspen as you descend. There are more mosquitoes here than in the open parks!

1.8 Photo op . . . great views! **N38 55.9715' / W108 06.5450'**

2.3 Point Cow Camp at **N38 55.5676' / W108 06.4538'.**

2.5 Porter Reservoir #4 at **N38 55.5834' / W108 06.5043'.** Meander back to the cow camp cabin and backtrack toward the trailhead.

5.0 Arrive back at the trailhead.

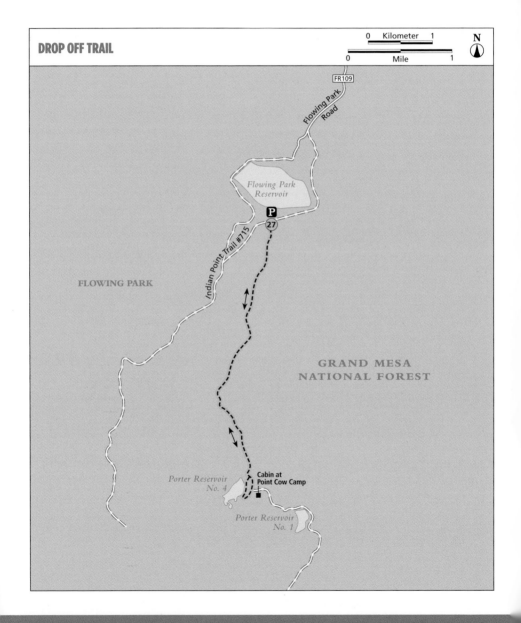

DROP OFF TRAIL

0 Kilometer 1

0 Mile 1

N

FR109

Flowing Park Road

Flowing Park Reservoir

P

27

Indian Point Trail #715

FLOWING PARK

GRAND MESA NATIONAL FOREST

Porter Reservoir No. 4

Cabin at Point Cow Camp

Porter Reservoir No. 1

BLACK CANYON OF THE GUNNISON

At its deepest near Warner Point inside Black Canyon National Park, the Gunnison River gorge is 2,772 feet deep. Yet, it's only 9 miles wide from rim to rim. That's one reason for the moniker *black*: Direct sunlight is limited to nonexistent at the bottom of this fascinating geologic spectacle.

The other reason is that dark 1.7-billion-year-old "granodiorite" rock forms the walls of this chasm. Granodiorite is an igneous rock that solidified from melting at great depth beneath the surface of the earth.

In his book *The Black Canyon of the Gunnison—In Depth*, geologist Wallace Hansen states, "Some are longer, some are deeper, some are narrower, and a few have walls as steep, but no other canyon in North America combines the depth, narrowness, sheerness and somber countenance of the Black Canyon of the Gunnison."

First published as USGS Bulletin #1191 in 1965, Hansen's book depicts a unique combination of geologic features that created this formidable canyon—hard rock uplifted, then carved by fast-moving debris-laden water.

The river first set its course millions of years ago over relatively soft Mesozoic and Cenozoic volcanic and sedimentary rocks. It then cut down to harder, older crystalline rock of the dome-shaped Gunnison Uplift. Once entrenched in its course, it continued cutting with turbid water carrying mud and debris, occasional rockfalls from high cliffs, and the relentless movement of landslides into the depths. This process took about 2 million years.

When we look at the canyon from its rim, we face a geologic mystery: There is a time gap of about 1.5 billion years between the crystallization of dark canyon-forming rocks and the deposition of the Mesozoic sediments. Whatever happened during that period is not preserved for us to see.

Other more subtle processes such as gullying, frost action, and chemical weathering (acid rain) continue to increase the material available for the river to wash away, according to the National Park Service's 2005 "Geologic Resource Evaluation Report."

The Gunnison River within the Black Canyon drops an average of 95 feet per mile (18 meters per kilometer). It's one of the greatest rates of fall for a river in North America. By comparison, the Colorado River through the Grand Canyon descends an average of 7.5 feet (2.3 meters) per mile.

This steep descent supplies the energy that propels a relentless stream of water and sediment that carves and polishes, providing incomparable scenery and deep pools that are home to great populations of hungry trout.

Hard rock uplifted, then cut through by fast-moving water: In just 48 miles through the Black Canyon, the Gunnison River loses more in elevation than the 1,500-mile Mississippi River does from Minnesota to the Gulf of Mexico.

28 DEADHORSE TRAIL— NORTH RIM OF THE BLACK CANYON OF THE GUNNISON

Hikes along the rim of the Black Canyon of the Gunnison River—and into the gorge itself—offer visitors spectacular views of some of the steepest cliffs, oldest rock, and craggiest spires in North America— one of our nation's most breathtaking geologic and scenic treasures. Deadhorse Trail is the least-used rim trail within this small national park (the third smallest in the United States), yet views here are spectacular. Easy terrain offers those who are not physically capable of the strenuous climbs into the inner canyon a glimpse into its rugged nature.

Start: At Deadhorse Trailhead 100 yards past Kneeling Camel Overlook on Rim Drive
Elevation gain: 8,345–7,855 feet (490 feet)
Distance: 5.0 miles out and back; 6.4 miles round-trip, including side loop
Difficulty: Easy to moderate
Hiking time: 2–3 hours
Seasons/schedule: Spring, summer, fall (closed for winter). The North Rim Ranger Station is open (sometimes) from mid-May to mid-Sept.
Fees and permits: None to hike on top; free backcountry permit required to hike into the inner gorge within National Park boundaries
Trail contacts: Black Canyon of the Gunnison National Park (visitor center located on the South Rim); (970) 641-2337; www.nps.gov/blca
Canine compatibility: No dogs allowed within National Park boundaries

Trail surface: Double-wide dirt track for first stretch, singletrack backcountry dirt trail from there
Land status: National Park Service, Black Canyon National Park
Nearest town: Crawford
Other trail users: None
Nat Geo TOPO! map (USGS): Grizzly Ridge
National Geographic Trails Illustrated map: Black Canyon of the Gunnison National Park #245
Special considerations: A vault toilet is located at the ranger station and water is also available from the ranger station from mid-May to mid-Sept. Bring your own water at all other times. If you're planning a hike/climb into the canyon, you must obtain a free permit here. Maps also are available.

FINDING THE TRAILHEAD

From Crawford drive south on CO 92 for 3 miles to the Black Canyon Road. Following the signs from here, turn right and drive 4 miles. The Black Canyon Road then splits. Turns right and drive another 0.8 mile, and the road turns left. In another 0.7 mile, the pavement ends and 1.2 miles beyond that point, turn right and continue on Black Canyon Road. You'll reach the park boundary in another 1.7 miles. The road will fork 3.3 miles into the park, approximately 15 miles from Crawford to this point. A NPS sign instructs visitors to turn right here onto Rim Drive and continue 0.5 mile to the North Rim Ranger Station and campground check-in. If you don't need to go to the ranger station, turn left on Rim Drive and continue to the Kneeling Camel Overlook on the south (right) side of the road in another 3.6 miles. This smooth dirt road ends 0.2 mile beyond Kneeling Camel Overlook at a roundabout and vault toilet.

Trailhead GPS: N38 33.7316' / W107 40.5972'

THE HIKE

The trailhead for Deadhorse Trail Overlook is located about 100 yards beyond Kneeling Camel Overlook, to the east and on the opposite side of the road. It begins on a gravelly doubletrack former jeep trail and is the least-traveled rim trail in this unpopulated park. It leads to spectacular views of the inner gorge.

From the high North Rim along Deadhorse Trail, hikers can scan the country on the opposite side of the canyon above the South Rim to view the dome-shaped rise of the Gunnison Uplift.

In a tenth of a mile, the trail splits. To the left, you'll find an old Quonset hut and a few tiny shelters, once used by Park Service rangers in the 1930s and 1940s. Veer to the right here along a smooth former four-wheel-drive road.

This broad sagebrush flat holds little appeal to some, but following a summer rain it comes alive with wildflowers—reddish Indian paintbrush, bluestem beardtongue, yellow thrift mock goldenweed, and sulphur flower, whose yellow petals fade to reddish-cream after a while.

At a little more than 0.6 mile, you'll pass a fence line and continue into the gully. The trail now becomes more of a singletrack. In another tenth of a mile, you'll pass a Park

Deadhorse Trail leads hikers across the top of the Black Canyon on its northern rim, with breathtaking views into the depths below.

Service "No Shooting" sign. The trail leads to the right here and up the other side of the gully, to a fenced spring-fed pond at 0.9 mile.

While humans may shun this trail, wildlife abound, from chipmunks to marmots, ground squirrels to ermine (small short-tailed weasels). Tracks along the trail indicate that bobcats and mountain lions visit this area. Coyotes are often heard at night, and their hair- and fur-filled scat can easily be seen on the trail. Elk occasionally graze on the tall grasses and mule deer browse on the sagebrush and serviceberry found throughout this area. Black bear roam the upper reaches of this magnificent canyon, in search of acorns from Gambel oak and high-calorie wild serviceberries found throughout the area in the fall.

At 1.2 miles the trail splits. To the right is a loop trail that extends the length of this hike by 1.4 miles, and offers incredible views into the bottom of the canyon.

This is a good birding trail, since it receives little human use. Don't be surprised to see towhees, western tanagers, pinyon and scrub jays, and black-billed magpies along with mountain bluebirds. You may even see a peregrine falcon, the fastest bird in the world, swooping down on other birds at 200 mph, their balled-up claws shattering the bones of its prey like bludgeons in midair.

At 2.6 miles, the loop winds back to the main trail. Go right here and hike 0.3 mile to the fence line. Go right again and hike another 0.9 mile to the end of the trail.

The cliffs here are home to white-throated swifts, violet-green swallows, golden eagles, pitch-black ravens, huge turkey vultures, and red-tailed hawks. You can often see the eagles, hawks, and vultures circling and soaring with updrafts. At the bottom of the canyon, you can see the operations below Crystal Dam, although you can't quite see the dam.

Return the way you came, including the loop, for a 6.4 mile trip, or shorten it by skipping the loop.

MILES AND DIRECTIONS

- **0.0** Start 100 yards east, on the opposite side of the road from Kneeling Camel Overlook, at Deadhorse Trail Overlook.
- **0.1** Take the right fork at structures once used by Park Service working crews.
- **0.5** Crest hill.
- **0.6** Pass the fence line, then drop farther into the gully.
- **0.7** Park Service "no shooting" sign; the trail cuts to right at this point, leading up the other side of the gully.
- **0.9** Reach a pond with a natural spring above, fenced off from the cattle; trail follows the fence line until it takes a right and away from spring at the 1-mile mark.
- **1.2** Trail splits; the path to the right takes hikers to the Overlook Loop; continue forward along the main trail. (Go right to extend the length of this hike.)
- **1.6** Trail pops out of the woods to a spectacular view of the canyon.
- **2.6** End of the loop; hikers are now back on the main trail. Go right and up the hill.
- **2.9** Reach the fence line and go right at the carsonite post.
- **3.8** The trail ends at the edge of the canyon, under a couple hundred-year-old pinyon and juniper trees.
- **4.0** Head away from the fence on the way back.

The power of fast-falling debris-laden water enabled the river to erode tough granite over a 2-million-year period.

5.0 Back to the loop.

5.2 Back to the first loop cutoff.

5.4 Back to the spring.

5.7 Back to the fence.

6.3 Back to the Quonset hut.

6.4 Back to the trailhead in 2–3 hours.

While the depth of the canyon at Werner Point inside the Black Canyon National Park is 2,772 feet deep (845 meters), the Painted Wall itself, near this trailhead, is the highest cliff in Colorado. From river to rim it stands 2,250 feet (685 meters) and is 1,000 feet (304 meters) taller than the Empire State Building.

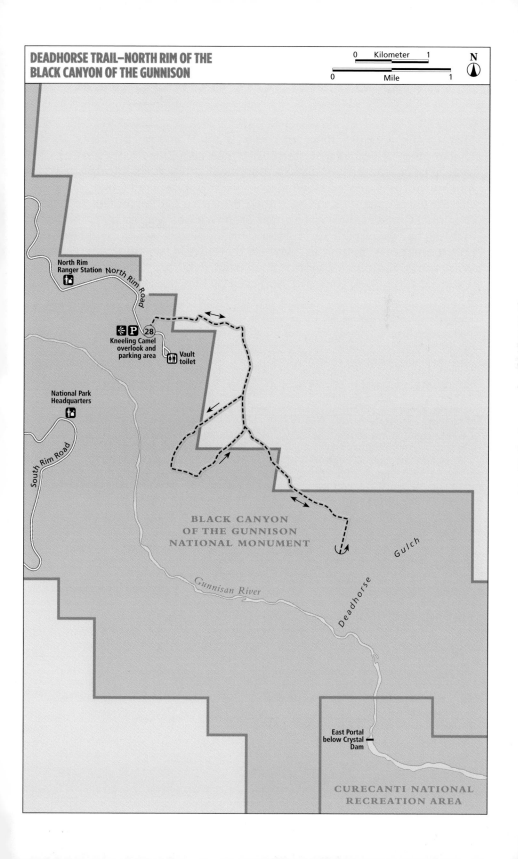

0   Kilometer   1

0   Mile   1

N

North Rim Ranger Station

North Rim Road

Kneeling Camel overlook and parking area   28

Vault toilet

National Park Headquarters

South Rim Road

BLACK CANYON OF THE GUNNISON NATIONAL MONUMENT

Gunnisan River

Deadhorse

Gulch

East Portal below Crystal Dam

CURECANTI NATIONAL RECREATION AREA

29 UTE PARK—SOUTH RIM INTO GUNNISON GORGE NCA

This is the longest hike into the Black Canyon, but the least challenging—if you've got stamina. It also provides nearly 2 miles of river access—more river access than most other trails into this magnificent gorge. Located downstream from Bobcat Trail (Hike 30), the Ute Park Trail also lies inside the 62,844-acre Gunnison Gorge NCA (National Conservation Area). This area was designated by Congress in 1999 to "recognize its outstanding geologic, scenic, wilderness and recreational resources." Within the NCA is the Gunnison Gorge Wilderness, famous for world-class trout fishing, challenging whitewater boating, rock climbing, and spectacular geology.

Start: From Ute Park Trailhead
Elevation loss: 6,538 feet at rim to 5,213 feet at river's edge
Distance: 9.0 miles out and back (7.0 miles out and back to the river)
Difficulty: Moderate to strenuous, depending on your stamina
Hiking time: 4–5 hours
Seasons/schedule: Best in spring, summer, fall (access very limited during winter months)
Fees and permits: $3 per person day-use fee ($15 annual day-use pass); $10 per person camping fee ($15 per person for 2 nights max. stay) Self pay at trailhead.
Trail contacts: BLM Uncompahgre Field Office, 2505 S. Townsend Ave., Montrose, CO 81401; (970) 240-5300; https://www.blm.gov/programs/ national-conservation-lands/ colorado/gunnison-gorge-nca
Canine compatibility: Dogs permitted under strict control (do not allow pets to chase wildlife!)
Trail surface: Singletrack dirt trail
Land status: BLM, Gunnison Gorge NCA
Nearest towns: Olathe, Delta, Montrose
Other trail users: Horseback riders
Nat Geo TOPO! map (USGS): Black Ridge
National Geographic Trails Illustrated map: Black Canyon of the Gunnison National Park
Other maps: BLM Gunnison Gorge Recreation Area map
Special considerations: The Peach Valley Road leading to this trail is impassable when wet.

FINDING THE TRAILHEAD

From US 50, 1 mile south of the stoplight in Olathe, take Falcon Road east toward the Gunnison Gorge National Conservation Area. Travel on paved Falcon Road for approximately 4 miles, then on dirt another 0.4 mile to the Peach Valley Recreation Area. Continue for another 6.5 miles on Peach Valley Road to the Ute Park Trail turnoff. (It's 3.8 miles past the Bobcat Trail turnoff. You'll also pass Chukar Trail Road and Wave Road parking area along the way down this very much misnamed road.)
Trailhead GPS: N38 40.9329' / W107 51.8395'

UTE PARK–SOUTH RIM INTO GUNNISON GORGE NCA

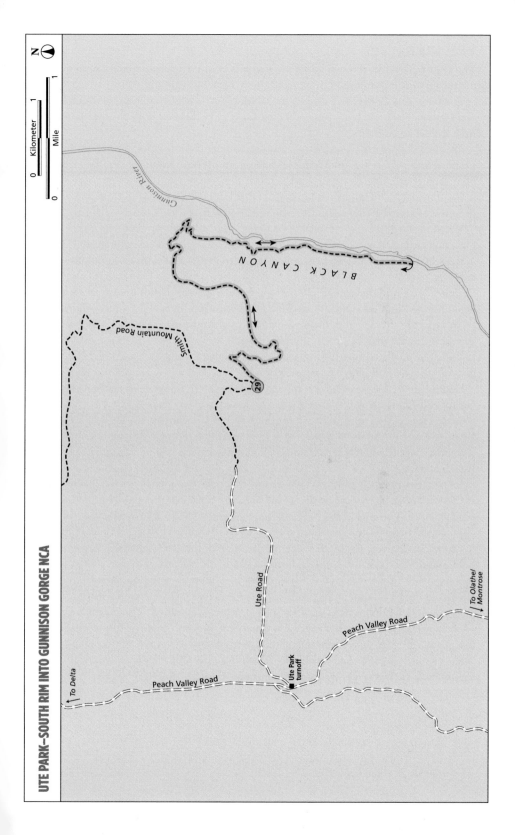

THE HIKE

The Gunnison River through Black Canyon National Park drops an average of 95 feet per mile—one of the steepest descents of any river in North America.

The Gunnison Gorge, managed by the BLM, is just downstream from the Black Canyon National Park and encompasses approximately 57,725 acres of public land in Montrose and Delta Counties.

User fees ($3 per day per person for day use; $10 per night for camping) are utilized to maintain and protect this wonderful resource from overuse, and this place has certainly been discovered. The first time I went down this trail more than 40 years ago, it was nearly impossible to find the road to the rim that leads here, let alone the trail down. Not so today. The road is easy to find, and the trail is easy to follow.

Those user fees paid to enhance the parking area and maintain the trail. Along with management fees, however, come rules designed to protect the area's natural and wilderness qualities, as well as to address visitor health and safety concerns and minimize user conflicts.

Unlike the "dispersed camping" ethic appropriate in other environments, BLM uses a "concentrated use" ethic here. "Overflow use into surrounding areas," according to one BLM brochure, "results in permanent damage to critical topsoil, riparian, or streambed vegetation, and sensitive fish and wildlife habitat."

With the increased use, leaving trash, litter, cigarette butts, garbage, toilet paper, or human waste is "unhealthy and unacceptable."

Hikers can use existing toilets at the Ute Park trailhead. There's also a primitive toilet facility at the bottom of Ute Park Trail.

From the trailhead, this trail leads north for 0.3 mile to its first switchback, dropping about 150 feet in elevation. In 1.5 miles, however, the trail begins to climb again. That climb may agitate some hikers at this point, but this stretch will be well appreciated on the way out.

In 2.4 miles, the main trail will cross a game trail that's also used by anglers and wildlife enthusiasts intent on photographing mule deer or, perhaps, chukar, peregrine falcons, or canyon wrens. The chukar partridge—*Alectoris chukar*—is a Eurasian upland game bird in the pheasant family, introduced into western Colorado in the 1940s and 1950s.

At the 3-mile mark, hikers are treated to great views downstream, where deep emerald pools swirl below tall, dark, rugged canyon walls of Precambrian rock, and a long, scenic upstream view of the verdant Ute Park itself. The white teepee seen in the foreground is used by the BLM to store supplies and equipment for trail and campground maintenance.

At 3.6 miles, you'll reach the river's edge near a designated hikers' camping spot. Camping is allowed in designated spots only (see "About Camping in the Gunnison Gorge NCA"). The teepee you spied from above is located downstream from this point. You can continue upstream for another 0.9 mile before you're stopped by a very large Precambrian rock wall, preventing further upstream travel.

Steven Marshall of Grand Junction stops to take in the tranquil beauty of the Gunnison River as it flows through the Black Canyon National Conservation Area, just downstream from Black Canyon National Park.

While the three major dams upstream—Blue Mesa, Morrow Point, and Crystal—have tamed the river's flow, they also created 26 miles of gold medal fishing water. Here in Ute Park, 2 miles of river access is available to stouthearted anglers and hikers.

MILES AND DIRECTIONS

0.0 Start from Ute Park Trailhead.

0.3 First switchback.

0.4 Continue right and stay on the trail, don't follow the wash.

0.7 Cross main drainage and continue heading down the right side of the wash.

0.9 Come to a trough once used to scrub ore. The trail cuts into the bottom of the gully.

1.2 Trail leads up to a sagebrush flat to the left and away from gully.

1.5 The trail leads to a white sandstone bench with bluish bentonite (Caution: muddy when wet) and continues climbing to the left around this sandstone bench.

1.7 Trail descends slightly through a lightning-struck area with blackened pinyon and juniper.

1.9 The trail climbs a little more to an excellent view site before descending to the next bench.

2.4 You'll cut across another well-used game trail/anglers' trail. Continue on the main trail to the right.

2.5 Another spur trail leads to the left. Continue forward.

3.0 Beautiful views looking both up and down river. Upstream is Ute Park.

3.2 Cross the gully and climb up the other side.

3.6 Take a hard left turn to Hiker's Camp Spot #20 and refresh yourself at The River.

3.8 Continue upstream to the old stone house. The well-traveled trail winds through pinyon and juniper and leads to a couple other boater campsites.

4.2 There's a small outdoor toilet here to accommodate all the hikers and boaters, however WAG bags (dog bags for humans) are strongly encouraged!

4.5 The trail ends at a large Precambrian rock wall, preventing further travel.

9.0 After backtracking, arrive back at the trailhead.

ABOUT CAMPING IN THE GUNNISON GORGE NCA

River corridor camping is allowed only in designated hiker or boater campsites identified on BLM maps and signs. Visitors must purchase camping permits and register and reserve campsites at wilderness trailheads or the Chukar boat launch. Maximum stay length in the wilderness and upstream of the Gunnison Forks for hikers is 2 nights/3 days. Boaters must move on after 1 night; no layover days.

Numerous other camping opportunities exist within the NCA, however. Camping is allowed in the remainder of the NCA for up to 6 consecutive nights, unless otherwise posted. Check BLM maps, signs, and website (https://www.blm.gov/programs/national-conservation-lands/colorado/gunnison-gorge-nca) for complete camping information.

30 BOBCAT TRAIL INTO THE BLACK CANYON OF THE GUNNISON RIVER

Full confession: I'm addicted to both hiking and fly fishing, and this is my power spot!

It's a short hike, but it's aerobically challenging, descending 880 feet from ridgetop to river in 1.1 miles. The bottom quarter-mile is very steep—so steep there's a 20-foot rope anchored to a juniper tree to assist in the climb down. It's not OSHA approved!

This trail is not for those afraid of heights or of climbing down backward on rock walls. But the hiking is great, the scenery is fantastic, and the fishing . . . well, it's OK I guess.

Start: From Bobcat Trailhead, at the southeast corner of the kiosk and check-in

Elevation loss: 6,259 feet at trailhead to 5,379 feet at river edge (880 feet)

Distance: 2.2 miles down and back (another 3.5 miles of river is accessible to hiking)

Difficulty: Difficult, strenuous, some rock-climbing and path-finding skills necessary

Hiking time: 40 minutes to 1 hour down; 45 minutes to 1.5 hours return

Seasons/schedule: Spring, summer, fall (road not passible when wet!)

Fees and permits: Special Recreation permit, $3 per person day use; $10 per person 1-night camping; $15 per person 2-night camping (limit: 2 nights). Annual Day Use Pass, $15. Self pay at trailhead.

Trail contacts: BLM Uncompahgre Field Office, 2505 S. Townsend Ave., Montrose, CO 81401; (970) 240-5300; https://www.blm.gov/programs/national-conservation-lands/colorado/gunnison-gorge-nca

Canine compatibility: Dogs allowed under control

Trail surface: Narrow, dirt, and rock backcountry trail; rock scramble on hard granite in bottom 0.25 mile

Land status: BLM, Gunnison Gorge National Conservation Area

Nearest towns: Delta, Olathe, Montrose

Other trail users: Some horseback riders on the rim.

Nat Geo TOPO! map (USGS): Black Ridge

National Geographic Trails Illustrated map: Black Canyon of the Gunnison National Park

Other maps: BLM Gunnison Gorge Recreation Area map

Special considerations: This trail is not for the faint of heart. While short, it is aerobically challenging, and the last 0.25 mile to the river requires some rock-climbing and bouldering skills. Note: Six rescuers and 2 horses spent a hot day in June 2024 rescuing 1 hiker who fell and broke an ankle here!

Other: The Colorado Canyons Association fosters community stewardship of National Conservation Lands with a focus on Dominguez-Escalante, Gunnison Gorge, and McInnis Canyons National Conservation Areas in western Colorado; 543 Main St. #4, Grand Junction, CO 81501; (970) 263-7902; https://www.coloradocanyonsassociation.org.

FINDING THE TRAILHEAD

Drive south from Olathe about 1 mile from the stoplight on US 50 and turn east on Falcon Road, following the signs toward the Gunnison Gorge National Conservation Area. Travel 4 miles to the end of the pavement, and another 0.4 mile on the dirt road to Peach Valley Recreation Area. Continue on this dirt road, now called Peach Valley Road, for another 2.8 miles to the Bobcat Trail turnoff. You'll pass both Chukar Trail Road and Wave Road parking areas. Turn right (east) at the Bobcat Trail turnoff and continue on a rugged four-wheel-drive road to its terminus at the top of the ridge in 1.5 miles.

Trailhead GPS: N38 37.7855' / W107 52.1847'

THE HIKE

At its deepest near Warner Point inside the Black Canyon National Park, the Gunnison River gorge is 2,772 feet deep. It's not quite that deep at the point where Bobcat Trail enters it. Nonetheless, you'll drop 880 feet into the gorge from this trail. It's one of four trails into the canyon from the south side of the BLM's Gunnison Gorge NCA and Wilderness.

The NCA is adjacent to and just downstream from Black Canyon National Park. The other three trails include Chukar, Duncan, and Ute Trails. All four are accessible from the misnamed Peach Valley Road east of the towns of Olathe and Delta.

This road is narrow and gets very slick if it's wet, so be careful on the drive. To reach the rim, you'll need a high-clearance, four-wheel-drive vehicle. You might make it in an old beater pickup to within 0.2 mile of the rim; then hike from there.

From the trailhead, the first few hundred yards along Bobcat Trail drops through a mix of yucca, mountain mahogany, pinyon, and juniper, with a spot of Mormon tea.

The trail then descends into the inner gorge's harder black igneous rock. Keep your eyes open for small groups of chukar at the rim. Along the way, you also may see elk, mule deer, Steller's jays, ravens, and turkey vultures.

Looking across the canyon on the way down, notice the dramatic, steep walls of the rock cleavage near the river.

This Precambrian rock is very hard and erosion resistant compared to the sandstone and other sedimentary rock above it. It's much older, too—formed around 1.7 billion years ago (see the "Black Canyon of the Gunnison" introduction).

As you near the river, you'll hear the sweetly haunting call of canyon wrens. If the wind isn't too heavy, you may also watch as white-throated swifts live up to their name, swiftly and expertly feeding on flying insects.

The last half-mile is the steepest, and one drop has a sturdy 20-foot rope anchored to a juniper tree to assist in the descent.

This rope, however, would certainly not be OSHA-approved, or BLM-approved, or Mom-approved, so you decide whether it will "assist" you or not.

Rock-climbing and bouldering skills are necessary to navigate this last stretch. Also, this trail is not as clearly distinguishable as others and some path-finding skills may be necessary.

The trail ends at river's edge near an official campsite. (Remember: A special permit is required that you should have gotten at the top of the trail!) Take a break here and enjoy the sounds of the river. Look for slicks left by frolicking river otters, reintroduced into the canyon by the Colorado Division of Parks and Wildlife (formerly Division of Wildlife) in the late 1970s and early 1980s.

Make sure you take plenty of water for this trip, and wear boots. This is not a hike for tennis shoes.

But once you're there, and if you're equipped, wet a line. This river is labeled "gold medal water" by the Colorado Wildlife Commission and is considered a world-class rainbow and brown trout fishery by anglers everywhere. Special regulations apply. Make sure you know them and keep in mind that this river is patrolled by wildlife officers in kayaks.

If you do some rock scrambling and one serious climb over the rock formation across from Buttermilk Rapids, you can hike downriver as far as the Duncan Trail. Keep an eye out for poison ivy.

MILES AND DIRECTIONS

0.0 Start at Bobcat Trailhead, just behind the BLM kiosk and check-in (6,260 feet).

0.2 Drop through a wooded area with mix of yucca, mountain mahogany, pinyon, and juniper into a grassy bowl, then into the next layer of pinyon/juniper.

0.6 Stay right at the top of this gully (an old, abandoned trail leads to the left).

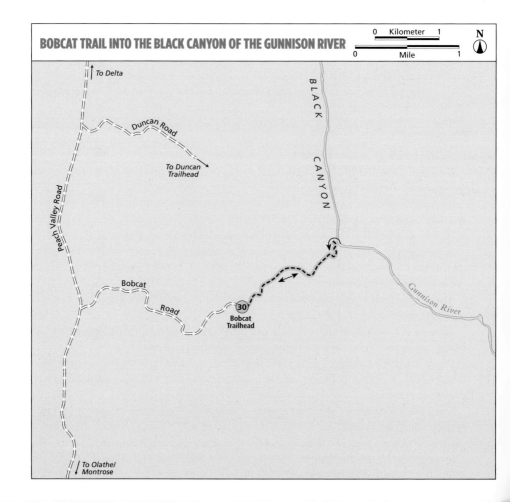

BOBCAT TRAIL INTO THE BLACK CANYON OF THE GUNNISON RIVER

0.7 Cross along the top of the Precambrian (granite) rock gully and stay right.

0.9 You can hear the river from here; in less than 0.1 mile, drop into the gully. Be careful. The top of this last descent consists of loose, slick dirt and rock. Below this, the final pitch is granite bedrock. It's steep, and some path-finding skills may be needed to find the 20-foot stretch of rope to assist in your descent.

1.1 Arrive at river. Scramble back up that rock wall to return to the trailhead.

2.2 Arrive back where you started.

Looking down on rafters

Bobcat Trail is a primitive trail that drops 880 feet in a little over a mile. The last half-mile requires basic rock-climbing skills, but for those adventurous few, the trip is well worth it.

Three major dams now block the upper reaches of the Gunnison Gorge—Blue Mesa, Morrow Point, and Crystal Dams (between the towns of Gunnison and Montrose). All three lie within the Curecanti National Recreation Area, established in 1965 with the completion of Blue Mesa Dam. This created the largest body of water in Colorado, Blue Mesa Reservoir—20 miles long with 96 miles of shoreline.

All three dams make up the Wayne N. Aspinall Storage Unit, one of four main units of the Upper Colorado River Storage Project (UCRSP). The other large dams in this project include Navajo Dam in New Mexico, Flaming Gorge Dam in Utah, and Glen Canyon Dam in Utah. The primary purpose of the project is to provide water storage to the Upper Colorado River Basin states of Colorado, Wyoming, New Mexico, and Utah.

The three dams in Curecanti each serve a specific purpose: Blue Mesa stores the water, Morrow Point produces electricity, and Crystal Dam regulates water flow for downstream irrigation, flood control, and habitat mitigation.

One reason the canyon and river below Crystal Dam is considered "gold medal water" for trout fishing is because it's a "tailwater fishery." Since the river's flow is now controlled by the dam and not by nature, fish don't have to battle immense spring runoff or late fall drought to survive.

There is no question the dams have altered the natural environment. According to the National Park Service, "The effects can be judged both positive and negative."

SOUTHERN ROCKIES

Telluride, Silverton, and most towns in the Southern Rockies were built as mining towns.

The youthful topography of the San Juan Mountains, with a total relief of almost 5,000 feet between the peaks and the bottoms of the canyons, is the result of massive and repeated volcanic activity followed by periods of glaciation that formed a fretted upland.

Volcanic activity persisted in the form of hydrothermal vents and hot springs laden with minerals. Gold, pyrite, quartz, clay minerals, and silver are all found within the mix here, and that's what brought about the mining boom of the late 1800s and early 1900s:

- Native gold. Much of the gold mined in the area is not visible to the naked eye and occurs either as very small particles, or included within pyrite and the other sulfide minerals.

Geologist Ray Pilcher, left, and his buddy Bill Haggerty enjoy the moment on top of 14,058-foot-tall Handies Peak

- Pyrite itself is not an ore mineral, but it carries gold or is closely associated with gold. Like quartz, pyrite is found in almost all the veins that fill fractures.

- Quartz is the most common vein mineral in the area south of Telluride. It fills fractures or parts of fractures of all different orientations and makes up part of every type of vein, excepting a few calcite veins.

- Clay minerals. A pure white or light greenish-gray claylike material is present in the veins in places, which suggests that it is a primary mineral rather than the result of weathering; this mineral is probably dickite.

- Native silver. A major amount of early mining was for silver. Wire silver is found with a mineral called argentite. It's a dark lead-gray mineral found in crystals and as formless aggregates.

When you see how sunlight and clouds play across these colorful mountains, you now know what early miners and prospectors were looking for!

31 POWDERHORN LAKES

Scoured by glaciation, the Calf Creek Plateau/Cannibal Plateau area—located in the heart of the 61,915-acre Powderhorn Wilderness—is one of the largest unbroken expanses of alpine tundra in the United States. Established in 1993, much of the wilderness sits above timberline at 12,000+ feet in elevation. The enchanted Powderhorn Lakes, however, are situated hundreds of feet beneath a giant talus ridge rising to the plateau's northeastern rim. Partly surrounded by dense Engelmann spruce forest, with that huge, glaciated wall of rock flanking its southern edge, these pristine lakes are the destination for this trip.

Start: From Powderhorn Lakes Trailhead

Elevation gain: 11,116 –11,885 feet (769 feet)

Distance: 8.0 miles out and back to Lower Powderhorn Lake; 9.8 miles out and back to Upper Powderhorn Lake

Difficulty: Moderate to strenuous due to both elevation and elevation gain

Hiking time: 2 hours to lower lake; 2.5 hours to upper lake from trailhead

Seasons/schedule: Late spring to early fall

Fees and permits: None

Trail contacts: Gunnison Ranger District, 216 N. Colorado St., Gunnison, CO 81230; (970) 641-0471; www.fs.usda.gov/recarea/gmug/recarea/?recid=80862; Bureau of Land Management, 2500 E. New York Ave., Gunnison, CO 81230; (970) 642-4940; https://www.blm.gov/visit/powderhorn-wilderness-area

Canine compatibility: Dogs permitted, under control

Trail surface: Dirt and rock backcountry singletrack trail

Land status: Wilderness area (southern 25 percent managed by Gunnison National Forest; northern 75 percent managed by BLM)

Nearest towns: Lake City, Gunnison

Other trail users: Some horseback use

Nat Geo TOPO! map (USGS): Powderhorn Lakes

Other maps: USFS Gunnison Basin Public Lands map

Other: The Gunnison Public Lands Initiative is a coalition of diverse stakeholders "working together to create a forward-thinking, well-balanced legislative proposal to keep our air and water clean, our local economy vibrant, and our heritage intact for generations to come." www.gunnisonpubliclands.org.

FINDING THE TRAILHEAD

From Gunnison, drive 9 miles west on US 50 to the Lake City turnoff, CO 149. Turn left (south) and continue for 20.1 mile to Gunnison CR 58, the Indian Creek Road. (It's just past mile marker 97.) Turn left (east) and drive 10 miles on a somewhat-rough two-wheel-drive dirt road. The trailhead sign and parking area are at the end of the road.

Trailhead GPS: N38 10.6047' / W107 09.9009'

THE HIKE

This is the most crowded trail in the Powderhorn Wilderness Area? I saw only six people when I backpacked into Powderhorn Lakes over a Labor Day weekend. Maybe its remoteness keeps the crowds away, but it's less than 40 miles south of Gunnison. Maybe the 10 miles of two-wheel-drive dirt road keep people away. A couple miles of that road are a little rough, even though those other six people made it in a Subaru Outback, a Toyota Corolla, and an old lightweight pickup.

The fact is, most people just don't know about this out-of-the-way geologic wonderland.

The southern quarter of Powderhorn Wilderness is managed by the Gunnison National Forest. The northern three-quarters is managed by the BLM. About 45 miles of trails access this seldom-visited area.

The "most popular" trail, Powderhorn Lakes Trail #3030, begins at 11,116 feet in elevation. The first 1.5 miles of trail provides a long, steady climb through a thick Engelmann spruce forest to 11,750 feet. Huge downed trees are strewn throughout this area. Gunnison National Forest forester Arthur Haynes speculates these fallen trees have been there since a couple old fires back in the 1950s. If it had been a blowdown, he says, all the trees would probably be lying in generally the same direction, whereas the trees in this area have fallen every which way.

While this is a healthy forest, Haynes and other foresters are keeping their eye on a very invasive spruce beetle epidemic that's wreaking havoc in the South San Juan Mountains, to the south and west of here (see sidebar to Hike 1, North Lake Trail on spruce beetle/pine beetle infestations).

At 1.5 miles, you'll come to a grassy high-mountain meadow full of colorful wildflowers in the summer and an expansive view of the La Garita Wilderness to the southeast. Its thick grass is grazed by herds of elk, especially in the early mornings and late evenings. During the daytime, watch for elk along the edges of this half-mile-long meadow.

The trail crosses the upper reach of the meadow, and then skirts the far side through heavy timber heading south. At 2.0 miles, the trail begins to climb away from the meadow.

About a mile and a half from the trailhead, you'll reach a grassy high-mountain meadow where you can see all the way to the La Garita Wilderness far to the southeast.

Upper Powderhorn Lake fills the entire western end of a spectacular glacial cirque beneath Calf Creek Plateau.

In another 0.7 mile, it skirts a small pond and crosses the drainage above it. This stretch may be wet in the late spring and into early summer. Don't be surprised by elk, deer, or even moose wandering through the woods here. Keep pets on leash and out of trouble.

At 3.1 miles, the trail takes a marked turn to the southwest, then up. At 3.5 miles, the trail levels a bit and soon you'll spot a small trail sign with arrows pointing to Hidden Lake (left) and Powderhorn Lakes (right).

The small pond you passed about a mile back is actually Hidden Lake. This trail leads to the far side of that pond and into the Middle Fork of Powderhorn Creek on Middle Fork Trail # 3020.

Continue to the right for 0.4 mile to Lower Powderhorn Lake. There are a handful of quality camping spots here, and fishing for cutthroats and brookies is considered good for a finicky high-mountain lake. The trail continues for another 0.9 mile as it follows the northern shoreline of Lower Powderhorn Lake. Soon, it veers southwest along the West Fork of Powderhorn Creek, a fine little brook trout stream. The path is relatively easy to follow along the north side of the creek, but don't worry if you feel you've lost the little-used main trail. The upper lake, which is about three times the size of the lower lake, fills the entire western end of a spectacular glacial cirque beneath Calf Creek Plateau, so you can't miss it. (The fishing at this upper lake, however, is marginal due to occasional winter kill.)

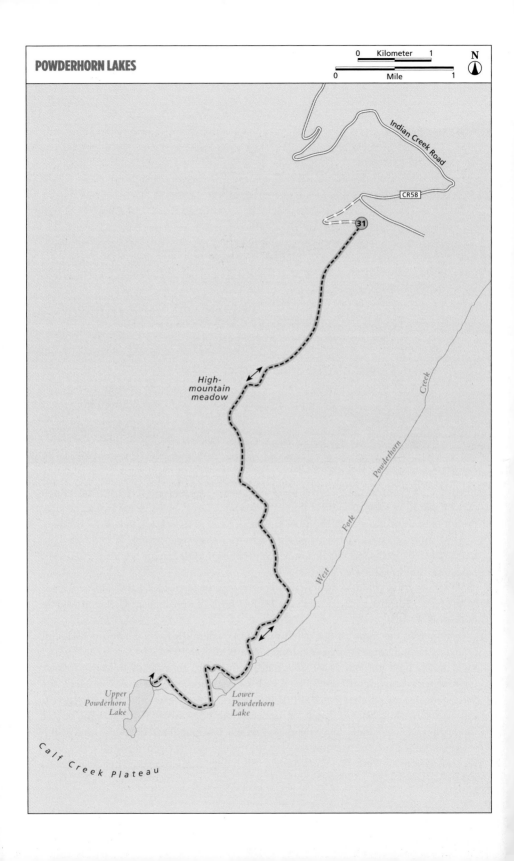

MILES AND DIRECTIONS

0.0 Start at the Powderhorn Lakes Trailhead #3030, to the right of the informational kiosk and begin a long, slow climb.

0.2 Powderhorn Wilderness Boundary and BLM sign-in.

1.2 Continue steady climb on a 10.2 percent grade; you'll drop a few feet in elevation here before climbing again.

1.5 You'll reach a large, broad meadow. The trail crosses the upper end of this meadow and continues south; trek quietly and watch for elk around the edges.

1.7 Back into the dark timber, the trail skirts the meadow, generally heading south.

2.0 Begin climbing away from the meadow to the west.

2.7 Skirt the small pond and cross a small drainage.

3.1 The trail now turns to the southwest, then up.

3.5 The trail mellows slightly here and soon emerges from the dark timber into a high-mountain meadow where the trail splits. A sign points to Hidden Lake to the left, and to Powderhorn Lakes to the right. Stay right and travel around a willow-filled meadow.

3.9 Reach the shores of Lower Powderhorn Lake. Continue skirting the lakes' western shore if you're headed to Upper Powderhorn Lake. Elevation 11,663; **N38 08.0667' / W107 10.8958'**

4.9 Reach the shores of Upper Powderhorn Lake. Elevation, 11,885; **N38 08.0317' / W107 11.4572'**

9.8 After backtracking, arrive back at the trailhead.

A faded sign leads to a secluded trail

Cannibal Plateau was named for Colorado's famous man-eater, Alferd Packer, who supposedly dined on five friends while lost and starving near here during the winter of 1874. Found guilty of manslaughter in 1883, he spent the next 16 years behind bars before being paroled in 1901. Maintaining his innocence until death in 1907, he insisted someone else murdered four of his companions, and he shot the fifth, Shannon Bell, in self-defense.

He confessed to being a cannibal, but was Packer really guilty of murder? Dave Bailey, curator of history at the Museum of Western Colorado, doesn't think so.

Alferd Packer was born "Alfred" but he preferred "Alferd," Bailey said. In 1994, while cataloging firearms in the museum, Bailey uncovered an 1862 Colt Police Model pistol with an accession card claiming it had been found in 1950 at the site Packer killed his traveling companions—"Cannibal Plateau." (Accession cards assign items to a particular collection within a museum.)

The gun was in poor shape but still had three of five bullets in the chamber. For the next 5 years, Bailey tracked the history of the gun and dug up every diary, document, and deposition of the Packer case. One lost journal depicted the crime scene, proving that Bell's body had been found some distance away from the others, supporting Packer's final story of Bell's attack on him. The journal said Bell had been shot two times. Bailey and a team of scientists from Mesa State College forensically matched the lead from the gun's remaining bullets to microscopic fragments in Bell's bullet wounds, thus possibly corroborating Alferd's own story.

There are lots of good sources for Alferd Packerd "stuff." Start here: https://en.wikipedia.org/wiki/Alferd_Packer
www.lakecitymuseum.com

32 FALL CREEK TRAIL

The Forest Service describes Fall Creek as a "typical mountain creek." While there are numerous "Fall Creeks" in Colorado and across the nation—just Google it—this Fall Creek is anything but typical. The trail along Fall Creek leads into the Uncompahgre Wilderness Area between Ridgway and Cimarron. It's an easy trail leading to an intriguing waterfall—a trail the entire family can enjoy. Of course, you can't see the waterfall from the trail, but that's OK. You can hear it, feel its pulse, and marvel at the spectacular granite canyon it tumbles through—even in a hailstorm.

Start: Fall Creek Trailhead #231 at the end of Gunnison CR 864
Elevation gain: 10,916–11,303 feet (387 feet)
Distance: 4.4 miles out and back
Difficulty: Easy
Hiking time: 2–2.5 hours
Seasons/schedule: June to Oct
Fees and permits: None
Trail contacts: USFS, Gunnison District Office, 216 N. Colorado, Gunnison, CO 81230, (970) 641-0471; www.fs.usda.gov/recarea/gmug
Canine compatibility: Dogs allowed under strict voice command or on a leash; it is illegal for dogs to chase wildlife!

Trail surface: Dirt singletrack
Land status: Gunnison National Forest, Uncompahgre Wilderness Area
Nearest town: Ridgway, Cimarron
Other trail users: Open to hiking, horseback riding
Nat Geo TOPO! map (USGS): Sheep Mountain, CO
National Geographic Trails Illustrated map: #146, Uncompahgre Plateau South
Other maps: Uncompahgre National Forest map
Special considerations: Weather changes quickly in this country! Be prepared!

FINDING THE TRAILHEAD

From Gunnison, travel west US 50 for approximately 26 miles to the intersection with Gunnison CR 864, the Little Cimarron Road. (From Montrose, travel east on US 50 for approximately 14 miles past Cimarron to CR 864, the Little Cimarron Road.) Turn south (left if coming from Gunnison, right if coming from Montrose) on CR 864 and continue for approximately 16 miles to the Fall Creek Trailhead (CR 864 eventually turns into CR 865).
Trailhead GPS: N38 11.4613' / W107 25.3925'

THE HIKE

Broad open meadows lined with spruce and fir lead hikers along one creek—Firebox Creek—into the next drainage, which is Fall Creek. A short detour from there takes you to the top of Fall Creek Falls. In the heart of the Uncompahgre Wilderness Area, the falls spill nearly 900 feet down a gnarly granite crack through the massive ridge that separates the Little Cimarron drainage from the Big Blue Creek drainage.

You can feel its power and hear its roar, but you can't see the falls, standing on the top of it. Nonetheless, it's well worth a short trip.

The Fall Creek Trail usually doesn't see much human activity since the trailhead is located on a remote dead-end road. Geoff Tischbein photo.

This trail continues another 8.5 miles to the south, connecting to Big Blue Trail #232. Big Blue Trail then connects to Uncompahgre Peak Trail #239, leading to the top of 14,309-foot Uncompahgre Peak.

The Fall Creek Trail usually doesn't see much human activity as the trailhead is located toward the end of CR 865. This wide dirt road was built by the Forest Service for the timber industry, but no company bid on the timber in this area because it's just too hard to retrieve. Thus, it is underused, much to the pleasure of hikers and horseback riders.

The trail leads downhill for a short distance through a coniferous forest of spruce, pine, and fir as it parallels Firebox Creek. In a little more than 0.1 mile, you'll come to the wilderness boundary and all wilderness regulations apply. "These regulations are necessary to protect the physical and biological resources of the Uncompahgre Wilderness and to protect the human experience of Wilderness character, solitude, and the untrammeled condition of the landscape," according to the Forest Service.

This area is certainly untrammeled. At 0.3 mile, you'll cross beneath a small rock field to your left, with the creek on your right. At 0.8 mile, you'll come to a natural ridge where the earth was pushed up by glaciation at the top of a long draw. In less than a tenth of a mile, you'll be walking down the other side of this dike and encounter two more such landforms as you head due south. Firebox Creek goes to the far right of the meadows you're hiking through, and the trail keeps to the far left. Notice the different year-classes of Engelmann spruce as you pass through this area. There are many different sizes—a good sign for the future of this forest.

At the 1.1-mile mark, you'll climb another short rise with a 4.7 percent grade to reach a broad meadow just below timberline. Wildflowers abound here in June and July. Even

Geoff Tischbein from Ridgway can grin and bear it . . .
he and his group were prepared for this summer storm!

into August, mountain gentian that is blue in color and numerous yellow composites line the trail.

You'll reach the high point on this trail at 11,303 feet in elevation at 1.8 miles, before dropping into the Fall Creek drainage. The trail winds through dark timber for a short distance before entering this drainage and you'll be greeted with another spectacular high-mountain meadow that seems to continue forever to your right (southwest).

Fall Creek Trail leads in that direction for another 8.5 miles to meet Big Blue Trail #232. As you exit the trees, however, you'll want to get off the main trail and take a sharp left, heading east. The top of the falls is only 0.2 mile from this spot. Pick your way across

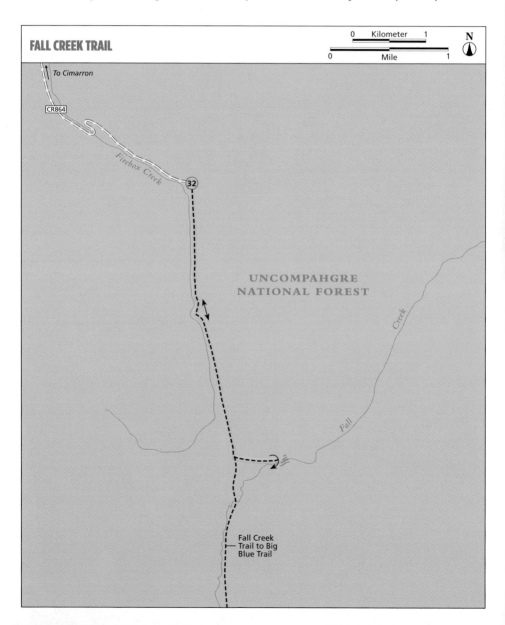

Fall Creek Trail connects with Big Blue Trail #232 in another 8.5 miles.

the meadow and head toward the water. You'll soon be standing on an incredible granite structure that was cut over millions of years by the constant effects of water as Fall Creek drops through a series of cascades from this spot nearly 900 feet to the valley below.

MILES AND DIRECTIONS

0.0 Start from Fall Creek Trailhead #231.

0.1 Uncompahgre Wilderness boundary.

0.3 Skirt beneath a rock field on your left; the creek is on the right.

0.8 Cross a small land ridge caused by glaciation on top of the draw you just hiked through.

0.9 Walk down the other side of this ridge, then up to the next little dike pushed up by glaciers.

1.1 Reach another little rise leading to a broad meadow just below timberline.

1.8 High point at 11,303 feet. Drop into Fall Creek Drainage from here.

2.0 Leave main trail, go left (east) toward the water.

2.2 Don't get too close to the edge!

4.4 Arrive back at the trailhead.

There are eighty-nine peaks that rise to more than 14,000 feet above sea level in the United States. California has twelve, Washington has two, and Alaska has twenty-one. The remaining fifty-three protrude from the rugged Rocky Mountains in Colorado (see sidebar). This is the only hike to a 14er in this book, and if you only plan to summit one 14,000-foot peak in your lifetime, Handies Peak is a great one! The panoramic views from the top of this 14,058-foot peak are fabulous. You're at the very heart—and top—of the Rockies!

Start: From the American Basin Trailhead
Elevation gain: 11,445–14,058 feet (2,613 feet)
Distance: 6.2 miles round-trip
Difficulty: All 14ers are strenuous, even though this is one of the easier ones!
Hiking time: About 5 hours
Seasons/schedule: July/Aug
Fees and permits: None
Trail contacts: BLM Gunnison Field Office, (970) 642-4940; 2500 E. New York Ave., Gunnison, CO 81230
Canine compatibility: Dogs permitted, but they'd better be in pretty good shape
Trail surface: Rocky dirt path through a couple snowfields
Land status: BLM Handies Peak Wilderness Study Area
Nearest town: Lake City

Other trail users: None
Nat Geo TOPO! map (USGS): Handies Peak, CO
National Geographic Trails Illustrated map: #141, Telluride, Silverton, Ouray, Lake City
Other maps: USFS Gunnison Basin Public Lands map
Special considerations: See sidebar on the dangers of climbing 14ers!
Other: www.14ers.org consists of volunteers who work to "protect and preserve the natural integrity of Colorado's 14,000-foot peaks through active stewardship and public education." www.14ers.com, in the meantime, provides a complete list of peaks, and discusses weather conditions, trailhead locations, maps, and tons of other useful information if you're thinking of bagging a 14er!

FINDING THE TRAILHEAD

From Lake City, drive 2 miles south on CO 149 (55 miles southwest of Gunnison) and turn right on the Lake San Cristibol Road (Hinsdale CR 30). This is the southern entrance to the "Alpine Loop" scenic byway. Follow the signs to Cinnamon Pass. In 4 miles, the pavement ends. Continue on the dirt road for another 16.3 miles to a signed fork in the road. Turn left to American Basin. (To the right is Cinnamon Pass.) If you do not have a four-wheel-drive vehicle with good clearance, park here. It's 0.9 mile to the trailhead. After 0.2 mile, cross a stream which can be fairly deep in spring. If you don't feel comfortable driving through the water, there are some parking spots in the area. Park when you cross the stream, and begin your hike on the trail marked: "This route open to horseback and hiking; closed to motorized vehicles." Or, you could continue on the rough four-wheel-drive road to its end at a large parking area. (The hike described here starts just after the road crosses the creek, adding about a mile to the trip.)
Trailhead GPS: N37 55.5280' / W107 30.8455'

THE HIKE

Handies Peak rises 14,058 feet above sea level and is the highest point of land managed by the BLM outside of Alaska. This Wilderness Study Area also hosts twelve other peaks that rise over 13,000 feet, three major canyons, numerous small drainages, glacial cirques, and three alpine lakes. The geomorphology shows a variety of volcanic, glacial, and Precambrian formations. A rock glacier formation is also located at the head of American Basin. You can't miss it because you must hike through it to get to the top.

From the summit, the Needles and Grenadier Mountains, the peaks of the Uncompahgre and Mt. Sneffels Wilderness Area, and the La Garita Mountains surround you. Redcloud and Sunshine Peaks are east of you, and in the far distance to the west, you can see the pointy top of Mt. Sneffels.

You can save yourself 0.8 mile of hiking if you have a big old four-wheel-drive vehicle that you don't mind banging up. Otherwise, start this hike just after the American Basin cutoff road fords the headwaters of the Lake Fork of the Gunnison River. You're right at timberline here, and there's a sign that says the trail is not accessible to motorized vehicles. It's referring to the trail that leads down into the little gully to the southwest of you, which may or may not be full of snow well into July. Hike up the road that some prefer to drive for 0.4 mile to the official trailhead. The trail cuts to the left of this upper parking area and heads due south into American Basin.

14,058-foot Handies Peak

By the time you reach the 1-mile mark, you'll have climbed to 12,000 feet in elevation. Don't forget to drink lots of water on this trail. You'll get dehydrated fast at altitude.

At 1.1 miles, you'll cross a glaciated stream that originates from Sloan Lake. There's a pretty little waterfall here. Have another sip of water and take a few pictures. You can't race up a 14er. Take it nice and easy. If you average a mile per hour on the way up, you're doing fine.

You'll hike toward a big honkin' cairn at 1.8 miles, where the trail takes a right turn. You're at 12,661 feet in elevation and you'll climb 300 feet in the next 0.2 mile to the bench where Sloan Lake lies. At this elevation, and lying in the shadow of an unnamed ridgeline that rises to 13,800 feet, this lake will remain frozen well into July.

You'll now get a short reprieve for about 0.2 mile, where the trail remains somewhat level, before beginning its next climb across a broad scree field, then you'll climb seven switchbacks to the 2.8-mile mark and 13,600 feet in elevation. There's a lovely saddle to Handies Peak here, as it looks off toward three unnamed 13,000-foot peaks to the southeast. Take another swig of water and have a granola bar. Get ready for the last push to the summit. It's only another 450 feet up in 0.2 mile. Feel the burn and enjoy the fragrance. Even up here, small tundra flowers bloom. The purple-colored sky pilot, *Polemonium viscosum*, in particular produces a sweet-smelling aroma that lifts your spirits as you trudge up this final ascent. Called skunkweed at lower elevations because its odor is a bit too pungent, it seems to smell sweeter the higher you go on the mountain.

The view of Sloan Lake from the top of Handies Peak

American Basin on the trail to Handies Peak

Or, maybe it's that sweet smell of success you're enjoying as you grin from ear to ear on top of 14,058-foot Handies Peak. Congratulations. You've just bagged one of Colorado's famous 14ers!

MILES AND DIRECTIONS

0.0 Start from designated hiking/horseback trail just across the creek at 11,445 feet; trailhead GPS: **N37 55.5280' / W107 30.8455'.**

0.4 Hike up the rugged jeep road to 11,589 feet and the official trailhead at: **N37 55.2169' / W107 30.9878'.**

1.0 You've hit 12,000 feet in elevation.

1.1 Cross a glaciated stream flowing from beneath Sloan Lake. There's a nice little waterfall here.

1.8 Waypoint: **N37 54.3730' / W107 30.7145'** You've reached 12,661 feet, near a large rock cairn; the trail heads south, climbing to the next bench.

2.0 Arrive at Sloan Lake: **N37 54.2757' / W107 30.7204'** at 12,954 feet.

2.2 A somewhat level trail now begins to climb again from 12,975 feet.

2.8 You'll have just climbed seven switchbacks up to 13,600 feet. Nice saddle here. Take a rest.

3.1 You're on the top at 14,058 feet above sea level. Congratulations! Lean on your hiking sticks and return the way you came.

6.2 Arrive back at the trailhead.

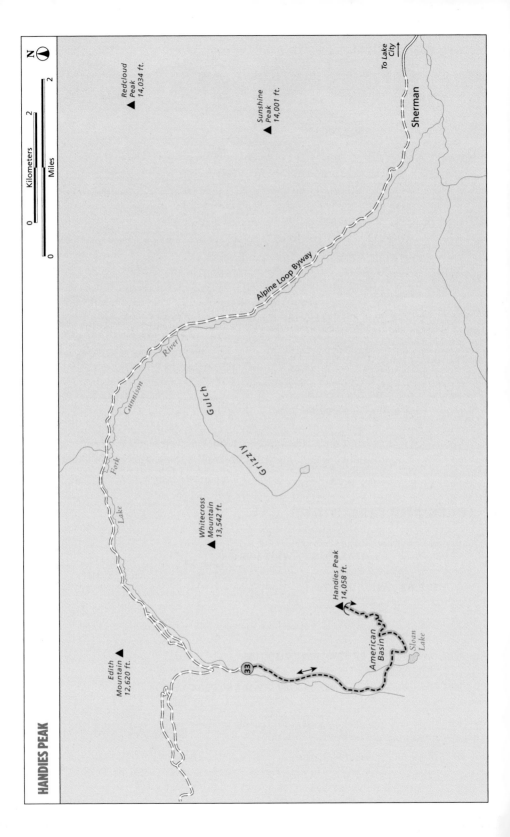

HANDIES PEAK

N

Kilometers
0   2

Miles
0   2

Redcloud
Peak
14,034 ft.

Sunshine
Peak
14,001 ft.

Edith
Mountain
12,620 ft.

Whitecross
Mountain
13,542 ft.

Handies Peak
14,058 ft.

American
Basin

Sloan
Lake

Lake Fork

Gunnison River

Grizzly Gulch

Alpine Loop Byway

Sherman

To Lake City

33

THE DANGERS OF CLIMBING 14,000-FOOT PEAKS IN COLORADO

1. Lightning is dangerous!
2. Lightning is the greatest external hazard to summer mountaineering in Colorado.
3. Lightning kills people every year in Colorado's mountains.
4. Direct hits are usually fatal.

PRECAUTIONS

1. Start early! Be off summits by noon and back in the valley by early afternoon.
2. Observe thunderhead buildup carefully, noting speed and direction; towering thunderheads with black bottoms are bad.
3. When lightning begins nearby, count the seconds between flash and thunder, then divide by five to calculate the distance to the flash in miles. Repeat to determine if lightning is approaching.
4. Try to determine if the lightning activity is cloud-to-cloud or ground strikes.
5. Get off summits and ridges.

PROTECTION

1. You cannot outrun a storm; physics wins.
2. When caught, seek a safe zone in the 45-degree cone around an object five to ten times your height.
3. Be aware of ground currents; the current from a ground strike disperses along the ground or cliff, especially in wet cracks.
4. Wet ropes are good conductors.
5. Snow is not a good conductor.
6. Separate yourself from metal objects.
7. Avoid sheltering in spark gaps under boulders and trees.
8. Disperse the group. Survivors can revive one who is hit.
9. Crouch on boot soles, ideally on dry, insulating material such as moss or grass. Dirt is better than rock. Avoid water.

34 PIEDRA RIVER TRAIL

You just may see a playful river otter sliding down a mudbank along this trail. This acrobatic aquatic mammal was once thought to be extinct in Colorado and most of the western United States. In an attempt to restore its populations, the Colorado Division of Wildlife (now called Parks and Wildlife) released more than a hundred river otters into the Piedra, Gunnison, Upper Colorado, and Dolores Rivers and at Cheesman Reservoir between 1978 and 1983. A total of twenty-four river otters were released into the Piedra River alone and by 2003, this population was considered "viable," or self-sustaining.

Start: Piedra River Trail/First Fork Trailhead
Elevation gain: 7,122–7,793 feet (671 feet)
Distance: 9.6 miles out and back
Difficulty: Easy first 2 miles; moderate beyond that due to elevation gain and loose gravel on trail
Hiking time: 5+ hours
Seasons/schedule: May to Oct
Fees and permits: None
Trail contacts: San Juan National Forest, 15 Burnett Ct., Durango, CO 81302; (970) 247-4874; www.fs.usda.gov/recarea/sanjuan/recreation
Canine compatibility: Dogs are allowed under voice or leash control. It is illegal for dogs to chase wildlife.
Trail surface: Rock and dirt singletrack backcountry trail; slippery due to loose gravel in spots after the second mile

Land status: San Juan National Forest
Nearest town: Bayfield, Pagosa Springs
Other trail users: Horseback riders
Nat Geo TOPO! map (USGS): Bear Mountain and Devil Mountain
National Geographic Trails Illustrated map: #140, Weminuche Wilderness
Other maps: San Juan National Forest map
Special considerations: While this area has been reopened after the Little Sand Fire, numerous hazards may still exist, including dead and dying trees and trail washouts. Use extra caution when entering this area.
Other: Special fishing regulations are in effect for this stretch of river: Licensed anglers may use artificial flies and lures only and all trout must be returned to the water immediately.

FINDING THE TRAILHEAD

From Bayfield, travel east for 19 miles on US 160 to First Fork Road (FR 622, also known as Archuleta CR 166) which is the first road directly after the highway passes over the Piedra River. Turn left (north) and travel 12 miles on this well-maintained dirt road to where the road crosses the Piedra River. The trail starts just north of the river on the right side of the road. Parking is available on the left.
Trailhead GPS: N37 21.2336' / W107 19.4500'

THE HIKE

The destination of this hike is the confluence of Sand Creek and the Piedra River—the original reintroduction site in this drainage for the threatened North American river otter (*Lontra canadensis*) (see sidebar), One of the reasons for this release site, other than its remoteness and clean water, is its abundance of fish since that's what otters eat.

The Piedra River flows low and clear in the late summer but it doesn't look like this during the spring runoff!

Deep pockets and holes on the Piedra River provide perfect holding and feeding spaces for wild fighting trout—and great swimming holes for playful river otters.

From the trailhead, you'll travel upstream through a tall ponderosa pine forest on a small doubletrack jeep trail. Motorized vehicles are no longer allowed in this area. Within 30 yards you'll cross a cattle fence and the trail leads northeast and away from the river. Be prepared for cattle here as the trail changes to a backcountry singletrack dirt/rock trail.

In 0.5 mile, you may notice poison ivy. Be careful: "Leaves of three—let them be! If it's hairy it's a berry; if it's shiny, watch your hiney!" The trail remains level for a mile, with a little bit of elevation gain here and there, hovering about 80 to 100 feet above the river. By 1.5 miles, you'll begin to notice vegetation changes with more grasses and forbs as the trail leads through open mountain meadows.

At 1.7 miles, you'll have crossed your second "seep," a slow flow of water seeping through the marshes and porous rock draining down from the north. Sneakers are fine on this lower 2-mile stretch, but you may have to do a little hopping here to get across.

In 1.9 miles, the trail splits. The main trail continues to the left (northeast). The lower (right) trail leads to a great camping spot and access to the river. This is also a good lunch spot or turnaround spot for those who don't wish to venture farther.

From here, the trail gets a little tougher. One of two relatively steep climbs comes just past the trail-split when you gain about 300 feet in elevation before crossing Davis Creek at 2.4 miles.

The trail now travels above Second Box Canyon, where the river flows beneath a steep-sided granite canyon that's accessible by boat, but not by foot.

At 2.8 miles, you'll notice some spot burns—remnants from the lightning-caused Little Sand Fire in 2012. (The Little Sand Fire covered more than 25,000 acres, or 39 square miles.) In another 0.3 mile, you'll see a few waist-high ponderosa pines. Ponderosa pines possess major adaptations to fire. Their barks are extra thick and act as insulators against the heat of fire. Their cones also exhibit "bradyspory" (seed retention) and "pyriscence" (fire-stimulated seed release). This allows seeds to compete with other grasses and plants because they thrive on increased nutrient concentrations that exist after fire.

Throughout this stretch, the trail travels through Gambel oak, wild roses, even a few aspen along with violet fleabane, serviceberry, and numerous other flowers, grasses, and shrubs. This is the understory, growing back strong after fire, but this is also a steep southeast-facing slope. The loose gravel makes you pay attention to your feet. Here's where a pair of boots would be much better than the sneakers.

Soon, you'll reach a steep switchback that leads down another gully before continuing east to the confluence of Sand Creek at 4.8 miles. You can continue up this trail for another 6.4 miles to the upper Piedra River Trailhead located on the Piedra River Road, 16 miles north of Pagosa Springs. If you've got a shuttle vehicle, this is a great 11.2-mile hike. Otherwise, search for those elusive river otters here, and then retrace your steps back to your vehicle.

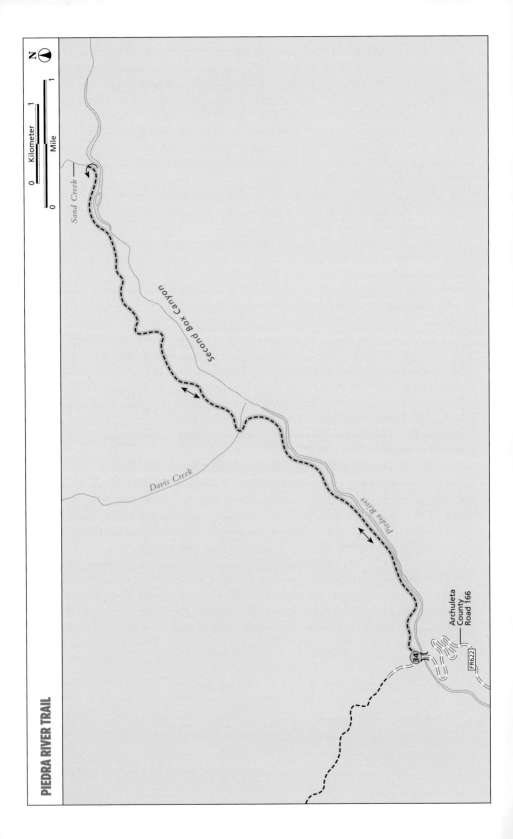

PIEDRA RIVER TRAIL

N

Kilometer
0   1

Mile
0   1

Sand Creek

Second Box Canyon

Davis Creek

Piedra River

Archuleta
County
Road 166

34

FR622

MILES AND DIRECTIONS

0.0 Start from Piedra River Trail/First Fork Trailhead.

0.5 Small clumps of poison ivy grow next to the trail. Remember: "Leaves of three, let them be."

1.5 The vegetation changes here with more grasses and an open canopy.

1.7 The trail cuts through a second seep from the left (northwest). Are you wearing sneakers?

1.9 The trail splits; **N37 22.0047' / W107 17.8034'.** The main trail goes to the left, while a great camping and lunch spot lies to the right.

2.0 Reach the river for lunch; go back to the trail split to continue upstream.

2.3 Trail climbs its steepest slope up the side of the Davis Creek drainage.

2.4 Cross the head of the Davis Creek drainage; it's probably muddy!

2.6 Climb steadily out of Davis Creek drainage at 7,519 feet in elevation..

2.8 Spot burns from 2012 Little Sand Fire.

3.1 Baby ponderosa pine almost waist high line the trail.

3.3 View the opposite side of Second Box Canyon of the Piedra River.

3.5 Major switchback heading down from 7,768 feet in elevation.

4.8 Reach Sand Creek. **N37 23.0710' / W107 16.0843'**

9.6 After backtracking, arrive back at the trailhead.

Trapping in the 1800s was the predominant cause of initial river otter population declines in Colorado. By 1882, as Native Americans were placed on reservations, western Colorado was then settled by miners, farmers, and ranchers with hundreds of thousands of livestock. River otter populations that survived the trapping onslaught then faced major changes in aquatic habitats with heavy-metal pollution from hard-rock mining and agricultural dewatering of rivers.

By the early 1900s, the North American river otter (*Lontra canadensis*) was thought to be "extirpated" from Colorado.

That all changed in the 1970s when Coloradoans, through the Colorado Division of Wildlife (now Parks and Wildlife), got serious about threatened and endangered species along with all nongame wildlife. Nongame wildlife includes 800 species of wildlife that cannot be hunted, fished for, or trapped.

Coloradoans began helping these species by voluntarily donating all or a portion of their tax refunds to the Colorado Nongame and Endangered Wildlife Fund. The money is earmarked for projects that manage or recover wildlife such as river otter, lynx, black-footed ferret, greenback cutthroat, and others.

You can also contribute by sending money directly to the Nongame and Endangered Wildlife Fund. To learn more, go to: http://cpw.state.co.us/about us/Pages/Tax-Checkoff.aspx.

The river otter was downlisted from "endangered" to "threatened" in Colorado in 2003. That means the species is not at immediate risk of extirpation in the state but remains vulnerable. Today, one of the biggest problems for river otter is "harassment" from dogs. Please keep that in mind as you hike this drainage.

A technical conservation assessment of Colorado's river otter may be found at: www.fs.usda.gov/Internet/FSE_DOCUMENTS/stelprdb5210168.pdf.

The hike becomes more rugged after the second mile.

35 FOURMILE TRAIL TO FOURMILE FALLS

Hiking this scenic trail is a great way to experience the wonders of the Weminuche Wilderness—its vast spaces, rugged cliffs, and lush forests—and its serious waterfalls. The first two waterfalls are 3 miles from the trailhead, but you can keep hiking to find more. Early spring brings heavy snowmelt and runoff. That's when the waterfalls thunder! Yet, because of its lower elevation and its lower longitude, bordering New Mexico, this trail stays snow-free later in the fall and melts out earlier in the spring than most treks into this wilderness.

Start: Fourmile Trailhead
Elevation gain: 789 feet to first two falls (8,970–9,759 feet); 1,572-foot gain to upper falls at 10,542 feet
Distance: 8.2 miles out and back (6.0 miles out and back to the two main waterfalls)
Difficulty: Moderate because the trail rises and falls, sometimes quite steeply
Hiking time: 4–6 hours
Seasons/schedule: Late Apr–late Oct most years
Fees and permits: None
Trail contacts: 180 Pagosa St., PO Box 310, Pagosa Springs, CO 81147; (970) 264-2268; https://www.fs.usda.gov/sanjuan

Canine compatibility: Dogs are allowed under strict voice control or on a leash; it is illegal for dogs to chase wildlife.
Trail surface: Rocky dirt trail
Land status: USFS, San Juan National Forest, Weminuche Wilderness Area
Nearest town: Pagosa Springs
Other trail users: Hikers and horseback riders
Nat Geo TOPO! map (USGS): Pagosa Peak, CO
National Geographic Trails Illustrated map: #145, Pagosa Springs, Bayfield
Other maps: San Juan National Forest map

FINDING THE TRAILHEAD

From US 160 in Pagosa Springs, turn north on Lewis Street, and then take an immediate left onto 5th Street, then a right onto Four Mile Road, or Archuleta CR 400. This county road soon becomes FR 645. Drive 8 miles and turn right, continuing on FR 645 for another 4.7 miles to a vault toilet and horse trailer parking area at Fourmile Stock Drive Trailhead. Continue another 0.1 mile to a second vault toilet at the Fourmile Trailhead to Fourmile Falls.
Trailhead GPS: N37 24.5596' / W107 03.1682'

THE HIKE

This hike features two great waterfalls on two different creeks. The elevation gain from the trailhead to the base of them is only 780 feet in 3 miles, but this trail goes up and down and up and down all the way to the falls. There are even more waterfalls above as you continue north up Fourmile Trail and into the largest wilderness area in Colorado—the Weminuche (see sidebar).

This trail leads downhill from the trailhead. (The Anderson Trail #579 leads due west and uphill from this spot. It joins Fourmile Trail near Fourmile Lake in a little more than

Falls Creek spills over a massive conglomerate of rock and mud. Some call this the Side Canyon Falls since it's not actually on Fourmile Creek.

9 miles.) In 0.3 mile, you'll cross a small drainage where the trail leads into a large patch of wild raspberries. They are normally in full fruit by mid-August.

In another tenth of a mile, you've entered the wilderness, and you may notice a pale yellow flower that resembles a snapdragon. It's called "butter and eggs," or toadflax. It's a nonnative, toxic weed that's despised by land managers in the West because of its invasive adaptability.

The roller-coaster trail continues another 0.7 mile until you begin climbing in earnest. All along this trail you'll find wild raspberries, twinberry (honeysuckle), currant, elderberries, and an interesting woody plant with bright orange berries, an American ash. With this plentiful food source, you can see why birds and black bears roam these woods.

At the 2.2-mile mark, you'll reach a short uphill stretch before the trail levels near another broad raspberry patch. Watch closely in the timber for red-breasted nuthatches. These colorful flyers wedge seeds into cracks of trees and then hammer them open with their beaks. You should also catch your first glimpse of the waterfalls.

While hiking beneath 12,097-foot Eagle Mountain and 12,137-foot Eagle Peak most of the way (they're off to your right, or east), at 2.6 miles the trails winds to the west for a great view of Pagosa Peak (12,640 feet in elevation). In another 0.2 mile, the trail splits and you've come to Falls Creek, flowing down the side of Pagosa Peak to its confluence with Fourmile Creek, just downstream from where you're standing.

Take the left (west) trail and hike uphill along Falls Creek a short distance before crossing it. Continue heading upstream (west) to the first waterfall (some call this the side-canyon waterfall). Here, Falls Creek spills over a massive conglomerate of rock and mud that comprises the lower eastern flank of Pagosa Peak.

After a photo shoot, head down the trail on the west side of Falls Creek to the main Fourmile Trail leading to your left (north). Turn onto this trail and hike a short distance for your best views of the major Fourmile Falls. You can see the upper parts of this spectacular waterfall as it cascades nearly 300 feet. The vegetation is so overgrown, however, that you can't see it spill into the creek valley below.

You're welcome to bushwhack as far as you can, but an alternative (if it's not during spring runoff) is to continue north and up the main trail to the 3.5-mile mark before crossing Fourmile Creek near the site of an old steel bridge. (The bridge is marked on topographical maps, but it's long gone.) Cross the creek on logs and rocks at this spot and continue for another 0.5 mile. (There's another switchback in very short order.)

At the 4-mile mark, you'll spy another set of waterfalls (Upper Fourmile Falls) tumbling through a lush, dense forest of spruce, willows, subalpine bluebells, and rocks. This makes a good turnaround, unless you'd like to continue up to Fourmile Lake in another 1.3 miles.

MILES AND DIRECTIONS

0.0 Start from Fourmile Trailhead. The trail heads north and immediately downhill.

0.3 Cross a small tributary to Fourmile Creek; gorge on raspberries.

1.1 Climb begins in earnest now from 9,062 feet in elevation.

1.3 Cross this seep and look around for more wild raspberries.

2.2 Another short, strenuous stretch uphill before the trail levels out.

2.6 Pagosa Peak (12,640 feet in elevation) looms large in front of you.

Pagosa Peak

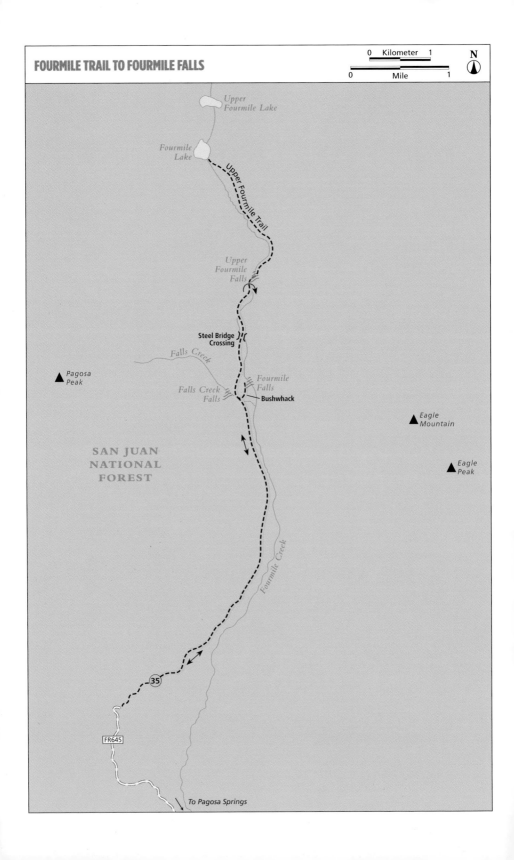

0   Kilometer   1

0   Mile   1

N

Upper
Fourmile Lake

Fourmile
Lake

Upper Fourmile Trail

Upper
Fourmile
Falls

**Steel Bridge
Crossing**

Falls Creek

▲ *Pagosa
Peak*

*Falls Creek
Falls*

*Fourmile
Falls*

Bushwhack

▲ *Eagle
Mountain*

**SAN JUAN
NATIONAL
FOREST**

▲ *Eagle
Peak*

Fourmile Creek

35

FR645

To Pagosa Springs

2.7 Trail splits. The lower (main) trail is blocked with gigantic downfall trees. Go left (uphill).

2.8 Reach the base of Falls Creek Falls and watch for white-throated swifts.

2.9 Returning to the main trail, turn left (north) and head upstream along Fourmile Creek (at an 18 percent grade).

3.0 Find your best views of the Fourmile Falls.

3.2 You're now above the last large waterfall (9,943 feet); head down to the creek bottom.

3.5 Cross on logs and rock above old steel bridge foundation.

4.1 Watch for American dippers (water ouzels) chasing food underwater in the stream and marvel at Upper Fourmile Falls just upstream. This is a good turnaround spot (or continue to Fourmile Lake in another 1.3 miles).

8.2 Arrive back at the trailhead.

The 499,771-acre Weminuche Wilderness (locals pronounce it WEM-in-ooch, named for a Native American band of the Ute Tribe) was designated by Congress in 1975, and expanded by two Colorado Wilderness Acts in 1980 and 1993. It spans the Continental Divide, North America's geological backbone, with an average elevation of 10,000 feet above sea level.

The area was uplifted by volcanic activity eons ago, then glaciers left sharp turrets and jagged peaks. Between them now lay turquoise-studded high-mountain lakes at the tops of spectacular alpine valleys. While three peaks, Eolus, Sunlight, and Wisdom, rise above 14,000 feet, many others reach above 13,000 feet in elevation and some of the most awesome and prominent ones, such as Eagle Mountain, Eagle Peak, and Pagosa Peak, are "only" 12,000+ feet, more than 2 miles above sea level.

There are hot springs scattered across western Colorado—from Steamboat Springs in northwest Colorado, to Glenwood Springs in west-central Colorado, to Dunton Hot Springs in southwest Colorado. Geyser Spring is Colorado's only true geyser, though. Located along the West Dolores River not far from Dunton in the San Juan Mountains, this geyser doesn't erupt like Old Faithful, but it does rumble to a sulfur-infused boiling point for 12 to 15 minutes every 40 minutes or so. The short hike to the spring is refreshing, even though you'll catch your first whiff of sulfur not far from the trailhead. If you're in search of easy, but weird, this is it!

Start: From Geyser Spring Trailhead (FS Trail #648)
Elevation gain: 8,559–9,110 feet (551 feet)
Distance: 2.4 miles out and back
Difficulty: Easy
Hiking time: 1.5–2 hours
Seasons/schedule: June to Oct
Fees and permits: None
Trail contacts: San Juan National Forest, Dolores Ranger District, 29211 Hwy. 184, Dolores, CO; (970) 882-7296; www.fs.usda.gov/detail/sanjuan
Canine compatibility: Dogs allowed under control. It is illegal for your dogs to chase wildlife!
Land status: San Juan National Forest
Trail surface: Backcountry rock and dirt singletrack path
Nearest towns: Cortez
Other trail users: Hikers, horseback riders, and mountain bikers, although horses are seldom seen

Nat Geo TOPO! map (USGS): Dolores Peak, CO and Groundhog Mountain, CO
Other maps: San Juan National Forest Service map; BLM 1: 100,000 Dove Creek, CO
Other: The San Juan Mountains Association (SJMA) promotes responsible care of natural and cultural resources through education and hands-on involvement that inspires respect and reverence for our lands. http://sjma.org; (970) 385-1210
The Canyon of the Ancients Visitor Center, 27501 Hwy. 184, Dolores, CO 81323, (970) 882-5600, is a museum of the Ancestral Puebloan (or Anasazi) culture and other Native cultures in the Four Corners region. https://www.blm.gov/learn/interpretive-centers/CANM-visitor-center-museum

FINDING THE TRAILHEAD

From Cortez, drive 22.4 miles from Cortez on CO 145 to the West Fork Road/Dunton turnoff. Continue on West Fork Road for 41.6 miles. The trailhead is just off the West Fork Road east of the Johnny Bull Trailhead. (Johnny Bull is marked on most maps, but Geyser is marked on only the newest ones.)
Trailhead GPS: N37 45.4321' / W108 07.6864'

THE HIKE

This is not a long hike, nor is it a strenuous hike. This is, however, a unique hike through a peaceful aspen/spruce/subalpine fir forest that leads to the only geyser in Colorado. And while it's certainly not "Old Faithful," it boils for about 12 minutes every 40 minutes, so you're bound to see the "eruption" if you linger long enough. Just be careful not to linger downwind, where the noxious fumes can make you sick.

The trail begins with a crossing of the West Dolores River, which used to be quite difficult until a new footbridge was installed in 2014. Once across the river, proceed on an old jeep trail that leads to the left (northeast) for a short distance before giving way to a singletrack dirt trail.

In 0.3 mile, you'll have to cross Geyser Creek. It can be wet in the spring, so be careful. There are a few old logs other hikers have placed across this stream, but they are slippery and they turn over easily. You may find a better place to cross just upstream where the creek isn't as wide. You'll have to cross once more in a very short distance, so make sure you have the proper footwear for this trip.

By the time you reach the half-mile mark, you'll begin to smell sulfur as it seeps out of the mountainside where mining activity a hundred years ago disturbed the area. Following a series of three gentle switchbacks, you'll smell that smell a few more times before the trail begins to level out at about 9,150 feet in elevation. Total elevation gain on this trail is 551 feet.

Just beyond the 1-mile mark, at waypoint **N37 45.1846' / W108 07.2260'**, the trail splits. Take the lower trail and soon you'll see Forest Service warning signs and smell that smell. Within 0.1 mile, you'll find the small white and turquoise-colored spring about 10

Robert Traylor checks the temperature at Geyser Spring, the only true geyser in Colorado.

feet wide by 14 feet long, lined with whitewashed rock, colored by the sulfur and other minerals in the water. Directly behind the pool is Geyser Creek.

The temperature of the spring is usually 82.4 degrees Fahrenheit, and the Forest Service issues the following warning: "Periodic eruptions of carbon dioxide and hydrogen sulfide gas displace oxygen near the water's surface. Swimming or bathing in the geyser exposes one to these gases and could cause a loss of consciousness, and potentially death. If you should feel light-headed or nauseous while viewing the geyser, you should leave the area immediately."

Yes, it's stinky. But it's cool—and it's the only geyser in Colorado, situated in a drop-dead beautiful forest deep in the San Juan Mountains. Hold your nose and enjoy it!

MILES AND DIRECTIONS

0.0 Start from trailhead, cross the footbridge over West Dolores River, then head northeast on an old jeep road.

0.1 Jeep track turns into singletrack winding back to southeast.

0.3 Cross Geyser Creek; be careful on wet logs. You may get wet in spring.

0.4 Head into the long draw due east.

0.5 There's a rock pile off the trail at an old mining site; you can smell the sulfur.

0.6 The first of three switchbacks leads up an old mining road.

1.0 Trail splits at waypoint **N37 45.1846' / W108 07.2260'**.

1.2 The sign reads, "Sensitive area, Foot traffic only." Follow your nose! This is your turnaround point.

2.4 Arrive back at the trailhead.

Springtime is a beautiful time to be on this trail as the aspen are beginning to leaf out!

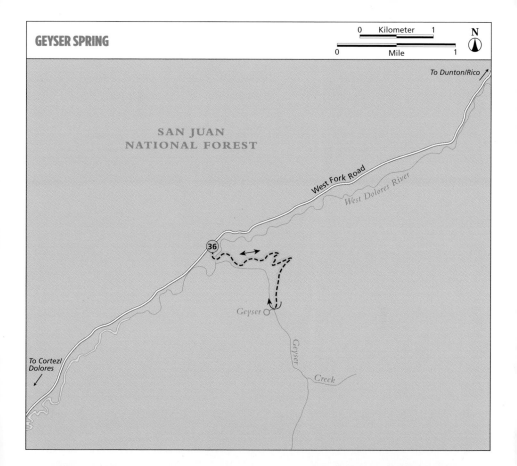

GEYSER SPRING

SAN JUAN
NATIONAL FOREST

West Fork Road

West Dolores River

To Dunton/Rico

36

Geyser

Geyser

Creek

To Cortez/
Dolores

Mule deer may be spotted all along the trail.

As rare as a geyser, a phone booth in the wilderness.

FOUR CORNERS AREA

These four corners are the only place in the United States where four states meet at one geographic point. Long before surveyors drew perpendicular lines to create Colorado, New Mexico, Arizona, and Utah, however, this center of the Colorado Plateau was well defined by millions of years of uplift and remarkable erosion.

The sandstone geology of this high-desert red-rock country has left bare slot canyons, natural bridges, hoodoos, reefs, goblins, and river narrows. And, as you'll see in the following hikes, ancestral Puebloan people lived in this region from around 2,000 to 700 years ago.

In the past century, the people of this region and their culture were referred to as "Anasazi," a name given to them by the Navajo, who were not their descendants. That

The Ute Mountains, collectively known as Sleeping Ute Mountain, can be seen from Sand Canyon. West of Mesa Verde National Park, these are sacred mountains to the ancestors of Ancient Puebloans—the Ute Mountain Ute Tribe—and are located on reservation land. Access by outsiders is severely restricted.

term was used to mean "ancestors of enemies." Most literature now refers to "Ancestral Puebloans" when speaking of the historical culture and architecture native to this region.

But, why did they live here, and why did they leave?

Water.

In these mazelike canyons of the Four Corners region, permeable Dakota sandstone rests on top of impermeable Burro Canyon shale. When it rains or snows, moisture soaks through the sandstone until it reaches shale. It then flows outward along the shale until it comes to the wall of a canyon, where it forms a spring.

Ancestral Puebloans knew these canyons with seeps and springs were ideal places to live. Perhaps that's why they built such sturdy towers. The masonry at Hovenweep is incredibly skillful and those structures may have been used for celestial observatories or storage facilities. Because of the value of water in this arid land, however, it is likely they were also used for defense.

With such structures in place, Ancestral Puebloans could protect their water—but they couldn't beat a drought that would dry up the seeps and springs.

Archaeologists speculate that a severe drought lasting a couple decades, possibly combined with overpopulation, resource depletion, factionalism, and warfare, eventually forced the Ancestral Puebloans to leave. Many migrated south to the Rio Grande Valley in New Mexico and the Little Colorado River Basin in Arizona. Today's Pueblo, Zuni, and Hopi people claim themselves to be proud descendants of this culture.

37 PETROGLYPH POINT—MESA VERDE NATIONAL PARK

While most tourists visit the large cliff dwellings found here, a hike to Petroglyph Point takes you away from the crowds and into one of the major canyons within Mesa Verde National Park. Its terminus is a large panel of petroglyphs, chipped and pecked through exterior desert varnish to the light sandstone beneath by 13th-century Puebloans. The trail begins below Chapin Mesa Archeological Museum and the famous Spruce Tree House. This 130-room cliff dwelling was closed to the public in 2015 because of unstable rock. Nonetheless, you get great views of it from this trail.

Start: From Petroglyph Point Trailhead below Spruce Tree House
Elevation loss: 6,731–6,937 feet (206 feet)
Distance: 2.6-mile loop trail
Difficulty: Easy to moderate
Hiking time: 1.5–2.5 hours
Seasons/schedule: Year-round, but some areas and accommodations are closed during winter months. Check NPS website (www.nps.gov/meve) for information about guided tours.
Fees and permits: $20–$30 per vehicle adjusted seasonally, $15 per person (motorcyclist, bicyclist and individual). NPS and Federal Recreational Lands Pass ($80 per year; $80 for lifetime senior pass) accepted.
Trail contacts: Mesa Verde National Park, (970) 529-4465, www.nps.gov/meve
Canine compatibility: Dogs are not permitted on trails within national park boundaries.
Trail surface: Paved for a short distance, and then it's a well-maintained singletrack dirt path
Land status: Mesa Verde National Park
Nearest town: Cortez

Other trail users: None
Nat Geo TOPO! map (USGS): Topo, Moccasin Mesa, CO
National Geographic Trails Illustrated map: Durango/Cortez #144
Other maps: Mesa Verde National Park map; BLM Cortez, CO 1:100,000 topo
Special considerations: Normally, this is a loop hike. Because of wintertime ice and snow, however, you may be directed to hike via the mesa top section of the trail, or the entire trail may be closed. Check first with park staff for trail conditions.
Other: The Mesa Verde National Park Visitor Center and Chapin Mesa Archeological Museum will both help you gain insights into the lives of the Ancestral Pueblo people. (970) 529-4465; https://www.nps.gov/meve/planyourvisit/museum.htm;

Also, the Anasazi Heritage Center, 27501 Hwy. 184, Dolores, CO 81323; (970) 882-5600, is open daily from 9 a.m. to 5 p.m. Mar–Oct; 10 a.m. to 4 p.m. Nov–Feb. Admission: $7 adults Mar–Oct; free Nov–Feb. Under 16 free. School groups free. The center honors Federal Recreational Lands Passes.

FINDING THE TRAILHEAD

 From Cortez, Colorado, head east on US 160 for 10 miles to the park turnoff. Proceed south on the Chapin Mesa Road through the Park Entrance for 22 miles (45 min) to the Chapin Mesa Archeological Museum. The trailhead is located just below the museum in front of the Spruce Tree House Overlook.

Trailhead GPS: N37 11.0505' / W108 29.2720'

THE HIKE

Mesa Verde National Park protects nearly 5,000 known archaeological sites, including 600 cliff dwellings. It's loaded with natural history and fascinating geology—but it's a human zoo in July and August. Approximately 3,000 people a day enter the park during the second week of August, alone. Most of them arrive on tour busses and pile into famous places like the Cliff Palace ruins. It's their chance to wander through a massive, reconstructed pueblo (150 rooms and 23 kivas [*kee-vahs*]) with a ranger and 150 of their closest buddies. Not necessarily a wilderness experience, it is nonetheless valuable for those who are unable to hike very far.

A short jaunt to Petroglyph Point, however, gets you away from the crowds. (USGS topographical maps show this trail leading to "Pictograph Point," and not "Petroglyph Point." The maps are mislabeled. Pictographs are painted on rock; petroglyphs are chipped or pecked into rock.)

The trail begins at the same trailhead with Spruce Canyon Trail, just below the museum and near one of those major attractions, the 130-room Spruce Tree House Pueblo. A Petroglyph Trail Guide, available at the trailhead, discusses the natural environment of Mesa Verde and how "The Ancient Ones" would have survived in this harsh environment. It's worth a 50-cent donation.

Spruce Tree House has been closed since 2015 due to continued rockfalls. Still, overlooks near the trailhead offer superb views of this impressive dwelling, constructed between AD 1211 and 1278 by ancestors of the Pueblo people of the American Southwest. Thought to have been home to sixty to eighty Puebloans, the dwelling includes eight kivas, or ceremonial chambers, and was built into a natural alcove measuring 216 feet (66 meters) across and 89 feet (27 meters) deep.

Spruce Canyon Trail and Petroglyph Trail begin on a short stretch of pavement with three switchbacks that remain open despite signs noting Spruce Tree House is closed. Within 0.1 mile, the pavement ends and shortly thereafter, the trails split. Continue forward and to the left on the well-marked Petroglyph Trail. Soon, you'll spot a large Douglas fir (*Pseudotsuga menziesii*) behind an informational post marked #1 (following the trail guide). When two local ranchers first discovered this cliff dwelling in 1888, they misidentified trees here as Douglas spruce, and not fir. Yet, it's not really a true fir either, but more closely resembles a hemlock.

Within a half-mile, you should be able to view other cliff dwellings far across Spruce Canyon to your right. They're located just below the rim and a large burned area, remnants of the 2,300-acre Long Mesa Fire that burned here in 2002 (see sidebar).

At 1.1 miles, you'll come to a small multiroom ruin. Notice nearby boulders with characteristic scrape marks, where ancient Puebloans sharpened their stone axes and knives. Please don't walk on the masonry walls or disturb this protected site.

You'll reach the rock art panel that this trail is named for in another 0.4 mile. In 1942, four Hopi men from northeastern Arizona visited this site and interpreted some of these

Thought to have been home to sixty to eighty native Puebloans, Spruce Tree House ruins have been closed to the public since 2015 due to continued rockfalls.

petroglyphs. These modern-day interpretations "may or may not have been the interpretations given them by the rock artists who produced them," according to the Park Service. You'll have to decide for yourself. They're outlined in the Petroglyph Trail Guide.

The trail now leads up a short, steep series of switchbacks and to the top of the mesa. It then winds its way back through a pinyon and juniper forest to the museum and parking area. Continue watching to your left (west) for other ruins just below the canyon rim.

MILES AND DIRECTIONS

0.0 Start from Petroglyph Point Trailhead below museum and Spruce Tree House on paved trail.

0.1 Pavement ends and soon Petroglyph Trail crosses the Spruce Canyon Trail. Stay on the well-marked Petroglyph Trail.

0.5 Look through the trees to your right. You may need binoculars to view other cliff dwellings across the canyon, just below the top ledge and below the large burn area.

1.1 Find a shaded grotto with remnants of a small multiroom cliff dwelling. Do not climb on any of the masonry walls!

1.5 **N37 10.3870′ / W108 29.5598′** Reach the rock art panel this trail is named for. Just beyond these petroglyphs, begin a short, steep climb up to a gravel trail that follows the mesa back to the museum.

1.7 Just beyond trail marker #33, look toward an alcove on highest rock ledge across the canyon to the southwest for another set of ruins.

2.6 Return to museum near trailhead and parking area.

Wildfire has played a major role in the ecology of Mesa Verde. In fact, 70 percent of the park has been burned by wildfires since it was established in 1906. About 95 percent of those fires were lightning caused. The largest was the Bircher Fire that consumed 22,400 acres in July 2000.

Due to increased fuel loading and recent extended drought conditions, fire continues to pose threats to the park's infrastructure, resources, and human safety. The park has implemented several strategies to help protect resources and human life, including prescribed, controlled burns and hazard fuel reduction.

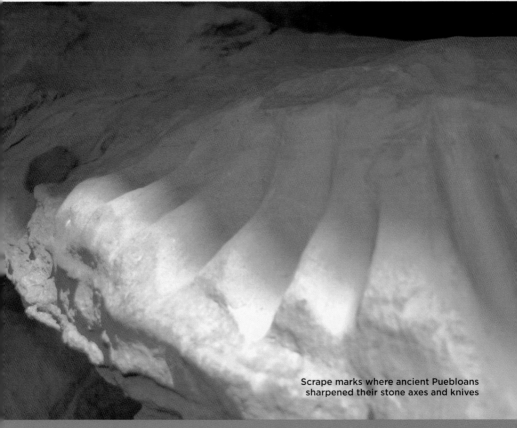

Scrape marks where ancient Puebloans sharpened their stone axes and knives

Petroglyphs on the rock art panel

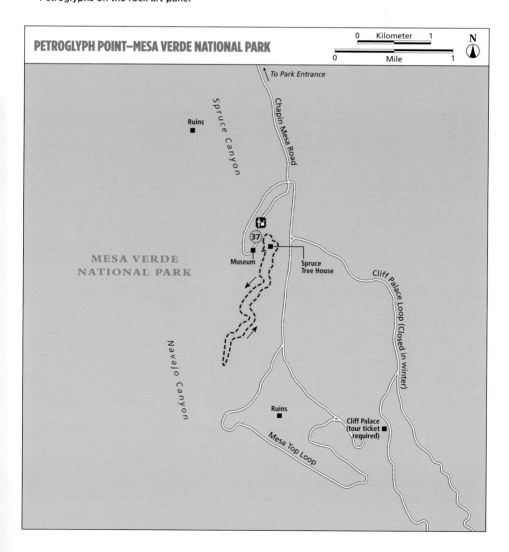

38 SAND CANYON—
CANYON OF THE ANCIENTS
NATIONAL MONUMENT

Remnants of Ancestral Puebloan homes are scattered throughout the incredible 171,000-acre Canyons of the Ancients National Monument, straddling the Utah border in the southwest corner of Colorado. A hike through Sand Canyon allows you to visit numerous 800-year-old archaeological sites. The Sand Canyon Trail is 6.5 miles (one way) from Sand Canyon Pueblo to the lower trailhead in McElmo Canyon. A vehicle shuttle is recommended. Otherwise, go to the lower trailhead and walk up. Other than the largely unexcavated Sand Canyon Pueblo at the upper trailhead, most of the accessible archaeological sites are within 2.5 miles of the lower trailhead.

Start: From upper trailhead at Sand Canyon Pueblo
Elevation loss: 6,827-5,454 feet (1,373 feet)
Distance: 6.5 miles one way
Difficulty: Easy to moderate
Hiking time: 3-4 hours
Seasons/schedule: Year-round but check on winter road conditions and accessibility at the Anasazi Heritage Center
Fees and permits: None
Trail contacts: BLM, 29211 Hwy. 184, Dolores, CO 81323; (970) 882-7296; https://www.blm.gov/office/tres-rios-field-office
Canine compatibility: Dogs are allowed on leash only. Keep dogs out of archaeological sites and springs and bring a plastic bag to scoop the poop.
Trail surface: Rock, sand, and dirt singletrack backcountry path
Land status: BLM, Canyon of the Ancients National Monument
Nearest town: Cortez

Other trail users: Horseback riders and mountain bikers. (The upper section is steep and rugged and not recommended for bicycles.)
Nat Geo TOPO! map (USGS): Battle Rock, CO and Woods Canyon, CO
Other maps: BLM 1:100,000-scale Dove Creek and Cortez maps; designated transportation system map online at: https://www.blm.gov/sites/blm.gov/files/uploads/Canyons_of_the_Ancients_Transportation%20map%20for%20web.pdf; trail map available at Anasazi Heritage Center
Special considerations: This is sacred ground to Native Americans and is their ancestral home. All cultural resources, structures, and artifacts are protected by federal law—and by the spirits of the Ancient Ones. Entering structures or canyon interiors is not permitted.
Other: Cellphone coverage? Forget about it! It's nonexistent, particularly in the canyons.

FINDING THE TRAILHEADS (PLAN ON 45 MINUTES FOR A VEHICLE SHUTTLE)

To reach the McElmo Canyon (lower) trailhead: From the intersection of US 491 and US 160 in Cortez, head south on US 491. In 2.5 miles, turn right (west) on CR G at the signs for the airport and Hovenweep National Monument. Go 12 miles on this paved road. Trailhead parking is an unimproved slickrock surface on the north (right) side of the road. No water, toilet, phone, or other services are available.
Lower Trailhead GPS: N37 20.4885' / W108 49.0395'

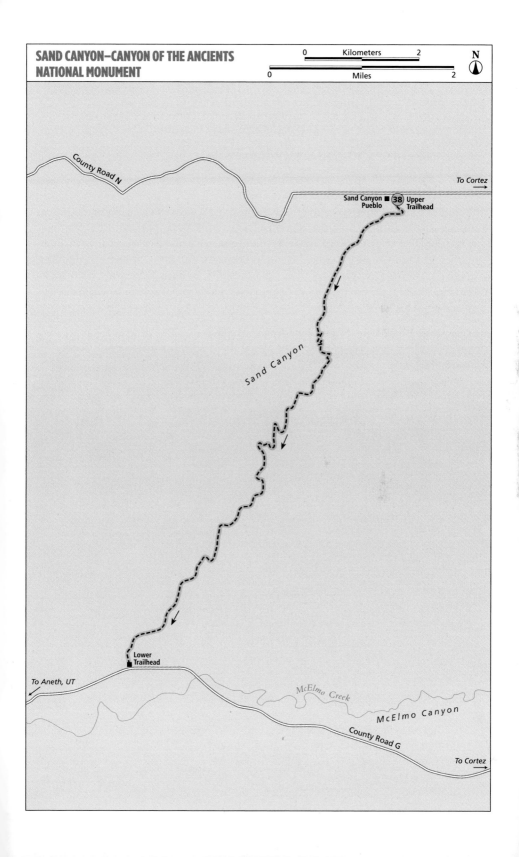

County Road N

To Cortez

Sand Canyon Pueblo ■ 38 Upper Trailhead

Sand Canyon

Lower Trailhead

To Aneth, UT

McElmo Creek

McElmo Canyon

County Road G

To Cortez

To reach the Sand Canyon (upper) trailhead: From the intersection of US 491 and US 160 in Cortez, drive north for 10.5 mile on US 491, then turn left (west) on Montezuma County (MC) Road P. This road eventually winds to P.5 Road. In 4.5 miles, turn left at 18 Road. In 0.5 mile, you're back on P Road, which will turn right (west). Go another 1.5 miles to 17 Road. Turn left as the road becomes N Road. You'll lose the pavement here, but it's a well-maintained dirt road. Continue for 2 miles to the trailhead, marked with a small "Canyons of the Ancients" sign on the left-hand side of the road.

Upper Trailhead GPS: N37 23.9829' / W108 46.5256'

THE HIKE

With 420 rooms, 100 kivas, and 14 towers the Sand Canyon Pueblo was about three times the size of Cliff Palace, the largest pueblo in Mesa Verde National Park, 50 miles to the east. The Canyons of the Ancients was designated a National Monument in 2000 by President Bill Clinton, partially because of the work done here. A number of rooms in this pueblo were excavated between 1983 and 1993. By then, most of the outer walls had crumbled since it was built on an open site with little protection from weather. What

Sunny Alcove Pueblo once included eight rooms and a kiva.

Saddlehorn Pueblo

was excavated was then backfilled to protect standing walls and preserve the site. Today, it appears as a pile of rubble about 0.2 mile west of the parking area near the upper trailhead.

However, the Sand Canyon Pueblo Project, a partnership between the BLM and Crow Canyon Archaeological Center, has created a detailed account of this ancient village and its residents. All artifacts found during the excavations at Sand Canyon Pueblo are curated at the BLM Canyon of the Ancients Visitor Center in Dolores, Colorado.

Information kiosks at the northern trailhead lead you about 0.2 mile from the parking area west to the original pueblo and discuss what happened here. The best standing ruins, however, remain along the lower stretch of this hike, so backtrack to the parking area and main trailhead, and head south.

Despite the lack of architectural "awe," the upper reach of the trail is charming in its own right.

You are hiking through the Great Sage Plain—an area between Cortez, Colorado, and Monticello, Utah, where deep soils hold winter moisture and have been used for dry land farming since the times of the Ancestral Puebloans.

Several thousand acres of mesa and canyon farmland would have been required to support the population of the Great Sage Plain in AD 1270. They grew corn, beans, squash, and other crops in small fields and terraces, using small check dams for irrigation. They used solar calendars and astronomy to calculate growing seasons. They also hunted and tended to large flocks of turkeys.

From the trailhead, you'll hike about 0.1 mile before dropping into a side draw of Sand Canyon. You'll follow along this side draw for another 2 miles before it drops into the main gorge. By the time you reach the bottom of the canyon, you'll have descended about 700 feet, down thirty switchbacks.

At 2.9 miles, you'll reach the first of the major ruins, called "House with Standing Curved Wall." You can see a 38-foot-long curved wall under a massive sandstone overhang, with a couple windows and other supporting walls nearby.

Not far from "House with Standing Curved Wall," is "Sunny Alcove." In 1965, researchers found corncobs, pottery sherds, and fragments of grinding stones. On the inside of these remarkably sophisticated double-layered stone walls are well preserved wall niches—little built-in shelves.

Today, many Native Americans consider this place their ancestral homeland. They don't consider this area abandoned. Rather, it's a living part of culture. Modern tribal people maintain close ties with the spirits of their ancestors who are buried on this landscape. Sites are visited often and blessings made on a regular basis.

As you continue down the canyon on this well-marked trail, you'll find at least six other ruins. Some, like Double Cliff House, were built in two ledges of an alcove. Others, like the Saddlehorn Pueblo, about a mile from the lower trailhead, have rooms in the alcove and structures on a pinnacle about 100 feet above the alcove.

At 5.9 miles, you can see the McElmo Canyon Road and verdant farms adjacent to the lower trailhead. Many more ruins are protected on private property in this area.

At 6.2 miles, a spur trail leads to Castle Rock Pueblo, the last archaeological site on the trail. It was built and occupied from around AD 1250 to the 1280s. In another 0.3 mile, you'll reach the lower trailhead.

MILES AND DIRECTIONS

0.0   Start from upper trailhead.

0.1   The trail drops into a short side draw with a couple short switchbacks.

0.2   Climb out of this side draw and continue south into main canyon.

2.4   The trail begins its descent into the main gorge with a series of switchbacks.

2.9   At the bottom of the canyon, you'll find your first spur trail to the right leading to "House with Standing Curved Wall."

4.7   Sand Canyon Trail meets Rock Creek Trail. Stay on the left (main) trail heading south.

5.3   Another spur trail leads to Saddlehorn Pueblo. **N37 21.1298' / W108 48.4718'**

5.9   You can see the road and verdant farms adjacent to the lower trailhead.

6.2   Spur trail to the left leads to Castle Rock Pueblo view site. **N37 20.6066' / W108 49.0482'**

6.5   Reach the bottom of the trailhead in McElmo Canyon along CR G. **N37 20.4885' / W108 49.0395'**

39 CUTTHROAT CASTLE— HOVENWEEP NATIONAL MONUMENT

Hovenweep is a native Ute/Paiute word meaning "deserted valley." That's what happened here. Archaeological evidence confirms that human life existed in these canyons more than 10,000 years ago. By AD 1250, approximately 2,500 Puebloans lived here. Yet, by AD 1300, the area was deserted.

This short trail leads to the remarkable ancestral ruins of Cutthroat Castle and a glimpse of Puebloan life in the arid Southwest 800 years ago. Approximately 0.5 mile from the Cutthroat Castle site is Painted Hand Pueblo, located inside Canyon of the Ancients National Monument. The drive here will lead you to both sites.

Start: From Cutthroat Castle parking area and upper trailhead
Elevation loss: 6,053–5,794 feet (259 feet)
Distance: 1.4 miles round-trip (to Cutthroat Castle Ruins)
Difficulty: Easy
Hiking time: 1 hour
Seasons/schedule: Open year-round, but best in spring and fall. It's extremely hot in the summer, and the road may be covered in snow in winter. Call the Hovenweep National Monument or Canyon of the Ancients Visitor Center to check on conditions in advance.
Fees and permits: None
Trail contacts: Hovenweep National Monument, McElmo Route, Cortez, CO 81321, (970) 562-4282; www.nps.gov/hove; 29211 Hwy. 184, Dolores, CO 81323, (970) 882-7296; https://www.blm.gov/office/tres-rios-field-office
Canine compatibility: Dogs permitted on leash only and their waste must be disposed of properly.
Trail surface: Rock and dirt path; parts of it are on an old jeep road.
Land status: The Cutthroat Castle group of ruins lies within Hovenweep National Monument, administered by the National Park Service; the Painted Hand Pueblo, 0.5 mile to the northeast, lies inside Canyons of the Ancients National Monument, administered by the Bureau of Land Management.
Nearest town: Cortez
Other trail users: Foot traffic only to the site, although the trail follows the four-wheel-drive road for a short stretch.
Nat Geo TOPO! map (USGS): Negro Canyon, CO
Other maps: BLM 1:100,000-scale topo: Cortez, CO
Special considerations: This is sacred ground to Native Americans and is their ancestral home. All cultural resources, structures, and artifacts are protected by federal law—and by the spirits of the Ancient Ones. Please, take only pictures. Leave only footprints. Entering structures or canyon interiors is not permitted.
Other: The Canyon of the Ancients Visitor Center and Museum, 27501 Hwy. 184, Dolores, CO 81323 (970-882-5600), is open daily from 9 a.m. to 5 p.m. Mar–Oct; 10 a.m. to 4 p.m. Nov–Feb. Admission: $7 adults, under 16 free. School groups free. The center honors Federal Recreational Lands Passes.

FINDING THE TRAILHEAD

From Cortez, drive north on US 491 for 19 miles to Pleasant View. Turn left (west) on Montezuma County (MC) Road BB and continue for 6 miles to MC Road 10. Turn left (south) and continue on MC Road 10 for 11.3 miles to the Cutthroat Castle/Painted Hand turnoff, Road #4531. Turn left (southeast) on this rough dirt road and continue 3.1 miles to the Cutthroat Castle upper trailhead. You will pass two pull-ins for the Painted Hand Pueblo. (Visit it on the way out!) Most SUVs can make it to the upper Cutthroat trailhead. Hardcore four-wheel-drivers could drive to the lower trailhead, but then you wouldn't get much of a hike!

Trailhead GPS: N37 26.7701' / W108 58.4112'

THE HIKE

Hovenweep National Monument includes six prehistoric villages built between AD 1200 and AD 1280. While National Monument headquarters are in Utah, three of the prehistoric villages, including Cutthroat Castle, rest inside Colorado's borders. A fourth, Painted Hand Pueblo, is 0.5 mile away in Canyons of the Ancients National Monument. You'll pass it on your way in and you'll have to stop on your way out, just to find the "Painted Hand!"

First, however, start with a hike to the Cutthroat Castle ruins. From the trailhead at 6,053 feet in elevation, the trail drops through some large cuts of easily navigable sandstone rock. Kids of all ages will love this spot. The trail then travels through pinyon and juniper woodlands, intermixed with sagebrush and Mormon tea, or *Ephedra nevadensis*. That's the shrub consisting of erect, segmented green twigs that age to a dull, cracked gray-green. In the springtime, it will produce yellow pods. Ancestral Puebloans drank a tea brewed from this plant to fight colds, kidney disorders, and other medical issues, as did early Mormon explorers who rediscovered this area in the 1800s.

In a little more than 0.1 mile, you'll cross the four-wheel-drive road that continued past the upper trailhead. In another 0.2 mile, you'll notice black-crusted cryptogamic soil. "Don't Bust the Crust!" As a living groundcover, these biological soil crusts are communities of living organisms consisting of fungi, lichens, cyanobacteria, bryophytes, and algae. Cryptogam is the foundation of high-desert plant life.

In 0.5 mile, pass through a fence at the Monument boundary. This is a small inholding within Canyons of the Ancients National Monument (see sidebar).

Soon, you'll find a lovely rock ledge the kids can hide under as they pretend to walk the paths of the Ancient Ones. You'll also get your first glimpse of the Cutthroat Castle complex in front of you and to your left.

Imagine ancient hunter-gatherers, initially mobile, taking temporary shelter beneath canyon overhangs and in shallow alcoves as they searched for food. They began cultivating corn, and eventually beans and squash, then built more permanent structures closer to their crops in valleys and on mesa tops.

By AD 1230, people began moving from mesa-top homes. Instead of small, scattered clusters of dwellings, larger villages were built around canyon heads containing water.

Continue on the trail for a short distance and you'll come to a spot just above the ruins where the lower and upper trails meet. Go left and explore the structures.

Some were built for housing, some for food storage, some for celestial observations and religious ceremonies, and some for defense.

The trail ends just below the largest structure, at 5,794 feet above sea level.

Some structures here were built for housing, some for storage, some for defense—and some for all these purposes.

Your first glimpse of Cutthroat Castle

After exploring, head back toward the lower trailhead. Following the sign, take this trail a few hundred feet until it reaches the four-wheel-drive road at 0.7 mile. Walk up this road, take a right at an intersection in 0.3 mile and continue on this road until you find the spot where the trail crossed it. Follow the trail back to your vehicle or continue up the road. Either way, the round-trip comes to 1.4 miles.

Since you've here, don't miss the Painted Hand Pueblo. Take one of the marked turns you passed on your way in. A 0.3-mile-long trail leads from the north end of the parking area to the Pueblo (0.6 mile round-trip). This was once a small village of about twenty rooms that still includes faint rock paintings (pictographs) and petroglyphs. Can you find the Painted Hand? Look, but don't touch! Skin oils damage ancient artwork. **(N37 27.2585' / W108 58.1697'.)**

MILES AND DIRECTIONS

- **0.0** Start from upper Cutthroat Castle trailhead.
- **0.1** Trail crosses the road.
- **0.3** Cryptogamic soils abound.
- **0.5** Trail passes through a fence line at **N37 26.5766' / W108 58.8641'.**
- **0.6** You're walking on the sand of the Ancient Ones.
- **0.7** After exploring, follow signs to the lower trailhead. In a few hundred feet, it reaches the four-wheel-drive road. Follow the road to the northeast.
- **1.0** Two four-wheel-drive roads converge. **N37 26.8170' / W108 58.7884'** Turn right (southeast) and up the hill toward your vehicle.
- **1.4** Trail crosses the road. Retrace your steps up the trail to your vehicle or follow the road. Your choice!

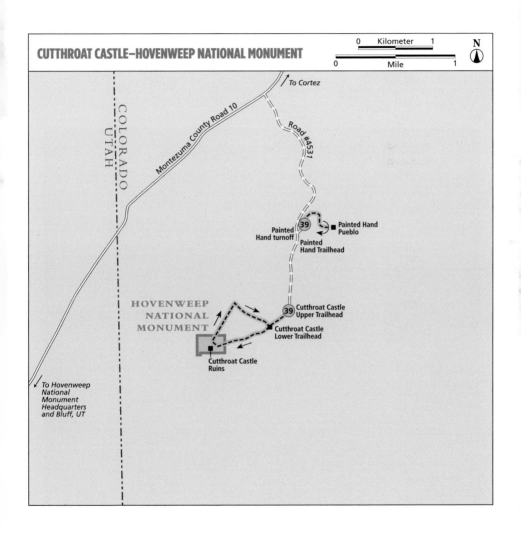

CUTTHROAT CASTLE–HOVENWEEP NATIONAL MONUMENT

0   Kilometer   1

0   Mile   1

N

To Cortez

COLORADO
UTAH

Montezuma County Road 10

Road #4531

Painted
Hand turnoff

39

Painted Hand
Pueblo

Painted
Hand Trailhead

HOVENWEEP
NATIONAL
MONUMENT

39

Cutthroat Castle
Upper Trailhead

Cutthroat Castle
Lower Trailhead

Cutthroat Castle
Ruins

To Hovenweep
National
Monument
Headquarters
and Bluff, UT

Was the top tower used for celestial observations or defense? How about the lower section? You can look inside, but don't touch! Even skin oils damage ancient artwork.

This short hike includes an even shorter side trip to the Painted Hand Pueblo. Only 0.5 mile from the Cutthroat Castle Complex in Hovenweep Canyon, Painted Hand Pueblo sits outside Hovenweep National Monument boundaries and inside the Canyons of the Ancients National Monument. Hovenweep National Monument was created in 1923 by President Warren G. Harding and is managed by the National Park Service. Canyon of the Ancients National Monument was designated by President Bill Clinton in 2000, and is managed by the Bureau of Land Management. No matter the management, both are rare gems of the American Southwest that preserve a link to our past.

The Painted Hand

HIKE INDEX

THE TEN ESSENTIALS OF HIKING

American Hiking Society

American Hiking Society recommends you pack the "Ten Essentials" every time you head out for a hike. Whether you plan to be gone for a couple of hours or several months, make sure to pack these items. Become familiar with these items and know how to use them. Learn more at **AmericanHiking.org/hiking-resources**

 1. Appropriate Footwear

 6. Safety Items (light, fire, and a whistle)

 2. Navigation

 7. First Aid Kit

 3. Water (and a way to purify it)

 8. Knife or Multi-Tool

 4. Food

 9. Sun Protection

 5. Rain Gear & Dry-Fast Layers

 10. Shelter